DIY HYDROPONIC GARDENS

The Complete Guide to Setting Up and Create DIY Sustainable Hydroponics Garden With The Best Techniques For Growing Fresh Vegetables, Fruits, Herbs Without Soil

CONTENTS

1
INTRODUCTION 6
What Is Hydroponics? 7
Advantages of Hydroponic Growing 8
Key Features of a Hydroponic System 13

2
EQUIPMENT 18
Irrigation 19
Pots and Trays 22
Substrates and Growing Media 24
Equipment for Growing Indoors 28
Grow Lights 29
Pest-Management Products and Equipment 32
Meters 35

3
HYDROPONIC GROWING SYSTEMS 38
How to Choose a System 39
Bottle Hydroponics 42
Floating Rafts 50
Wicking Bed 60
Nutrient Film Technique (NFT) 69
Top Drip System 83
Media Beds 92
Flood and Drain 99
Aeroponics 106
Vertical Gardens 115

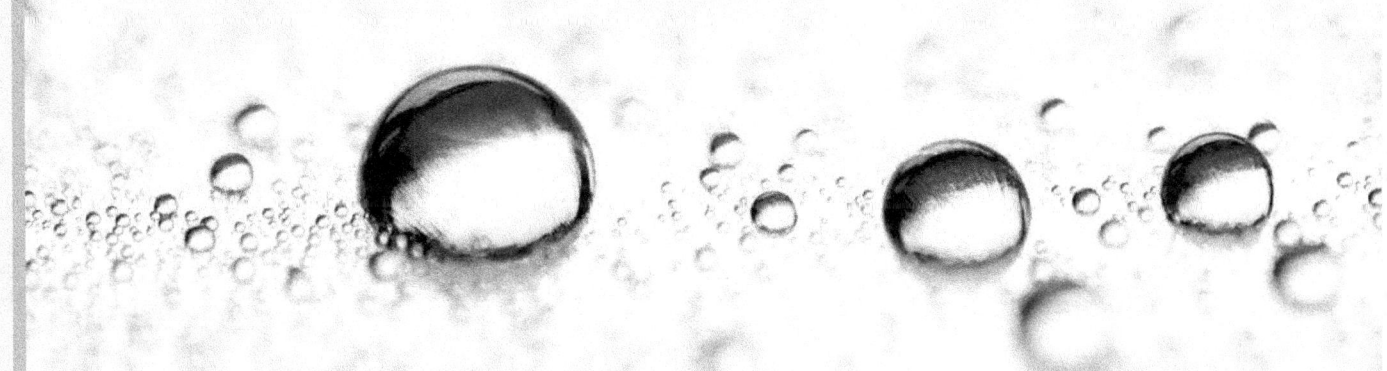

4
STARTING SEEDS and CUTTINGS 136
Starting Seeds in Stone Wool 138
Rooting Cuttings in Stone Wool 142
Rooting Cuttings in a Hydroponic Cloner 146
Transplanting Plants Started in Soil 148

5
PLANT NUTRITION 150
Plant Nutrient Uptake 151
Fertilizers 152
Measuring Fertilizer Concentration 154

6
SYSTEM MAINTENANCE 156
Managing the Nutrient Solution 157
Flushing 160
Cleaning 161

7
COMMON PROBLEMS and TROUBLESHOOTING 162
Nutrient Deficiencies 163
Infestations 166
Seedling Problems 168

Glossary 170
Appendix: Crop Selection Charts 172
Metric Conversions 186
Index 188

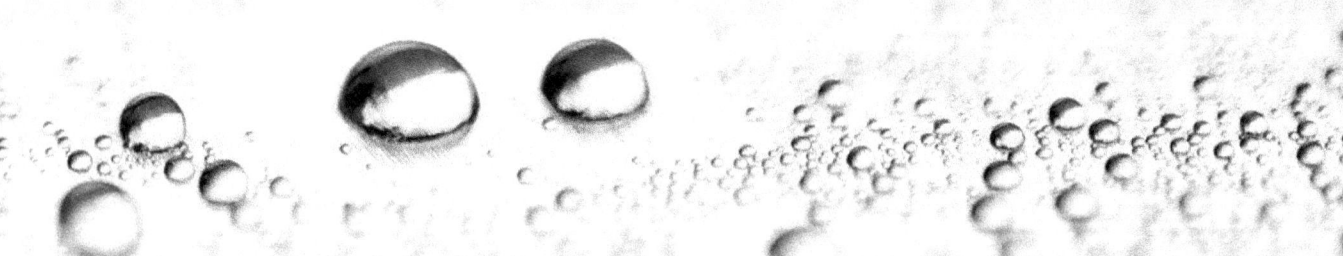

1
INTRODUCTION

THIS BOOK MAKES HYDROPONICS ACCESSIBLE to gardeners of any experience level. You'll learn both the science of hydroponics and its practical applications and see that DIY hydroponics is not just a way to avoid purchasing expensive hydroponic systems; it's also a way to create a beautiful garden better suited to your needs. Offering build guides for hydroponic gardens that range from simple to complex, this book shows systems suitable for nearly any environment or application. The build guides include many options for customizing the design so you can create a garden catered to your space, crop selection, and budget. Additionally, this book offers invaluable seed variety recommendations that can save new hydroponic gardeners time and money that could have easily been wasted on poorly suited crop selections. Avoid the costly mistakes commonly made by new hydroponic growers. The more you know, the better you grow!

WHAT IS HYDROPONICS?

Put simply, hydroponics is growing plants without soil. Most people assume that soil is indispensable for plant growth, but if you have this book, you probably already know that isn't so. The various functions of soil can be recreated using other materials. Soil provides support for the plant because it creates a physical structure for the roots to grasp. Tall trees would be unable to hold themselves upright on a windy day without a firm grip in the soil. In a hydroponic system, the physical support provided by soil can be replicated with a variety of materials and trellis structures.

Soil also provides essential nutrients for plant growth. These same nutrients can be supplied using alternative methods, however. Hydroponic systems dispense water-soluble nutrients derived from both organic and conventional sources. Soil can also provide a home for essential microbial populations that create beneficial relationships with plant roots. These same microbes can live and thrive in a hydroponic environment. So, if hydroponics is simply recreating the role of soil, why not just use soil?

ADVANTAGES OF HYDROPONIC GROWING

1. **Doesn't require quality soil**

   Gardening is often thought of as an activity limited to those fortunate enough to have a lawn. Hydroponics greatly increases gardening options for those in homes without lawns or those with lawns that have soil poorly suited for edible crops. Hydroponics combined with indoor growing techniques gives gardeners even more options by expanding the potential garden space to nearly anywhere in the home.

2. **Potential for faster crop growth**

   Plants rarely maximize their full growth potential in soil. There is almost always some limiting factor slowing down their growth. In soil, the plant roots need to search for nutrients that are often unevenly distributed and possibly inaccessible because they are bound to various soil particles. Some nutrients are inaccessible because the microbes in the soil have yet to break down the nutrient source (for example, manure) into a form that is available to the plant's roots. It is also possible for the plant growth to be constrained by a lack of water or too much water. Too much water can reduce the amount of oxygen available to the roots and inhibit biological processes necessary for the roots to uptake nutrients and water. Hydroponics bathes the roots in a precise blend of essential nutrients with a balance of water and oxygen. Many of the constraints on a plant's potential growth can be eliminated or reduced using hydroponics and indoor growing techniques.

3. **Requires less space**

   A plant must spread its roots far and wide in the process of searching for water and nutrients. By eliminating the need for the plant roots to find water and nutrients, the spacing of plants is only limited by the area needed for the plant canopy.

4. **Less constraint on growing season**

   Obviously, growing indoors permits gardeners to extend the growing season. Less obviously, hydroponics specifically can extend the growing season even when placed outdoors. Often the temperature of a plant's roots is more critical to its health than the leaf temperature. It is possible to grow winter crops in 100°F if the root temperature is kept in an optimal range closer to 65° to 75°F. It is also possible to grow crops that prefer warm temperatures in cold climates by increasing the root zone temperature. Hydroponics increases the ability to precisely adjust the root zone temperature. Through use of heaters, chillers, or simple practices like burying a hydroponic reservoir, a hydroponic gardener can increase or decrease water temperature and improve crop growth.

5 Can be used in any location

Hydroponics allows gardeners to grow in areas that do not possess quality soil. Hydroponics also allows gardeners to grow in locations that would be unsuited for crops due to inhospitable climate or limited water access. One of the biggest opportunities for hydroponics is growing in deserts. Deserts often have a wonderful climate for growing crops, with lots of light and little pest presence, but they are limited in access to water. Hydroponics uses substantially less water than traditional methods and can make farming in deserts a viable option. Hydroponics is also the primary method used to grow plants in space. Many crops, including lettuce, have been grown in space using hydroponic methods.

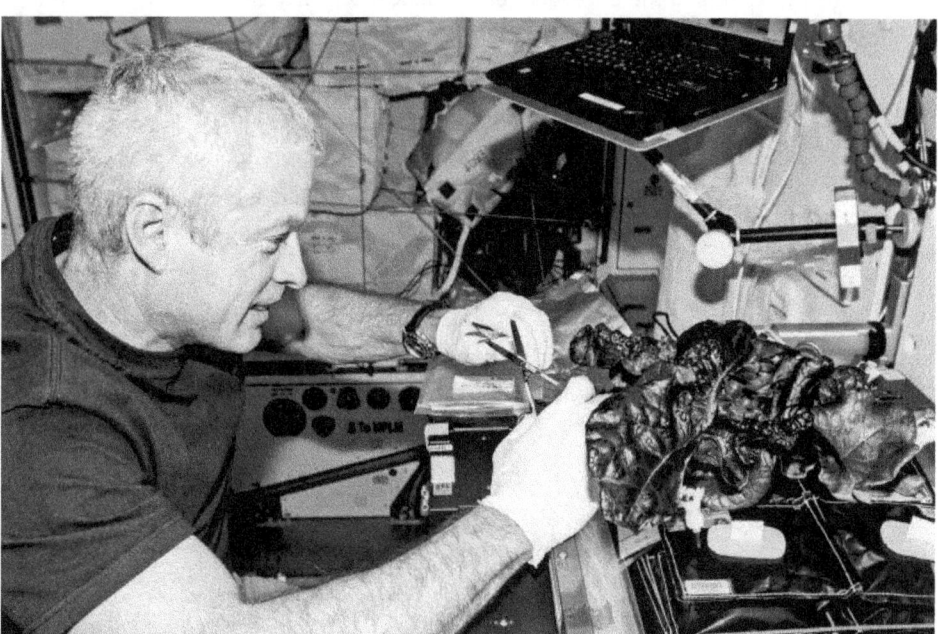

Leafy vegetables can be grown hydroponically in outer space. Photo courtesy of NASA.

6 Uses less water

Hydroponics uses less water because you may reuse any irrigation water not directly taken up by the crop. In soil, much of the water is lost to evaporation and drainage. In hydroponics, evaporation can be reduced or eliminated by covering the water reservoir, and all drainage water is collected to be reused.

7 No weeding and no herbicides

No weeding. It may seem like a small point at first, but after a season of pulling garden weeds, most traditional soil gardeners would love to have spent that time doing something more fun, like preparing dishes from their harvest. Hydroponic growers also have no need to purchase herbicides. Furthermore, hydroponic growers never have to face the potential crop damage of herbicide drift when a breeze accidentally blows herbicide onto your garden and injures or kills your precious plants.

8 Can reduce or eliminate need for pesticides

Hydroponic gardens, especially those outdoors and in greenhouses, are rarely pest free, but hydroponics does have the potential to reduce pest pressure. Hydroponic gardens present fewer hiding places for pests that will burrow into soil or hide in decaying plant debris. When hydroponics is combined with indoor growing techniques it is possible to have a completely pest-free garden if the gardener practices preventive pest control techniques. Preventive pest control techniques are covered in the Equipment for Growing Indoors section of the Equipment chapter.

9 Can reduce or eliminate agricultural runoff

It is difficult to manage runoff in a traditional garden. The gardener may fertilize the garden and the next week a rainstorm washes away much of the nutrients. It is also possible that the nutrients will be carried away by normal irrigation. Using advanced hydroponic techniques it is possible to have zero runoff. This is a practice best suited for professional hydroponic growers as it involves advanced water testing, chemistry, and an extensive knowledge of a crop's specific nutrient requirements. For home hydroponic gardeners, it is common to flush or dump out the nutrient solution in the hydroponic system every few weeks to avoid potential nutrient disorders in the crop created by an imbalance in nutrients. Plants do not consume all nutrients at the same rate, so over time some accumulate and some become deficient. Periodic flushes, or changes of the nutrient solution, help reset the system and ensure the crop has access to the correct balance of nutrients. This wastewater does not have to be simply flushed down, though; most hydroponic gardeners use this water for their outdoor garden or potted plants. A traditional soil-based garden is a great companion to a hydroponic garden.

10 Ability to manipulate nutrient content

One of the most common misconceptions surrounding hydroponics is that hydroponic produce has a lower nutrient density than soil-grown produce because hydroponic crops are grown in water. There have been many studies comparing the nutrient density of hydroponic and soil-grown produce and the results are evenly mixed. There are so many factors that affect the nutrient density of a crop, and although fertilizer does play a role in which nutrients are present, the environment has a huge role in which nutrients the plant actually uptakes. Light intensity and specific colors of light can affect antioxidant content. Stress due to irrigation practices can affect antioxidant content. Temperature can affect sugar concentration. There is a long list of factors that affect the nutrients present in a crop but, overall, these vegetables are nutritious. The differences are very minute and it is difficult to go wrong when eating a vegetable. Nearly all plants will show visible signs of nutrient deficiency if their nutrient density is significantly off from normal levels, so if the plant looks good it more than likely is going to have a nutrient profile comparable to a similar-looking plant regardless of the environment in which it was grown.

That said, there are some unique methods that hydroponic growers are using to manipulate their crop. Many commercial hydroponic tomato growers purposely stress their plants with high nutrient levels at key stages in their development to induce an increase in sugar content in the tomatoes. The growers can spike the nutrients to induce the sugar increase and then reduce the nutrients to a normal level to maintain healthy growth. For lettuce, the Oizumi Yasaikobo Co., Ltd., in Chichibu City, Japan, has developed a method for growing low-potassium lettuce using hydroponic methods. The farm grows these specialty lettuces for customers suffering from kidney disease who are getting treated with dialysis and are restricted from consuming vegetables with a high potassium content. This effort to grow produce with a custom nutrient content is one of many similar projects being developed around the world as growers gain the ability to precisely control every aspect of a crop's growing environment.

11 Increased ability to direct crop growth for specific characteristics

Not only can nutrient content be manipulated, but other characteristics, such as leaf size, leaf color, root size, and plant height, can also be manipulated when hydroponics is combined with indoor growing. Indoor gardeners can use various colors of light to induce specific characteristics. A popular practice is the use of blue light to grow more compact plants indoors to reduce the vertical space required for a crop.

12 Clean and low mess

Soil gardening can be messy. This is not bad, but not always ideal. The most extreme example is the International Space Station. A floating cloud of soil would be a disaster around that sensitive equipment. For those of us not growing

plants in space, the benefit of soilless growing is a cleaner crop. Crops grown hydroponically often require little or no washing. Hydroponic gardens can be a great way to expose kids to plants in a classroom or home without bringing in the potential of a big muddy mess. One of my favorite kid-friendly systems is the hydroponic fairy garden described in the Media Beds section of the Hydroponic Growing Systems chapter.

13 Can be easier and less work than growing in soil

Easy to use fertilizers, easy to automate, and no weeding are just a few of the reasons hydroponic gardening can be far simpler than traditional methods. Hydroponics may seem intimidating to beginners, but after a crop or two most hydroponic gardeners are hooked.

14 Easy to master and replicate results

Hydroponic crops grow quickly, allowing growers to get more experience in a shorter period of time. The best teacher is experience, and faster-growing crops allow hydroponic growers to learn quickly. Once a grower figures out the right recipe for that environment and selected crop, it is easy to replicate the process. Hydroponics gives the grower the power to replicate the exact nutrients available and irrigation frequency. When hydroponics is paired with indoor growing techniques, growers increase their control even further. Indoor gardeners can replicate light intensity, light duration, temperature, humidity, carbon dioxide levels, and airflow to grow consistent crops year-round without the seasonal and yearly fluctuations experienced by traditional gardeners.

15 Increases ability to manage soilborne pathogens like root rots and bacterial wilts

Some of the most aggressive plant pathogens are soilborne. Any grower who has battled root rot or bacterial wilt in a traditional garden knows that is it very difficult to eradicate the problem. Many of these pathogens hide in the soil until the conditions are right, and then they spring into action. In hydroponics, the gardener can completely clean out the hydroponic system if there is a case of a soilborne pathogen. This allows the gardener to quickly remove the old crop, clean and sterilize the system, and then start up a new crop.

16 Reduces potential of contaminating crops

Several of the national foodborne disease outbreaks have been traced back to manure. Animal manure, one of the primary nutrient inputs on traditional farms, is a potential source of harmful pathogens, including *E. coli*, Listeria, and Salmonella, if not properly prepared before application. The problem is that not all manures present in agricultural fields are applied by the farmer. In 2011, an *E. coli* outbreak in Oregon was believed to be due to deer feces found on the suspected farm. It is rare to see any manure-derived fertilizers in hydroponics, and contamination from wildlife is very uncommon, as most hydroponic farms are in controlled environments that exclude wildlife. Another potential source

> ### History of Modern Hydroponics
>
> There are historic records of crops grown in floating rafts made of reeds and other modes of farming with hints of hydroponics that date back thousands of years; however, the fundamentals of modern hydroponics started to take shape around the 1920s at the University of California with Dr. William Frederick Gericke. Dr. Gericke developed some of the original hydroponic nutrient recipes and growing methods that laid the foundation for further development by other hydroponic researchers. Dennis Hoagland and Daniel Arnon continued to develop Gericke's recipes at the University of California. Versions of their recipes are still used today under the name "Hoagland solution."

of contamination is heavy metals present in soil or irrigation sources. Hydroponic growers can easily filter their water source to reduce heavy metals, but removing heavy metals from soil can be very difficult. There is research indicating that edible crops can uptake heavy metals that could lead to slow heavy metal poisoning if they are grown using contaminated soil or contaminated water sources.

KEY FEATURES OF A HYDROPONIC SYSTEM

Hydroponic systems are quite simple. To create one, you will need some kind of waterproof reservoir to contain the nutrient solution and, in some cases, the plants themselves. You'll also need a growing area, which is the place the plants will live. The size and type of growing area defines the kinds of plants you can grow and how much they will yield. You will also need, in most cases, lighting and ventilation systems. Finally, growing medium is needed to store and release nutrients to the plant roots.

The Reservoir

Most hydroponic systems have a reservoir that is filled with a nutrient solution, a mix of fertilizer and water. There are many options for nutrient sources in hydroponic gardens. Most nutrient solutions can be used for a wide variety of plants or they can be catered to specific crops. Feeding plants in a hydroponic garden is as easy as making iced tea from concentrate. Simply mix in the powder or liquid concentrate, stir, and done! Reservoirs can be created by repurposing common household items like storage totes; they can be constructed with wood and a plastic liner; or they can be purchased. Reservoirs can be as simple as a plastic or glass bottle.

The Reservoir

The Growing Area

The growing area in a hydroponic garden can be adjusted to grow nearly any plant. By adjusting irrigation frequency, pot/tray size, substrate, and environment, hydroponic gardeners can create optimal growing conditions for any crop they desire. Some crops are more practical than others; for example, hydroponic wheat and corn are possible but they often require large areas for proper pollination, and the economic value of their yield is low and difficult to justify with a capital-intensive growing method. Most hydroponic gardeners, however, find many advantages over traditional growing methods when they devote their growing area to vegetables and flowers. The growing area design is the biggest difference between the various hydroponic growing methods covered in this book. Recirculating hydroponic systems, like those described in this book, have a growing area that drains back into the reservoir. The reuse of irrigation water in hydroponics can greatly reduce the water required to grow a crop compared to the water use required in traditional growing methods.

The Crop

Plants grown in hydroponic systems can grow faster and yield more. Hydroponics eliminates the need for herbicides and can reduce or eliminate the need for pesticides when combined with indoor growing methods. With reduced sprays and no dirt, hydroponic produce is often cleaner than produce grown with traditional methods. Many people know that hydroponics can reduce water use during the growing cycle, but it is less commonly known that some produce, like lettuce, often uses more water for washing than the entire water requirement to grow the crop.

The Growing Area

The Crop

The Lights

Hydroponics is a popular growing technique indoors because it is clean and very productive. When gardeners decide to grow indoors they often want to maximize the yield in their limited growing area, and this goal is generally accomplished with hydroponic growing techniques. The primary equipment required to grow indoors is a grow light. There are many options for indoor lighting and each option has its advantages. Depending on light intensity, duration, and color, a grow light can stimulate a wide range of desirable plant traits, including enhanced flavor, increased nutrient content, increased plant pigmentation, reduced or increased plant height, earlier or delayed flowering, and increased yield. Nearly all the systems in this book can be used indoors when paired with an appropriate grow light.

The Growing Medium

Soil gardening and soilless hydroponic gardening are not enemies; each has its strengths and weaknesses. Blindly stating that one is better than the other may be tempting for those deeply invested in one method or the other, but doing so ignores the fact that both of these methods are very diverse.

The fertilizers used for hydroponics are usually very different from those used by soil gardeners. Hydroponic fertilizers need to provide everything required for healthy plant growth, whereas fertilizers intended for use in soil will just focus on a few of the major nutrients because it is assumed most of the other nutrients will already be present in the soil. Hydroponic fertilizers will work in soil, but fertilizers intended for use in soil will rarely work in hydroponic gardens. Not only would the fertilizer intended

Many Hydroponics Methods

It is hard to make blanket statements about hydroponics because there are so many different growing techniques that are considered hydroponic. Let's start with a few definitions:

True hydroponics: Hydroponic methods that use no substrate. Deep water culture (DWC), nutrient film technique (NFT), and aeroponics are a few techniques that can be classified as true hydroponics.

Recirculating: A hydroponic system that reuses irrigation water. Every DIY garden in this book is a recirculating system.

Drain-to-waste: A hydroponic system that does not reuse irrigation water after it is delivered to the crop. This method is sometimes used in top drip hydroponics.

It may seem strange that a drain-to-waste garden would be classified as hydroponic, but the only characteristic of a hydroponic system is that it does not use soil and receives its food through a nutrient solution. Drain-to-waste hydroponics can be as simple as a traditional garden pot filled with coco coir, peat, and/or perlite that is hand watered with a nutrient solution. Drain-to-waste hydroponic systems are great for certain situations, but the benefits that many associate with hydroponics, like water savings, may not be so great. Hydroponics is diverse and there are pros and cons to each method.

for soil not have all the required nutrients, but the nutrients are usually derived from sources that can foul the water in a hydroponic garden. For example, manure is commonly used for soil-based gardening but is almost never used in hydroponics. Most animal-derived fertilizer sources like manure, blood meal, bone meal, fish meal, and feather meal will create horrible odors when used in a hydroponic garden. One of the major advantages of soil gardening is the ability to use these animal-derived fertilizers, which are generally by-products of the meat industry. Soil gardening provides a great opportunity to use these by-products for a great purpose (growing plants) instead of going straight to a landfill.

Most hydroponic fertilizers, and fertilizers in general, are created using mined minerals and products from energy-intensive methods, such as the Haber-Bosch process, which converts atmospheric nitrogen gas (N_2) into ammonia (NH_3). This ammonia is used to create fertilizers like urea ($CO(NH_2)_2$) and ammonium nitrate (NH_4NO_3). Modern agriculture heavily relies on mined and synthetic fertilizers. It is estimated that half of the nitrogen fertilizer applied to crops comes from chemical sources. These fertilizers are growing crops that feed billions of humans.

The pros and cons of synthetic versus natural fertilizers are incredibly nuanced. When focusing on one attribute, it can appear that one fertilizer source is far superior to another, but the whole picture is far more complicated. For example, the manufacturing of synthetic fertilizers has a significant carbon footprint. Synthetic fertilizers, however, are far more concentrated than natural fertilizers and can be shipped more efficiently. Synthetic fertilizers are very clean and precise, which is great for hydroponics. The use of synthetic fertilizers makes it possible for some

The Lights

farms to never dump any wastewater, resulting in huge water savings compared to traditional soil farming. The back and forth of advantages and disadvantages proves to me that no one has it perfect yet. There is plenty of opportunity to learn from other growing methods and pool their advantages to create increasingly sustainable methods of farming.

2
EQUIPMENT

THE EQUIPMENT YOU'LL NEED FOR a hydroponic growing system depends, of course, on what kind of system you want to create. Except for the most basic systems, hydroponics usually includes a pump to recirculate the mixture of water and fertilizer. The recirculating water is important because it is through movement, and in some cases an airstone with tubing, that oxygen from the ambient air is supplied to the liquid and then to the plants. These pumps, along with the tubing and joining connectors, are the heart of the system and probably the most important equipment you will buy.

IRRIGATION

Irrigation is just a fancy word for *watering*, but when you are talking about a hydroponic growing system, defining it can get tricky. Whether you think of irrigation as providing nourishment or providing an infrastructure, the equipment you need to create the irrigation function really boils down to a couple basic items: a pump (with or without a filter) to propel and circulate the water through the system, and a series of tubes to convey the liquid.

Water Pumps

The major factors to consider when selecting a water pump are delivery height, target flow rate, and output tube size. Most systems simply need a pump powerful enough to deliver water to a specific height. For example, a grower selecting a pump for a flood and drain system can primarily focus on whether that pump has a maximum delivery height greater than the distance from pump outlet to flood tray. Some systems perform best when water is delivered at a target flow rate. A couple systems that depend on target flow rates are NFT and aeroponics. For these systems it is important to consider how delivery height will impact flow rate. A pump that delivers 600 gallons per hour (GPH) at 4 feet high only delivers 200 GPH at 10 feet high. The number of emitters will also impact flow rate. It is generally better to select a pump that may be slightly overpowered than a pump that could be underpowered. It is possible to reduce flow using valves, but it is not possible to increase flow.

Air Pumps

Air pumps are primarily used to aerate but they can also be effective for keeping nutrients evenly mixed in a reservoir. Aerating the nutrient solution can increase the dissolved oxygen. Although plants produce oxygen, they also use oxygen to perform a variety of tasks. One of these tasks is moving water through a filtration process in the roots. If a plant does not have adequate oxygen around its roots, then the plant will begin to wilt because it cannot perform the task of moving water through the filtration process and up to the leaves. Increasing oxygen in the root zone often increases crop yield and improves plant health.

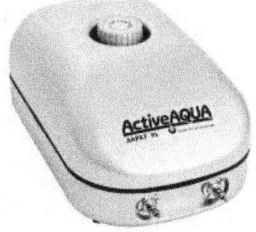

Two-outlet air pump

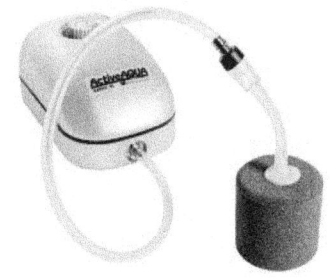

Adding a check valve between the air pump and the air stone is an inexpensive way to protect your system from a potentially expensive failure. In the event of a pump failure, generally due to a power outage, water may siphon out of the reservoir down through the ¼" tubing to the air pump. This can destroy the air pump and flood the area around the pump.

A 2' flexible air stone

Many large pumps have multiple outlet sizes. Small pumps are very useful in DIY hydroponic gardens but they may only have one outlet size. This small pump only connects to 5⁄16" tubing.

This exploded view of a 400 GPH pump shows the mesh filter, adjustable intake, impeller, suction cups, and two outlet attachments.

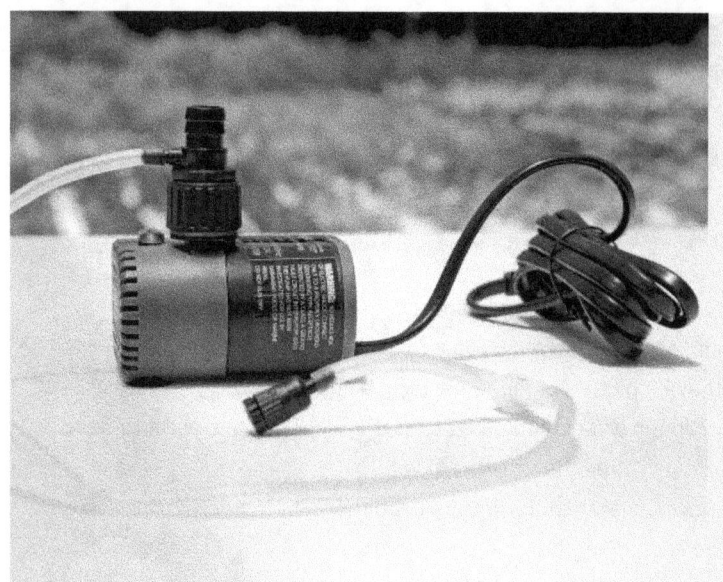

Venturi Pumps

A venturi attachment is a simple way to aerate a hydroponic system without adding an air pump and air stones. A venturi can attach directly to a pump or be installed inline in a section of tubing. Venturis take advantage of a phenomenon called the Venturi effect, which occurs when a liquid or gas flowing through a pipe moves through a constricted section, resulting in increased velocity and decreased static pressure. The venturi pump attachments have an intake tube positioned in the area of lower pressure. The decreased pressure creates a suction, which is used to pull air into the pipe. A pump with a venturi attachment can be placed on a reservoir wall to both circulate and aerate the nutrient solution.

Air pumps are rated by airflow measured in liters per minute (L/min). The target liters per minute for each hydroponic system depends on many factors, including reservoir size, water temperature, crop, and crop age. In my experience, 1 L/min per 5 gallons is generally sufficient for most applications.

Air Stones

Air pumps deliver air through air stones, which come in a variety of shapes and sizes. Air stone preferences vary greatly by grower. I personally prefer flexible air stones and round air stones with bottom suctions. There are other ways to aerate a nutrient solution besides air pumps with air stones or water pumps with venturi attachments. Cascades or waterfalls are often the sole method of aerating nutrient solutions in NFT systems. Other more advanced methods include ozone generation and liquid oxygen injections.

A 100' roll of ½" black vinyl tubing

Tubing

Not all irrigation tubing is the same. Traditional irrigation tubing used in landscaping is often very stiff and difficult to use in most hydroponic applications. Black vinyl tubing is generally the standard choice for hydroponic irrigation because it is flexible, is strong, and easily connects to the standard fittings used in hydroponic gardens. The most common sizes for black vinyl tubing are ¼, 5/16, ½, ¾, and 1 inch.

Clear tubing is not recommended for irrigation lines. There is always the potential for algae growth when the nutrient solution is exposed to light. Clear tubing can be a hot spot for algae and is difficult to clean once algae develops. Clear tubing is popular in aquariums because it is nearly invisible and is more aesthetically pleasing. If aesthetics are not a major concern, ¼-inch black tubing will work just as well as ¼-inch clear tubing.

A sample of ¼" clear vinyl tubing

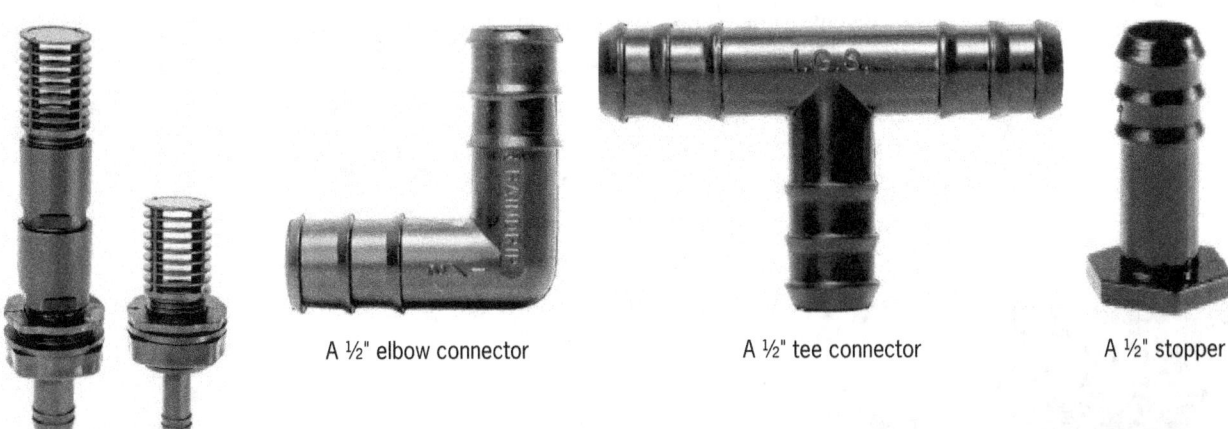

Flood and drain combo kit   A ½" elbow connector   A ½" tee connector   A ½" stopper

A ½" rubber grommet

Ball valves (or shutoff valves) restrict or stop flow. They are useful for balancing flow in NFT and vertical hydroponic gardens that may have multiple irrigation zones with various flow rates.

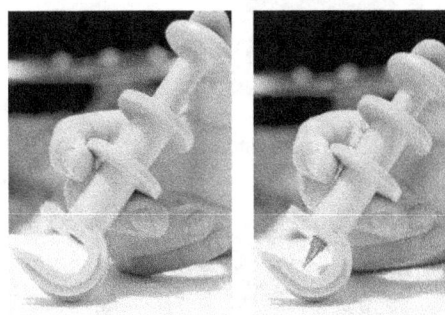

An irrigation line hole punch is used to create small holes in ½" or ¾" vinyl tubing for the insertion of ¼" barbed connectors.

Fittings

Flood and drain fittings allow DIY gardeners to create their own flood trays from household materials like plastic storage totes. Generally, these fittings come in a set that includes a ½-inch fill fitting, a ¾-inch drain fitting, extensions, and two screen fittings.

Grommets are one of the most useful irrigation fittings in DIY hydroponics. Grommets create a watertight seal around irrigation fittings. They can transform PVC pipes, plastic totes, buckets, and more into hydroponic growing areas or reservoirs. Commonly available in ½ or ¾ inch.

Tubing connectors function and look very much like the plumbing connectors that anyone with experience doing home plumbing is accustomed to using (except, of course, that they are much smaller).

POTS AND TRAYS

Net pots can be square or circular and generally range from 2 to 10 inches wide. This book focuses on uses for 2- and 3-inch net pots, the most commonly used net pot sizes in DIY hydroponic systems.

Circular plastic pots are generally the easiest to find.

Square plastic pots can help maximize the space in a hydroponic garden by removing all gaps between pots. Square pots are a popular option in grow trays because they can be packed in tightly.

Grow bags have been used in commercial farms for a long time and are starting to make their way into home gardens. They can be difficult to reuse, but they are definitely one of the cheapest options for a pot. The side walls of grow bags can be rolled down to adjust the volume of the pot. Although the bag may look square when empty, it fills out to be a cylinder.

Fabric pots are great for hydroponics because they are quick draining but don't have large holes that can possibly let out substrate. They are perfect for flood and drain systems because it is easy for the water to soak into the substrate and then drain quickly. Fabric pots are easy to reuse too! Simply empty out the substrate, turn the bag inside out, let it dry, and brush off any remaining debris. They can even be put in a washing machine for a deep clean.

Terracotta pots are not commonly seen in hydroponics, but that doesn't mean they can't be used. Terracotta pots used in gardens are porous, allowing air and water to pass through the walls, traits similar to a fabric pot. Unlike a fabric pot, terracotta is heavy and fragile.

A 12" circular pot

Square pots are great for using space efficiently.

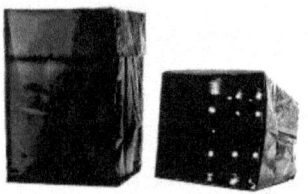

Low-cost grow bag

Flexible fabric pot

Classic terracotta pots

EQUIPMENT

Pot Color

Indoor growers often prefer white pots because they are reflective. White surfaces can help reflect light back into the plant canopy. White pots are also popular outdoors in warm climates because they tend to stay cooler than black pots. In cold environments, black pots may be advantageous to increase the temperature of the roots.

Right: A 2' × 4' tray stand with an attachable light support bar

Trays

Grow trays come in a various sizes, depths, and colors. The standard size options are 1' × 3½', 2' × 2', 2' × 4', 3' × 3', 4' × 4', 3' × 6', 4' × 6', 2' × 8', and 4' × 8'.

Reservoirs

Prefabricated reservoirs typically range from 20 to 115 gallons. Prefabricated plastic reservoirs are generally lightweight, lightproof, and available in kits that include lids and porthole covers.

A 20-gallon reservoir kit with lid and porthole cover

Shallow 4' × 4' tray. Shallow trays are generally about 3" to 4¼" deep. This is deep enough for top-drip gardens but may not be deep enough for other hydroponic garden designs.

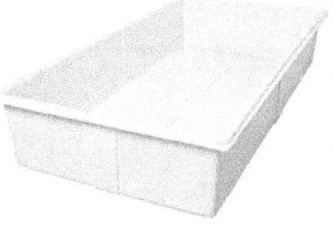

Deep 2' × 4' flood tray. Deep trays are generally between 7" and 8" deep. They are great for top drip, flood and drain, media beds, and floating raft gardens.

SUBSTRATES AND GROWING MEDIA

Hydroponic gardeners have a choice between high risk with fast growth and low risk with slower growth. The decision is primarily based on the porosity of the substrate and the ability of the roots to breathe. One of the most common mistakes made by new gardeners is overwatering. In a heavy soil or a poor-draining pot, an excess of water can drown the plant. Even though plants create oxygen, they also require oxygen. The roots especially need oxygen to perform a critical step in the uptake of water and nutrients. Without oxygen in the root zone, the plant cannot uptake water and the top of the plant starts to wilt. It is very counterintuitive to see a plant wilting when sitting in water. Excess water can also increase the chance of root disease.

Hydroponic gardeners can select substrates that hold very little water to increase the oxygen available to the roots, but this requires frequent or continuous irrigation. Some gardeners prefer to reduce the number of irrigation cycles required by using a substrate that holds more water. A substrate that holds more water adds some safety from power outages, pump failures, and other potential sources of delays in irrigation. A plant grown in a very porous substrate like clay pellets may be damaged or die after a couple of hours of no irrigation when grown in a warm, sunny environment. That same plant grown in coco coir, a substrate that holds a lot more water, may be able to go a couple of days without irrigation. Usually the trade-off for this increase in safety is slightly slower growth.

Substrates for Starting Seed

This book focuses on stone wool and polymer bound plugs made from peat moss and coco coir. There are many other options for start substrates, but these are two of the most beginner-friendly options because they have a good water-holding capacity yet are difficult to overwater.

Stone Wool Commonly called rock wool in the United States, stone wool is made by melting basaltic rocks and spinning the "rock lava" into fibers . . . similar to cotton candy but far less tasty. Disclaimer: Do not eat stone wool! Stone wool is one of the most popular hydroponic substrates in both commercial and hobby hydroponics. It has a nice balance of water retention and porosity, which makes it great for new hydroponic gardeners, who often tend to overwater plants. Some substrates are not very forgiving to overwatering, but stone wool in general will still function when overwatered—it might not have the best growth, but it usually won't kill the crop. Stone wool is available in blocks, slabs, and loose.

Coconut Coir Also called "coco" coir, coconut coir is a growing substrate made from the husks of coconuts. It is a popular substrate for both conventional and organic hydroponic growers. If coco is not properly washed during processing it can have high levels of salt, which may damage salt-sensitive crops. It is a good practice to wash any coco before using in a hydroponic garden to remove any remaining salts and wash out any tannins that may stain the reservoir or growing area.

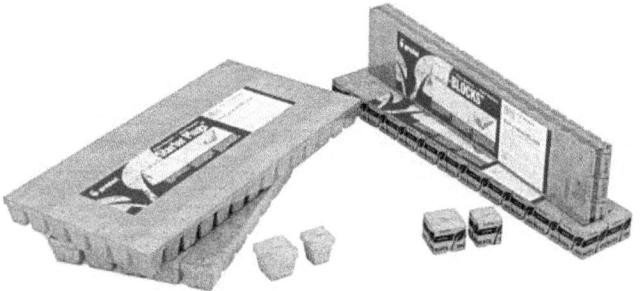
Stone wool seedling sheets

Polymer bound plug made of peat moss and coco coir fiber

Stone wool blocks

Fine coco peat

Coco chips

Perlite

Expanded clay pellets

Coco Peat A very fine coco, sometimes called coco pith or coco dust, coco peat can hold a lot of water. It is often used as a substitute for or mixed with peat moss. Coco peat, unlike peat moss, has a starting pH that is acceptable to most vegetables without needing to add lime. Coco peat, like peat moss, is often mixed with perlite or another porous substrate to lighten the mix and improve drainage.

Coco Chips A chunky coco, sometimes called coco croutons, coco chips have a good balance of water retention and drainage. They can be used as a standalone substrate or incorporated into a mix. When used as a standalone substrate, coco chips may need to be irrigated frequently, similar to growing in expanded clay pellets.

Perlite Perlite is made by heating volcanic rock until it pops like popcorn. This expanded rock is very lightweight and has many commercial applications, primarily in construction. Perlite is used in horticulture because it is cheap, organic, lightweight, and great for aerating heavy substrates like coco and peat. It comes in many sizes, from very fine to chunky, and can be used as a standalone hydroponic substrate.

Alternative Substrates

New hydroponic substrates are introduced every year. Some of these substrates are manufactured and some are repurposed by-products from other industries. The following substrates may not be as beginner friendly as the previously mentioned options but you may be able to find them for free. Each substrate has pros and cons along with specific best practices for their use; sometimes these best practices need to be developed for your specific crop and environment through trial and error.

Gravel: Performs similarly to expanded clay pellets.

Phenolic Foam: Oasis is one of the most popular brands for this substrate, which is a great alternative to stone wool seedling sheets.

Rice Hulls: Performs similarly to perlite.

River Rock: Performs similarly to expanded clay pellets.

Sawdust: Used as a substitute for peat and coco but can be very challenging.

Sand: Has a low water holding capacity and is heavy. Coarse builders' sand is the most commonly used sand for hydroponics.

Wood Bark: Popular in regions where it is easily accessible, but its successful use is very dependent on source and crop selection.

Peat/perlite mix

Peat Often called sphagnum peat or sphagnum peat moss, peat is partially decayed plant matter harvested from bogs. It has the ability to hold a lot of water yet is lightweight when dry, perfect for shipping. Peat generally has a very low pH around 4. It is often mixed with lime to raise the pH to a more acceptable range for vegetables. Peat can be used as a standalone substrate but it is more commonly used in a mix with perlite. Its availability is largely limited to North America, as the harvesting of this nonrenewable resource is severely restricted in most of the world.

Expanded Clay Pellets Sometimes called Hydroton after one of the original manufacturers, and also called LECA (which stands for light expanded clay aggregate), expanded clay pellets are pH neutral, inert, and one of the most popular substrates for both hydroponic and aquaponic media beds. The pores in the pellets can retain some water, yet it is difficult to overwater clay pellets because they are very quick to drain. Always rinse clay pellets before using them in a hydroponic garden.

Reusing Substrates

River rocks and clay pellets can be washed and reused, but other substrates are usually difficult to reuse in a hydroponic garden. Most hydroponic gardeners will mix used coco, peat, and perlite into their compost or directly into a traditional soil garden to improve water retention and drainage. Some hydroponic gardeners will also break up their used stone wool cubes and slabs into small pieces to mix into their traditional soil garden.

EQUIPMENT FOR GROWING INDOORS

Although hydroponic gardens do not need to be indoors, they are generally associated with indoor growing. Indoor growing may sound easier because there are fewer unpredictable events like bad weather and bugs, but indoor gardeners find there is a whole new list of challenges. Some of the most common mistakes for beginner indoor growers are lack of adequate airflow, poor temperature control, poor humidity control, and insufficient light. The proper equipment is essential to have a successful indoor garden.

Grow Tents

Grow tents provide an enclosed space for environmental controls, lights, and growing systems. Sometimes it can be difficult to create the proper growing climate indoors, or the ideal growing climate may not be the same climate you wish to have in the rest of your indoor space. Plants may like humidity ratios around 50 to 80 percent, but people often prefer to be in a humidity outside of that range. Grow tents are a great way to isolate the plants in an indoor environment. Besides keeping a separate climate from the rest of the indoor space, a grow tent can keep in the bright light required for plant growth. It is sometimes advantageous to run grow lights for 20 hours or more per day, but I imagine people living in a small studio apartment might not be too happy having a bright light on for 20 hours a day when they're trying to sleep. Grow tents can also allow gardeners to contain their pest-management strategies, whether that is spraying or releasing beneficial predator insects to protect the crop. Grow tents are perfect for renters who do not have the ability to modify a room for growing. I have lost a couple of security deposits through the years due to my excitement to create a grow room without considering that all the modifications I was making to the room might not make the landlord very happy. A grow tent can pay for itself when you consider the possible loss of a security deposit.

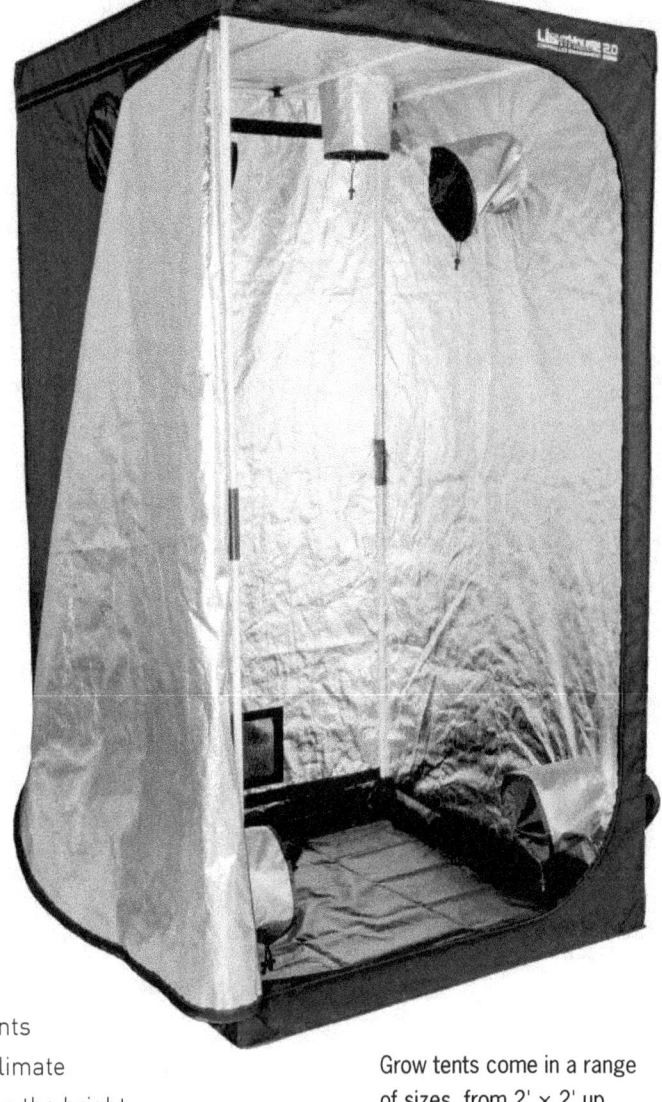

Grow tents come in a range of sizes, from 2' × 2' up to 10' × 20' (and bigger!). Ducting ports on grow tents make it easy to set up climate control and to hang lights. The tents' solid bottoms contain any possible leaks.

28 DIY HYDROPONIC GARDENS

Inline fans can be placed inside or outside a grow room.

A HEPA filter is capable of preventing insects, bacteria, fungi, and pollen from entering a grow tent.

Climate Control

Depending on the climate outside of a grow tent, a gardener may be able to control the inside climate with inline fans. Inline fans can be placed on the inside or outside of the grow tent. There are advantages to both of these setups. An exhaust fan placed inside a grow tent is great for containing crop odors because it makes sure any air leaving the grow tent passes through a carbon filter, which traps all odors. This setup is sometimes called a negative pressure grow room. Air passively flows into the grow room from ducting ports as the exhaust fan pushes air out.

Intake Fans An intake fan placed on the outside can save valuable grow space in the grow tent. In this setup, air is pushed into the grow tent and the exhaust passively escapes from ducting ports. This positive pressure grow room is great for pest management because the exhausting air makes it difficult for pests to get into the grow tent. A negative pressure grow tent can sometimes suck in pests near any possible openings, but a positive pressure grow tent will create an outward airflow that makes it difficult for pests to enter the grow tent from anywhere but the intake fan. There are many heavy-duty air intake filters, like the HEPA filter shown at left, that can prevent insects, bacteria, fungi, and pollen from entering a grow room.

Note: Grow lights can generate a lot of heat and it may be difficult to manage that heat with just ventilation fans. Air-conditioning units dedicated solely to the grow room are sometimes necessary for indoor gardeners using very powerful lights, using multiple lights, growing in warm climates, or growing temperature-sensitive crops.

Airflow

Inadequate airflow is one of the most common mistakes made by beginner indoor gardeners. Luckily, it is one of the easiest to remedy. Inadequate airflow may result in spindly, lanky plants, weak stems, tip burn, and an increased likelihood of fungal issues in the crop (i.e., powdery mildew). An easy trick to check whether a grow room has sufficient airflow is to look closely at the leaves to see if they are visibly moving. Visibly moving leaves is a sign that there should be sufficient airflow in that location, but there is always the potential for "dead air" spots in a grow room. Oscillating fans can help reduce the potential of these dead air spots.

GROW LIGHTS

Use of artificial light to grow plants can be traced back to the 1800s. Grow lights were not always a practical option, but in the past few decades there have been advances in lighting technology that have made the use of grow lights accessible to hobby gardeners with gardens of any size. There are many lighting options, but not all are well suited for your specific growing area; please review the many options before purchasing a grow light to avoid a potentially costly mistake.

Fluorescent These are probably the most beginner-friendly grow lights. They are also widely available and relatively cheap compared to other grow lights.

Compact fluorescent grow light

T5 fluorescent grow light

A powerful 1000-watt double-ended (DE) HPS light is great for greenhouses and grow rooms with high ceilings.

A 150-watt HPS light is great for grow tents and small growing areas that require high light levels.

A 315-watt ceramic MH grow light

They consume minimal electricity and are available in several spectrums, so you can grow a wide range of crops. They may not be ideal for crops that require intense light, such as peppers. Because they emit only small amounts of heat, they can be placed very close to the crop—within a couple of inches—which makes them great for seedlings and young plants.

High Pressure Sodium (HPS) These are one of the cheapest options for high-intensity lighting. HPS lights can generate a lot of heat, which is good in cold environments but difficult to manage indoors without proper ventilation and/or air-conditioning. They often are used for flowering crops indoors and are great for providing supplemental light in greenhouses. Usually they are positioned a few feet above a crop.

Metal Halide (MH) and Ceramic Metal Halide (CMH) MH and CMH are high-intensity lighting options often used for vegetative stages but are also capable of growing flowering crops. Light from MH bulbs appears blue and many gardeners find it pleasant to work under. The blue dominant light is also good for encouraging compact growth. Most grow light manufacturers are focusing production on the newer, more efficient CMH bulbs instead of the traditional MH bulbs.

Light Emitting Diodes (LEDs) LEDs are very efficient, using minimal electricity to generate a lot of light. They produce very little heat relative to their light output and are available in many different configurations, some suitable for mounting high above the crop and some suitable for placing very close to the crop. LEDs come in many different colors, which can greatly affect plant growth. The white LEDs are less efficient but more pleasant to work under than red and blue LEDS, which cast a purple light that is great for growing plants but some growers find aesthetically displeasing.

Additional Light Options Other options include induction lights, plasma lights, and lasers, as well as many other lighting technologies besides the ones listed above. Some of these newer lighting options can be very expensive and may not be well suited for the beginning hydroponic gardener. Lighting technology advances quickly, however, and many of these options may soon be the standard, just as LED lighting is quickly moving to the forefront among the traditional HPS, MH, and fluorescent lighting options.

Lighting Accessories

Hangers Lights can be hung with rope, cable, or chain or mounted directly to a crossbeam or the ceiling. Rope ratchets are very popular with indoor gardeners because they make moving lights up and down very easy.

Grow Room Glasses Some gardeners find it unpleasant to work under the orange light of HPS or the purple light of LED grow lights. Glasses with tinted lenses designed specifically for these light sources are a great way to make it more pleasant to work with these grow lights.

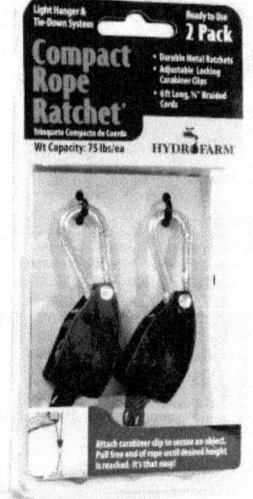

Rope ratchet for hanging grow lights

Grow room glasses made specifically to reduce the orange color produced by HPS grow lights

LED light bars in 1', 2', and 4' lengths

PEST-MANAGEMENT PRODUCTS AND EQUIPMENT

Hydroponics can have some impact on pest pressure but the bigger factor on pest pressure is environment. Hydroponic systems are often used in controlled environments like greenhouses or indoors. Growing in a controlled environment gives the gardener the potential to completely exclude pests from the crop, but achieving this can be very difficult. Generally, there are some pests that get into the garden and once they get in they can quickly multiply. A controlled environment garden is great for both plants and pests. When a bug gets into an indoor garden it finds itself in an environment with perfect weather and no predators . . . pretty much pest heaven. There are several tactics for controlling pests, but often the best defense is prevention. Most of the methods for pest management can be used in a controlled environment or outdoors.

Preventive Methods

Preventive methods include pest-exclusion techniques like positive pressure grow rooms and HEPA intake filters, described earlier in the Equipment for Growing Indoors section. Another exclusion practice is wearing clean clothes before entering an indoor grow room to avoid carrying in pests from outside. Preventive methods also include selecting plant varieties that are appropriate for the growing environment and have disease resistance, and giving these plants the water and nutrients they need to be healthy enough to resist diseases.

Physical If preventive practices don't keep pests out and a pest is found in the garden, physical pest-management practices are a great, nontoxic method for controlling pests. My favorite physical pest-management technique is using a vacuum to remove any bugs I spot. Additional physical pest-management techniques are removing entire plants and using sticky traps. Sticky traps are also used for monitoring pest levels.

Biological Biological pest management involves the use of predators, parasites, and diseases to control pest populations. One of the most popular biological pest-management strategies for gardeners is the release of ladybugs. Biological pest-management may not completely eradicate a pest population, but it usually can keep the pest population in check.

Organic Pesticides Organic pesticides are generally considered less toxic than conventional/synthetic pesticides, but they still should be used cautiously. Always check the label on pesticides, even organic ones, to see whether there is any recommended personal protection equipment like gloves, goggles, or a respirator. Most farms are able to completely manage pests using only organic pesticides.

Conventional Pesticides Conventional, or synthetic, pesticides are rarely required by home gardeners. Even commercial farms that are not certified organic will very

Yellow and blue sticky traps

Praying mantis eggs

Small portable vacuum

often solely use organic pesticides because they are very effective. Most of the conventional pesticides available to gardeners are just as safe as organic pesticides when used properly.

Pest-Management Tools

This is by no means a comprehensive list of pest-management tools, just a few of my favorite methods for managing pests in my garden.

Vacuum This is a pesticide-free method of removing insects.

Sticky Traps Yellow sticky traps are generally used to trap and monitor aphids, whiteflies, and fungus gnats. Blue sticky traps are generally used to trap and monitor thrips.

Beneficial Insects Successfully managing pests with natural predators can be tricky. There are many beneficial insect options; the following are a few of the most commonly used predators in home hydroponic gardens. Grow room climate and the presence of spray residues can impact the effectiveness of beneficial insects.

- Lacewing (*Chrysoperla carnea*): Primarily used to control aphids but also may be effective for controlling whiteflies and thrips.
- Ladybug (*Coccinella septempunctata*): Used to control aphids.
- Praying mantis (*Tenodera sinensis*): Eats a wide range of insects, including aphids.
- Predatory mite (*Neoseiulus cucumeris*): Used to control thrips and spider mites.
- Swirski mite (*Amblyseius swirskii*): Used to control thrips.

Essential Oils Essential oils can be very effective for killing or repelling pests like mites, thrips, and aphids. A few of the more commonly used essential oils are garlic, clove, mint, thyme, rosemary, and cinnamon.

Neem Oil An organic pesticide derived from the neem tree, this oil can repel insects and potentially kill them if applied directly onto the pest.

 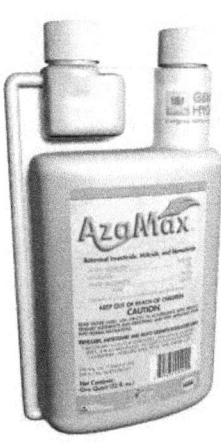  

Organic pesticide that includes garlic and clove oil

An organic pesticide containing azadirachtin

Bti can be used to control fungus gnats in hydroponic systems.

Insecticidal soap

Azadirachtin An extract made from Neem seeds that concentrates one of the most potent insecticidal compounds found in Neem oil. Azadirachtin repels insects similar to Neem oil, but it also disrupts the molting process in many pests. Azadirachtin keeps pests in their juvenile stage, preventing them from reaching adulthood and reproducing.

Organic Pyrethrins An organic pesticide derived from the chrysanthemum flower. One of the most powerful organic pesticides, it is capable of quickly killing most insects when applied at a strong concentration. Pyrethrins may potentially kill beneficial insects too.

Bacillus thuringiensis (Bt) A beneficial microbe primarily used to manage caterpillars.

Bacillus thuringiensis subspecies *israelensis* (Bti) A subspecies of Bt that can provide some biological control of fungus gnats.

Soap Insecticidal soaps, or even dish soap, can be very effective for controlling whiteflies and aphids.

Spinosad An organic pesticide derived from the bacterium *Saccharopolyspora spinosa*. Effective for controlling thrips and caterpillars.

Streptomyces lydicus A beneficial microbe effective against root rot and foliar fungi.

Potassium Bicarbonate A very effective organic fungicide capable of quickly knocking down powdery mildew issues. May also be used to raise pH in hydroponic systems.

Sodium Bicarbonate (baking soda) Very similar to potassium bicarbonate in effectiveness against powdery mildew. Plants can tolerate some sodium, but they will show nutrient toxicity or deficiency symptoms when exposed to excessive amounts. Many gardeners are able to use sodium bicarbonate to effectively control powdery mildew and other foliar fungi.

METERS

A variety of meters are employed in most hydroponic systems to monitor and help regulate the growing environment. The meters measure levels such as nutrient concentration and balance, pH balance, temperature, and light intensity. Some work automatically and others require the hydroponic gardener to create and uphold a regular monitoring program.

Electrical Conductivity (EC)

EC meters are used to estimate the fertilizer concentration in a nutrient solution. EC meters are not critical for growing hydroponically but they are definitely one of the most helpful tools. They are available in many shapes from many companies and in many price ranges. There are some very low-cost options available that I've seen work for growers and hold up for years. I personally am not always the most gentle with my equipment and prefer a robust meter that can tolerate some abuse. A truncheon EC meter is currently my go-to choice because it does not require calibration, is waterproof, and can handle abuse.

pH

Although pH meters are not critical for growing hydroponically, they are great for helping hydroponic gardeners understand the state of their nutrient solution. Understanding the pH of the nutrient solution is also useful when trying to diagnose potential nutrient deficiencies. However, pH meters are a bit more temperamental than EC meters and should be handled with care and well maintained or they can quickly become inaccurate or simply break. Always read the instructions on a pH probe to ensure you correctly calibrate it and perform the regular maintenance required to keep the probe accurate. There is a lot of variation between pH probes on the market and they are not all equal. I've tested many pH meters and currently my favorite is the Bluelab pH Pen.

The pH can also be tested with an indicator solution. These indicator solutions often come as part of a pH control kit that includes pH up and pH down solutions. A pH indicator solution can give an approximate pH but it will never be as accurate as a pH meter. Many new hydroponic growers start with a pH control kit with a pH indicator solution because it is an affordable option that can get the job done.

Light Intensity

Guessing light intensity is incredibly difficult, if not impossible. There are many meters available to help gardeners monitor their light levels to determine whether they are sufficient, adequate, or too intense for their specific crop.

Lux Meter Lux meters are generally the most affordable meter for measuring light intensity but not the most ideal. Lux meters measure light on a scale specific to

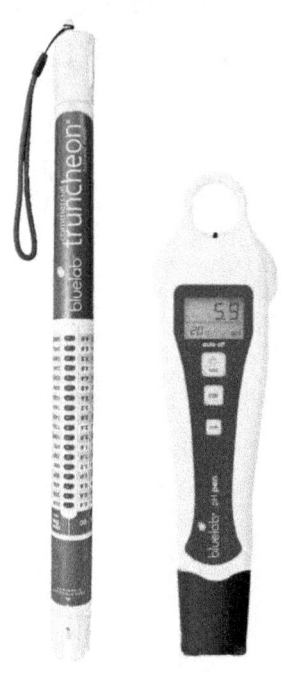

Bluelab truncheon meter (left) and Bluelab pH Pen (right)

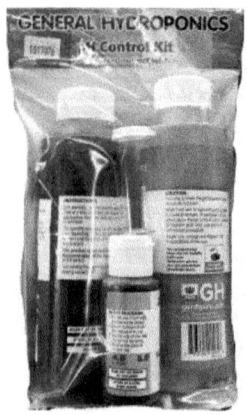

A pH control kit with pH indicator solution, pH up and pH down

Converting from Lux to PPFD

Multiply a lux reading by the following conversion factors to obtain an approximate PPFD (µmol/m2/s):

Light Source	SE HPS	DE HPS	Fluorescent	MH	CMH (4200K)	CMH (3100K)	Sunlight
Conversion Factor	0.012	0.013	0.014	0.014	0.015	0.017	0.019

Example: A reading of 10,000 lux measured under a metal halide (MH) lamp would be converted to PPFD by multiplying 10,000 lux by the conversion factor 0.014 to get an approximate PPFD of 140 µmol/m2/s.

how light is perceived by the human eye. The human eye is most sensitive to green and yellow, whereas plants are most sensitive to blue and red. Most of the light level recommendations for crops are not based on lux; they instead use photosynthetic photon flux density (PPFD), which is measured by photosynthetically active radiation (PAR) meters.

PAR Meter PAR is an acronym for photosynthetically active radiation. PAR light falls within a wavelength range that is visible to plants and that plants can use to power photosynthesis. PPFD is an acronym for photosynthetic photon flux density. PPFD measures how many photosynthetically active photons, measured in µmol, are landing in a square meter (m2) each second (s); the unit used is µmol/m2/s. PAR meters are the preferred meter for measuring light intensity in a horticultural environment but they tend to be more expensive than lux meters.

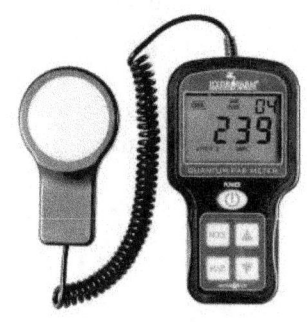

Daily Light Integral (DLI) Meter A PPFD measurement shows light intensity per square meter per second. A DLI measurement shows the light intensity delivered per square meter per day. DLI is a total of all the PPFD readings for each second throughout the day. The unit used is mol/m2/d. DLI does not use µmol because the number would be huge: 1 mol is 1,000,000 µmol. DLI is useful because it measures the light a plant has access to throughout the day, not just at a single moment. Indoors it is fairly easy to calculate the DLI with a single PPFD measurement because the light levels do not fluctuate throughout the day as they do outdoors. For example, a PPFD reading indoors of 100 µmol/m2/s is converted to DLI with the following steps:

DLI meter that measures total light delivered in 24 hours using mol/m2/day

1. Multiply PPFD by 60 seconds to get total µmol per m2 per minute.
   Example: 100 µmol/m2/s × 60 seconds = 6000 µmol/m2/minute
2. Multiply this number by 60 minutes to get µmol per m2 per hour.
   Example: 6000 µmol/m2/minute × 60 minutes = 360,000 µmol/m2/hour
3. Multiply this number by the number of hours the lights are on; in this example, the lights are on for 20 hours a day.
   Example: 360,000 µmol/m2/hour × 20 hours = 7,200,000 µmol/m2/day
4. Lastly, divide by 1,000,000 to convert µmol to mol.
   Example: 7,200,000/1,000,000 = 7.2 mol/m2/day

Outdoors a DLI can be measured using a DLI meter. A DLI meter is designed to total the PPFD measurements throughout the day to generate a DLI reading in mol/m2/day.

The reference chart below is based on personal observations and should only be considered a general recommendation.

Crop	Target DLI Range
Microgreens	6–12 mol/m2/day
Leafy Greens	12–30 (generally 17–25) mol/m2/day
Flowering Crops	17–45 (generally 25–35) mol/m2/day

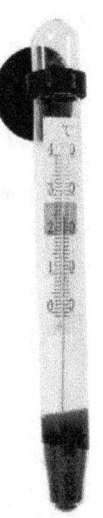

Floating thermometer for monitoring water temperature

Temperature and Humidity Monitoring Equipment

A simple aquarium thermometer is often sufficient for monitoring temperature in a hydroponic reservoir. The target water temperature for most hydroponic crops is 65° to 70°F but it is definitely possible to grow healthy crops outside of this range. Most pH and EC meters also measure water temperature. Water temperature affects the EC and pH readings, so these meters must factor in the water temperature before giving an accurate reading.

A thermometer with a hygrometer that records daily high and low points is great for monitoring conditions in a greenhouse or grow room. Gardeners may spend a lot of time with their plants, but they can't be there all the time; a thermometer/hygrometer that monitors the high and low points enables gardeners to make adjustments to day or night temperatures that they might not see when they're in the garden.

3
HYDROPONIC GROWING SYSTEMS

DIY HYDROPONIC SYSTEMS ARE A great way to create a custom garden catered to your location, crop, and desired aesthetics. Many beginning hydroponic growers decide to build their own systems because of the cost of retail systems, but from personal experience, I have found building DIY systems may not always be the cheapest option, especially if there are mistakes in the system design. I love creating original systems built for specific locations, *but* creating original systems can often involve a lot of expensive mistakes. I've purchased items that don't fit, or wouldn't hold after I glued them into place, or broke, or didn't provide enough light, or didn't provide enough drainage . . .

In the end, I learned a lot from my mistakes and I'm thankful for that, but I also spent a lot of money learning and making those mistakes. The following systems pull from my experience, and my mistakes, to save you time and money.

HOW TO CHOOSE A SYSTEM

Choosing which hydroponic system to install in your home requires you to take many variables into account and to decide which matters most to you. Among them are crop selection, preferred location of the hydroponic garden, maintenance demands, ease of use, and the amount of maintenance and upkeep each requires. Initial cost is important too, of course, as is the cost for energy consumption, inputs, and other ongoing maintenance expenses.

Choosing a System by Crop

Knowing what you want to grow should be the first consideration when choosing a hydroponic system. There are systems that can grow a wide range of crops (i.e., flood and drain) and there are some systems that work best for crops with specific growth habits. One of the first systems in this chapter is a hydroponic

bottle garden. This system works great for leafy green crops like lettuce and basil, but is horrible for larger crops like tomatoes. You should also consider the diversity of crops you want to grow. Do you want to grow crops with a wide range of nutrient requirements and desired pH ranges? The best option sometimes is to have multiple systems. The best part about growing plants is that they are generally easy to replace! Experiment with new crops and learn from experience. I offer a lot of guidelines in this chapter and useful crop selection notes in the appendix, but these guidelines are not meant to prevent you from experimenting. Many crops will grow in conditions outside of their ideal range. Plants are far more tolerant than we give them credit for. Don't be afraid to fail; there are always more seeds to plant!

Degree of difficulty is a primary consideration when choosing a hydroponic system. This recirculating trough system is relatively simple to make but requires regular monitoring and maintenance.

Choosing a System by Location

There are hydroponic systems for growing lettuce in space! No matter your location, there is potential to grow plants hydroponically. I even have a hydroponic garden in my RV. For each of the systems listed in this chapter I give location suggestions. Many of these systems can be modified for indoors, outdoors, small spaces, or large ones.

Choosing a System by Maintenance Requirements

The ratio of plants to volume of water is generally the biggest factor for estimating maintenance requirements. A system with a small reservoir and a lot of plants will need frequent maintenance because the grower will need to add water and amend the reservoir with fertilizer as the plants quickly reduce the water level in the reservoir.

Systems with a high plant-to-water ratio also tend to accumulate an imbalanced ratio of nutrients and require frequent full system flushes. Another factor that will influence maintenance requirement is crop selection. Crops like tomatoes, peppers, and cucumbers may require trellising and pruning depending on variety. Some crops grow very quickly and need to be replaced often, like microgreens, and they'll require a lot of work because they need to be seeded and harvested weekly.

Choosing a System by Difficulty

Although I would never stop someone from starting with an advanced hydroponic system, I am aware that many gardeners want to succeed from the start. Difficult-to-use systems may have a learning curve. I love learning! You might too. But you also might value simplicity and using a hydroponic system that has minimal moving parts and few opportunities for failure.

Bottle Hydroponics, Floating Rafts, and Wicking Beds are great beginner-friendly systems that don't require electricity. Media Beds and Flood and Drain are also beginner friendly, but they have some moving parts that require electricity. Nutrient Film Technique, Top Drip, Aeroponics, and Vertical Gardens are not terribly difficult, but they might not be the best option for a first-time hydroponic gardener. The difficulty of using a system is a personal opinion and it's possible you might find some of the less beginner-friendly systems easiest to use . . . The only way to find out is to build them all!

Featured DIY Hydroponic Systems

On the following pages you will see many of my favorite DIY hydroponic systems explained and built before your eyes. Along the way I have tried to give reasons why you might choose one system over another. Before you decide which one (or ones) you want to make for yourself, I suggest that you read through all the builds so you fully understand the pluses, minuses, and degree of difficulty of each system.

- BOTTLE HYDROPONICS
- FLOATING RAFTS
- WICKING BED
- NUTRIENT FILM TECHNIQUE (NFT)
- TOP DRIP SYSTEM
- MEDIA BEDS
- FLOOD AND DRAIN
- AEROPONICS
- VERTICAL GARDENS

GROWING SYSTEM

BOTTLE HYDROPONICS

A QUICK GOOGLE SEARCH OF "bottle hydroponics" will reveal the many ways to use bottles in hydroponics. Unfortunately, most of these are either complicated, ugly, or both. These simple hydroponic bottles are easy to build, low cost, low maintenance, require no electricity, and look great.

Hydroponic systems don't get much simpler than bottle hydroponics.

- **Suitable Locations:** Indoors, outdoors, or greenhouse
- **Size:** Small
- **Growing Media:** Stone wool
- **Electrical:** Not required
- **Crops:** Leafy greens and herbs

Kratky Method and Aeration

The Kratky method is the easiest hydroponic growing technique. No pumps, no complex irrigation systems . . . just plants sitting in water. Most of the early hydroponic research focused on static water systems like the Kratky method. These systems worked, but, as scientists tend to do, they kept experimenting and eventually found there was an increase in plant growth rate when the nutrient solution was aerated. This discovery spurred the development of circulating hydroponic systems with increased aeration, like nutrient film technique (NFT) and top drip irrigation.

Now most of the hydroponic research is focused on these circulating systems, but there are still horticulturists experimenting with static noncirculating hydroponics. One of the most vocal proponents of noncirculating hydroponics is Dr. Bernard Kratky of the University of Hawaii. He has done so much to continue the development of noncirculating hydroponics that his name has become synonymous with the technique . . . the Kratky method.

Crops

The Kratky method has been successfully used to grow a wide range of crops, from leafy greens like lettuce to flowering crops like tomatoes and potatoes. Most hydroponic gardeners prefer to grow leafy greens and herbs with the Kratky method because the larger crops may struggle with inadequate oxygen levels in their root

Red butterhead lettuce, Italian basil, and Thai basil grown in a hydroponic bottle garden.

It is possible to grow in a clear, unpainted bottle, but it may require frequent cleaning to remove algae buildup.

zone. The root zone oxygen demand for crops like lettuce is far less than it is for tomatoes.

The crops that are best for bottle hydroponics stay short or grow upright to mitigate the possibility of the system getting too top-heavy and falling over. Basil, kale, Swiss chard, and lettuce are my favorites for bottle hydroponics, but I've also had success with cilantro, dill, and other herbs.

Locations

The Kratky method can be used outdoors, indoors, or in a greenhouse. It may be difficult to use a Kratky-style garden outdoors in areas with heavy rainfall because the nutrient solution may be quickly diluted or washed away. Kratky-style gardens are great for off-grid gardens that do not have access to electricity.

The appropriate locations for bottle hydroponics are more limited. The black paint used in this build could lead to excessive heat buildup in the root zone. If you want to use bottle hydroponics outdoors you'll want to use a light-colored paint for areas with warm climates. My favorite way to use bottle hydroponic systems outdoors is with a wall-mounted bottle holder on a porch. This keeps the bottles in a semi-shaded area and it looks awesome. Indoors, bottle hydroponics can be placed nearly anywhere—a kitchen counter, desk, windowsill, or even wall mounted in a hallway with a grow light above . . . the only limiting factor when placing a bottle hydroponic system indoors is access to light.

HOW TO BUILD A BOTTLE HYDROPONIC GARDEN

This hydroponic bottle is the easiest hydroponic garden in this book and a great first step into hydroponics. I love building this system with kids from ages 8 to 18 when I do school visits. There are so many ways to customize the bottle with different paints and decorations, so it is easy to make this garden your own. To simplify the assembly of this system, you may wish to find a bottle with an opaque exterior to skip the painting process.

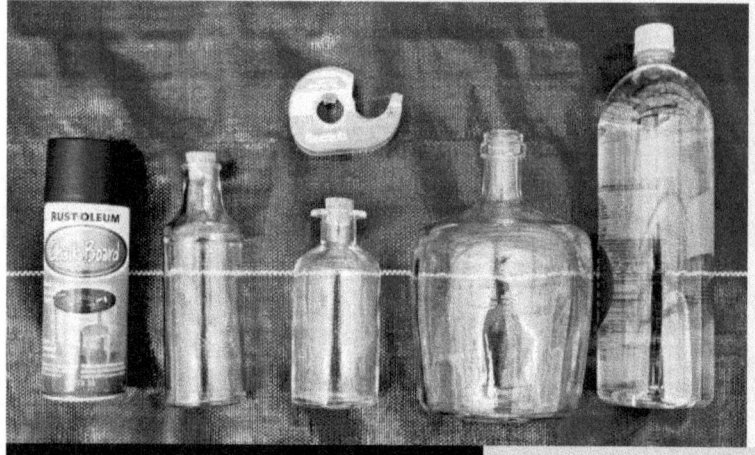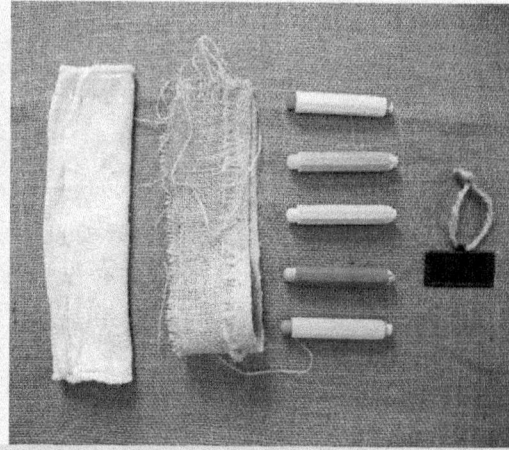

MATERIALS & TOOLS (as shown)

Required
Glass or plastic bottle
Stone wool seedling plug sized for bottle opening
Fertilizer

Optional
Scotch tape
Stake for mounting while painting
Blackboard spray paint
Chalk
Burlap or cloth
Bottle label
Grow light

Optional Tools
Scissors
Funnel
Hot glue gun

Bottle Preparation

The bottle selection is the most critical decision in this build. The ideal bottle has a short neck so the plug can quickly access the main body of the bottle. If possible, select a wide bottle. Wide bottles maintain their water level longer, giving the roots more opportunity to grow into the nutrient solution before the water level drops due to evapotranspiration. The following steps are for clear bottles, so please skip to the next section if using a nontransparent bottle.

1. Remove any labels from the bottle.
2. Add a strip of tape along the side. This will be removed later to create a viewing window for the roots. Fold the end of the tape strip on the bottom of the bottle to make removal easier after painting.

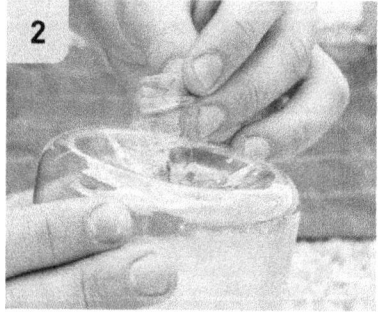

3. My preferred method for painting bottles is putting them on a stake, but I've also had success dipping bottles in paint. Make sure there are enough coats of paint that light will not penetrate inside the bottle.
4. Remove the tape strip once the paint dries.
5. It is best to do any chalk art at this point before filling the bottle with water.

Plug Selection

Either select a plug that fits snugly in the neck of the bottle or select a bottle with an opening suitable to your plugs. It is possible to cut a stone wool plug to fit a smaller bottle but this can potentially damage the seedling's roots.

6. The plug should be wide enough to hold itself firmly in the opening of the bottle.
7. Growing more seedlings than needed allows you greater options to select only the best seedlings for your hydroponic bottle.

Nutrient Solution and Transplanting

It is important to use a fertilizer designed for hydroponic gardens. In this garden I used FloraNova Grow, but there are many other options. Check out the Plant Nutrition chapter to learn more about hydroponic fertilizer options.

8   Mix fertilizer with water using the recommended rates listed on the fertilizer bottle or bag. Mix the water and fertilizer in a separate container to make it easy to check if the fertilizer has fully dissolved. Extra nutrient solution may be saved for a couple weeks if stored in an airtight container in a dark, cool environment.

9   Fully fill the bottle with nutrient solution. There is potential for some overflow when the seedling is inserted, but this is preferable to too little water.

10 If you do not plan on using a wicking strip (see next page), the seedling can now be transplanted into the bottle. The bottom of the plug should be sitting in nutrient solution; if needed, add more nutrient solution to make sure the plug is fully saturated. Make sure the bottle is completely full if you are not using a wicking strip because the plug will need access to the nutrient solution for several days until it can grow roots deep into the nutrient solution. The plug should not be placed too deep into the neck of the bottle. You will need to remove the plug to refill the bottle, so keep enough of the plug outside of the bottle to make removal easy in the future.

11 Check to see if the plug is dry during the first week. Depending on crop selection and environment, you may need to add more nutrient solution in the first few days to give your plant a chance to grow roots long enough to pull up water from the bottle. A wicking strip is not necessary, but it will help reduce the potential of your seedling drying out in the first week.

Leave enough stone wool above the neck of the bottle to make plug removal easy when refilling the bottle.

Optional Wicking Strip

A wicking strip is useful in bottles that are tall and skinny or with crops that grow slowly. The following steps use a clear bottle for demonstration purposes, but using a clear bottle for growing a crop is not recommended because it will encourage algae growth.

12. Cut burlap or cloth into a strip long enough to reach the bottom of the bottle and approximately as wide as the seedling plug (usually 1" to 2" wide).
13. String the wicking strip through the bottle opening.
14. Use the seedling plug to hold the wicking strip in place.
15. Leave enough stone wool exposed to make removal easy when refilling the bottle with nutrient solution.
16. A funnel can make it possible to refill the bottle without fully removing the stone wool plug. This can help reduce the potential of damaging roots when removing and reinserting a plug with a developed root system.
17. If not using a funnel, very carefully lift the plug out of the bottle.
18. Fill the bottle with nutrient solution. For young plants with poorly developed roots, it is best to fill to nearly the top of the bottle. For older plants with larger root systems, it is best to fill to three-fourths full so the roots have access to a balance of air and nutrient solution.

Very carefully reinsert the plug back into the bottle after refilling. Make sure the roots are submerged in the nutrient solution.

Maintenance

Most of the crops that are appropriate for hydroponic bottles are fast growing and may not require a lot of maintenance during their growth cycle. It is possible to grow longer-term crops that have multiple harvests, such as basil, as long as the bottle is kept over half full with nutrient solution. It is a good practice to clean out the bottle and refill with fresh nutrient solution every month to avoid nutrient imbalances in the solution.

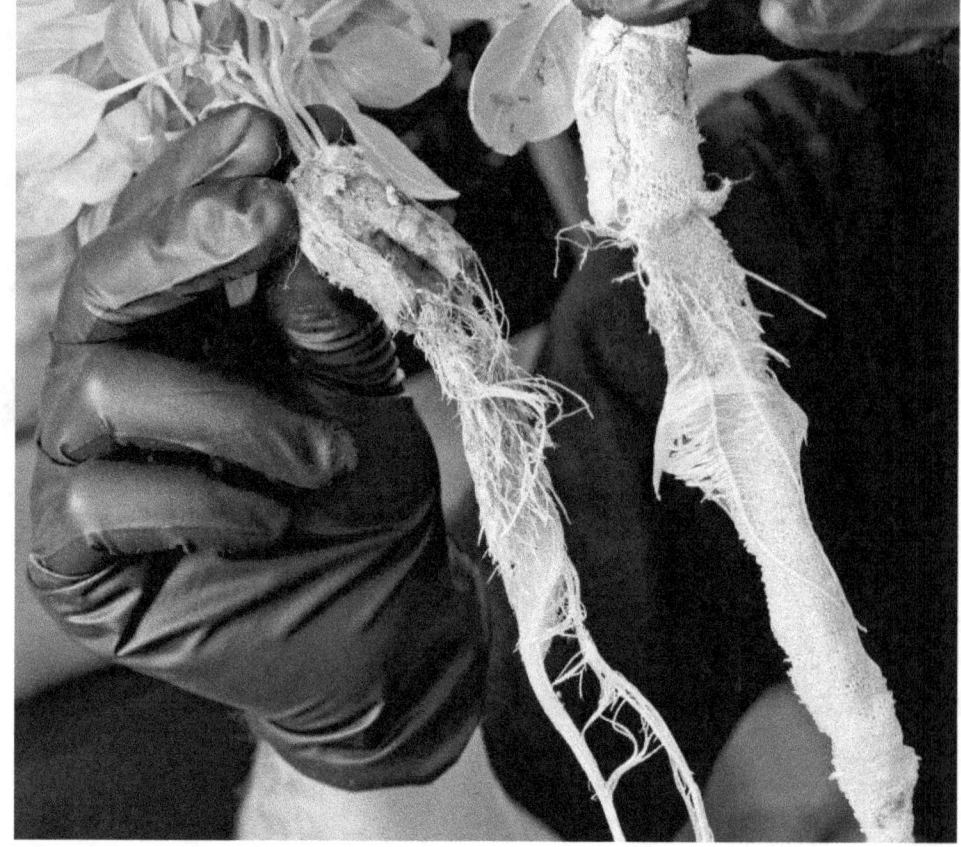

Some crops, like the basil on the left, can send roots into the nutrient solution faster than the nutrient solution is lost due to evapotranspiration. These crops may not require a wicking strip. Other crops, like the heirloom romaine lettuce on the right, grow slowly and greatly benefit from a wicking strip to assist with water uptake.

Additional Options

Decorations Besides chalk art, I like to decorate my hydroponic bottles with name tags and burlap scarfs. Covering the neck of the bottle with a scarf can help hide any potential algae growth on the surface of the seedling plug. I use a hot glue gun to secure burlap on the neck of the bottle.

Lighting Hydroponic bottle gardens are best suited for indoors. They can be placed on a windowsill and receive natural light or placed under a grow light. Hydroponic bottles under a small grow light are a great addition to a work desk.

Troubleshooting

Plants are wilting

- Check water level and add additional nutrient solution if water level is low.
- Water temperature or air temperature may be too high.
- Try adding wicking strip if roots are not reaching nutrient solution.

Plug is falling into bottle

- Try wrapping plug in cloth or burlap to create a snugger fit into neck of bottle.
- Place plug so more stone wool is exposed above bottle opening.

Plant is growing slowly or poorly

- The crop selection may not be appropriate for hydroponic bottle garden.
- Crop may not be receiving enough light.
- Use a fertilizer designed for hydroponics.

GROWING SYSTEM

FLOATING RAFTS

Floating raft hydroponics is a subtype of deep water culture (DWC) hydroponics. Most traditional DWC systems hold the plant at a set height and the nutrient solution is refilled to maintain contact with the roots. Floating raft hydroponics allows the plant to remain in contact with the nutrient solution even as the water level drops. Floating raft systems require very little labor and maintenance. It is common to not perform any maintenance on the system, not even adding water, from transplant to harvest when growing leafy greens.

CROPS

Floating raft hydroponics has been used for large flowering crops like tomatoes but it is most appropriate for shorter crops with lower oxygen requirements in their root zone. Traditional DWC systems are great for these larger flowering crops because they create space for the roots to access air and they often use air pumps to heavily aerate the nutrient solution.

I've trialed hundreds of crops in floating rafts and I'm amazed at the versatility of this growing method. The sidebar on the next page lists some crops that can be grown in floating rafts.

In a floating raft, the buoyant planting platform actually floats on the nutrient solution.

- **Suitable Locations:** Indoors, outdoors, or greenhouse
- **Size:** Small to large
- **Growing Media:** Stone wool seedling cubes
- **Electrical:** Optional
- **Crops:** Leafy greens and herbs

Colorful Swiss chard roots make chard a very fun plant to grow in a floating raft garden.

Great
- Basil
- Celery/celeriac
- Chives
- Dill
- Fennel
- Kale
- Lettuce
- Mustard greens
- Nasturtium
- Sorrel
- Swiss chard
- Watercress

Not Optimal, but Possible
- Arugula
- Beets
- Carrots
- Cilantro
- Dwarf peppers
- Dwarf tomato
- Marigolds
- Mint
- Parsley
- Radishes
- Spinach
- Strawberries

LOCATIONS

Floating raft gardens can be placed indoors, outdoors, or in a greenhouse. Outdoors they may have problems if not protected from rain. The rainwater will dilute the nutrient solution and wash away the nutrients. Floating raft systems often hold a lot of water, and this might not be ideal indoors. If the system is not properly placed or built there could be potential for leaks and flooding indoors. Water is very heavy too, so floating raft systems should not be installed on floors with weight limitations.

Floating raft systems benefit from aeration. but for most crops it is not necessary. I've grown beautiful heads of lettuce and basil in floating raft gardens with no aeration in 90°F weather. These crops will benefit from aeration, often with faster growth and reduced potential for root diseases and nutrient issues, but floating raft gardens can thrive without electricity. There are affordable options for solar-powered air pumps if you wish to keep your floating raft garden off-grid yet receive the benefits of aeration.

SIZING

Floating raft systems can be designed for countertops or large fields. Very small floating rafts have the potential of getting unstable when supporting large, top-heavy crops, but they are great for leafy greens. Large rafts are capable of holding more weight, but they should be handled with care when they are holding heavy mature crops because they can break under the weight when lifted out of the reservoir. Most rafts are made from 2 × 4-foot foam boards or 4 × 8-foot foam boards cut in half. Most floating raft gardens are thus rectangular with widths in increments of 2 feet and lengths in increments of 4 feet. Don't feel limited to rectangles, though; these foam boards can be cut to any shape. I've seen circular kiddie pools transformed into floating raft gardens with foam boards cut to size.

HOW TO BUILD A FLOATING RAFT GARDEN

This design can be used as a model for smaller or larger floating raft gardens. No matter the size there are several steps that will remain the same, including adding a liner and building rafts. You may wish to use an existing container, like a kiddie pool, as your reservoir instead of building one, in which case you can simply skip ahead to building the raft. This design worked great for me but there are many ways to add your own spin to it. I painted this garden white because it is in a greenhouse that can get very hot and I wanted to do everything possible to prevent the nutrient solution from getting extremely hot (over 95°F). You may wish to use a darker color if your garden will be placed indoors or in a cooler environment.

MATERIALS & TOOLS

Reservoir
- 4   2 × 12" × 8' lumber
- 2   1 × 2" × 8' furring strip board
- 1 gal.   White water-based latex primer, sealer, and stain blocker (KILZ 2 LATEX)
- 1 lb.   #10 × 2½" exterior screws
- 1 lb.   #8 × 1¼" exterior screws
- 1   6 × 100' black 6 mil. plastic sheeting

Safety Equipment
- Work gloves
- Eye protection

Raft
- 1   1" × 4 × 8' insulation foam board
- 18   2" net pot

Optional
- 18–72   2" net pots (additional pots to increase planting density)
- 1   Air pump with air stones
- 1   Small water pump with venturi attachment

Tools
- Circular saw
- Paint roller and/or paintbrush
- Rafter square
- Level
- Drill
- Drill bits matching screws
- Staple gun and staples
- Heavy-duty scissors
- Razor blade knife
- Sawhorses with clamps
- Tape measure
- Permanent marker
- 2" hole drill bit (if using net pots)

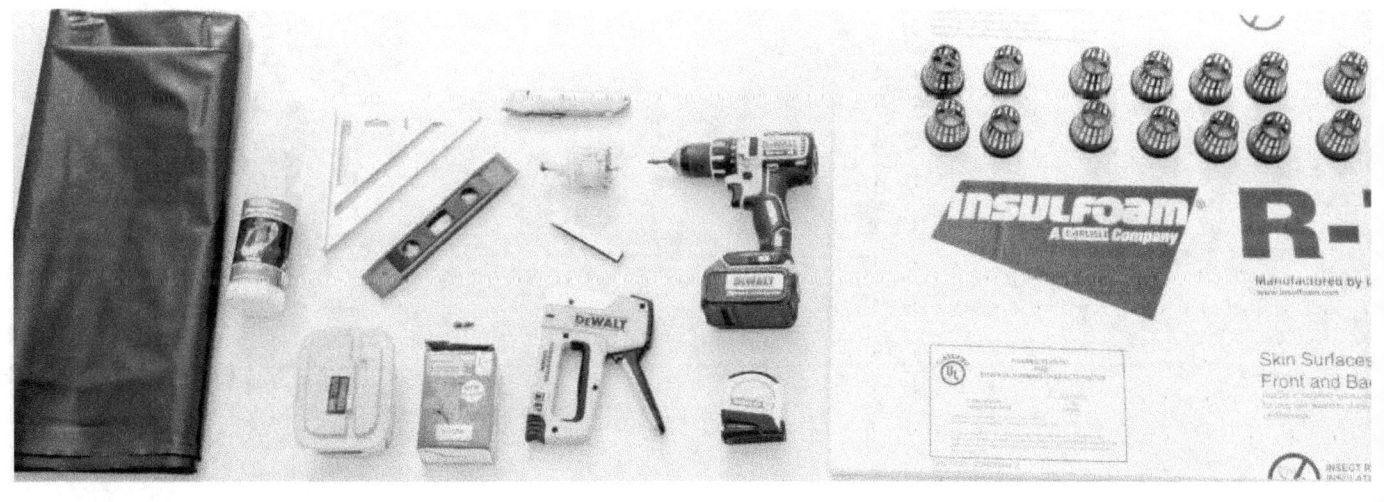

Assemble the Reservoir

There are many ways to make reservoir assembly easier. Most stores that sell lumber offer to cut the lumber to specific dimensions if requested. Request the dimensions listed in the steps below to skip the work of cutting the lumber and reduce the number of tools required. It is possible to buy prefabricated reservoirs for floating rafts; check out the Pots and Trays section in the Equipment chapter to see some of the options.

1. Wearing work gloves and eye protection, cut the four 2 × 12" × 8' boards into the following lengths:

    One board into 4'4" and 2'4" segments
    Another board into 4'4" and 2'4" segments
    One board into 2'1", 2'4", and 2'4" segments
    One board into 2'1" and 2'4" segments

    Cut a 4'1" and a 2'4" segment from each of the two 1 × 2" × 8' furring strips.
    Final lengths and quantities of cut lumber:

2	2 × 12" × 4'4" boards
5	2 × 12" × 2'4" boards
2	2 × 12" × 2'1" boards
2	1 × 2" × 4'1" strips
2	1 × 2" × 2'4" strips

    The lumber can be painted before or after assembly.

2. Lay the five 2 × 12" × 2'4" boards on a flat level surface. These boards will be the base of the system. It is possible to build the reservoir frame without a base, but a solid wood bottom can add a lot of strength to the structure. A base also helps reduce the chance of tears to the reservoir liner. Foam boards are also commonly used as a base to protect the liner from the ground.

3. Set up one of the 2 × 12" × 4'4" boards on its side running along the long side of the base and one of the 2 × 12" × 2'1" boards on its side running along the short side of the base. The 4'4" board should cover the end of the 2'1" board.

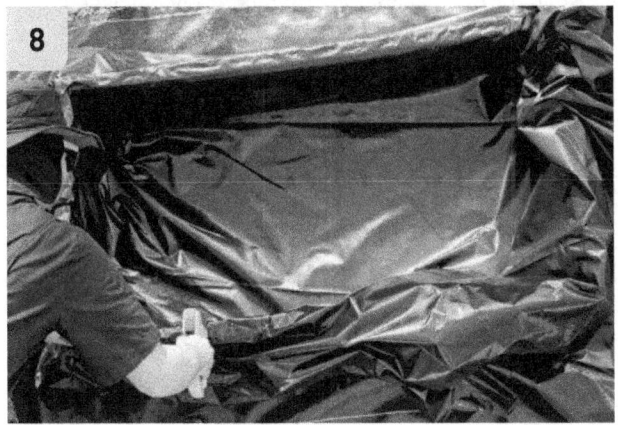 

See 3 and 5 for proper placement. Make sure they are square and level. Use two 2½" screws to fasten the boards together.

4   Place the other 2 × 12" × 4'4" board along the other long side of the base and fasten to the outside end of the 2'1" board from step 3 using two 2½" screws.

5   Place the remaining 2 × 12" × 2'1" board on the last open side of the base between the two 4'4" boards. Fasten into place with two 2½" screws on each end.

6   Flip over the frame and place the five 2 × 12" × 2'4" baseboards back into position. Fasten the base to the frame with two 2½" screws on each end of the 2'4" boards.

7   Flip the frame back over.

8   Adding the liner is one of the most difficult steps in assembling the reservoir. It is always best to have excess liner inside the reservoir instead of making the liner very taut. A very taut liner may be stressed by the weight of the water and could rip, creating leaks. For this reservoir, I used two layers of 6 mil plastic to add some leak security. Fold the liner at the reservoir corners to get the liner flush with the frame. Once the plastic is in place, staple it to the rim of the reservoir frame.

9   Cut away excess liner with scissors or a razor blade knife.

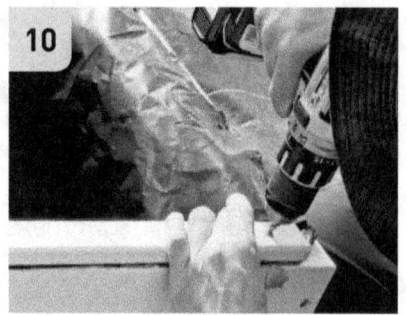

10 The furring strips are fastened along the rim of the reservoir to hide the ends of the plastic liner and to hold the liner securely in place. The furring strips are not completely necessary for the functionality of the reservoir but they add a lot aesthetically. Fasten the furring strips into place with 1¼" screws.

Assemble the Raft

Building a DIY raft is very easy. There are prefabricated rafts available, but they can be expensive. Many of the prefabricated rafts have holes created for specific seedling plug sizes and eliminate the need for net pots. It is possible to create a DIY raft with holes specific to your plug size, making net pots unnecessary, but for this floating raft garden I'm using net pots because they make the process far easier. The prefabricated rafts have a few other design features, like raised plug holders, that make them really nice to use, but for most applications a DIY raft is more than sufficient.

11 Cut a 2 × 4' section from the 1" × 4 × 8' foam board using a razor blade knife. Brush away any loose foam pieces from the cut edge.

12 Place the 2 × 4' section of foam board on sawhorses and fasten into place with clamps.

13 Most leafy greens are grown with 6" spacing in hydroponic systems. A 2 × 4' raft with 6" spacing holds 18 plants (3 rows of 6). Some greens, such as romaine and basil, grow upright and can be grown at a density of 36 plants per 2 × 4' raft. Some growers go even higher density (72 plants or more per 2 × 4' raft) to grow crops like baby kale, baby lettuce, spring mixes, and some herbs. Measure and mark the

DIY raft on the left and a prefabricated hydroponic raft on the right

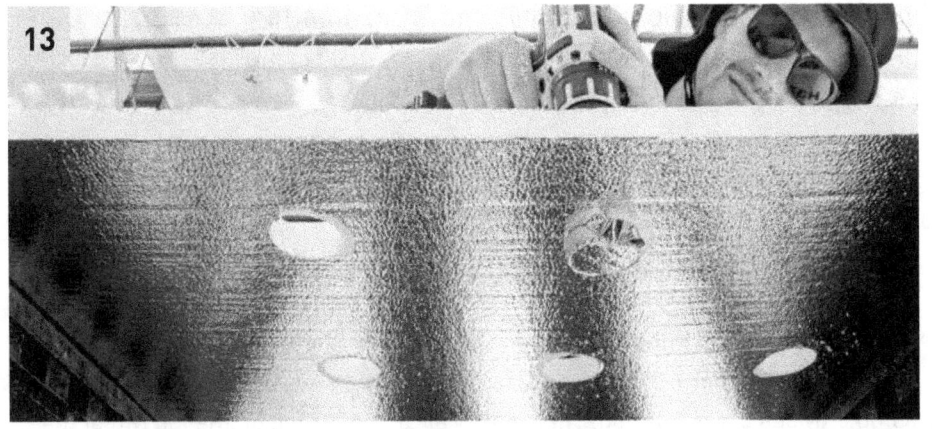

plant site positions on the raft and drill 2" holes with the 2" hole drill bit.

14. Some hydroponic growers leave the reflective surface on their DIY foam boards, but I prefer the look of clean white boards in my clean white reservoir.

15. Test to see if the raft fits in the reservoir. Make any additional adjustments to the raft size so it comfortably fits inside the reservoir. Too much exposed reservoir surface can encourage algae growth, but too snug of a fit makes it difficult for the raft to move downward as the water level drops over time.

16. Place the 2" net pots into the 2" holes in the raft.

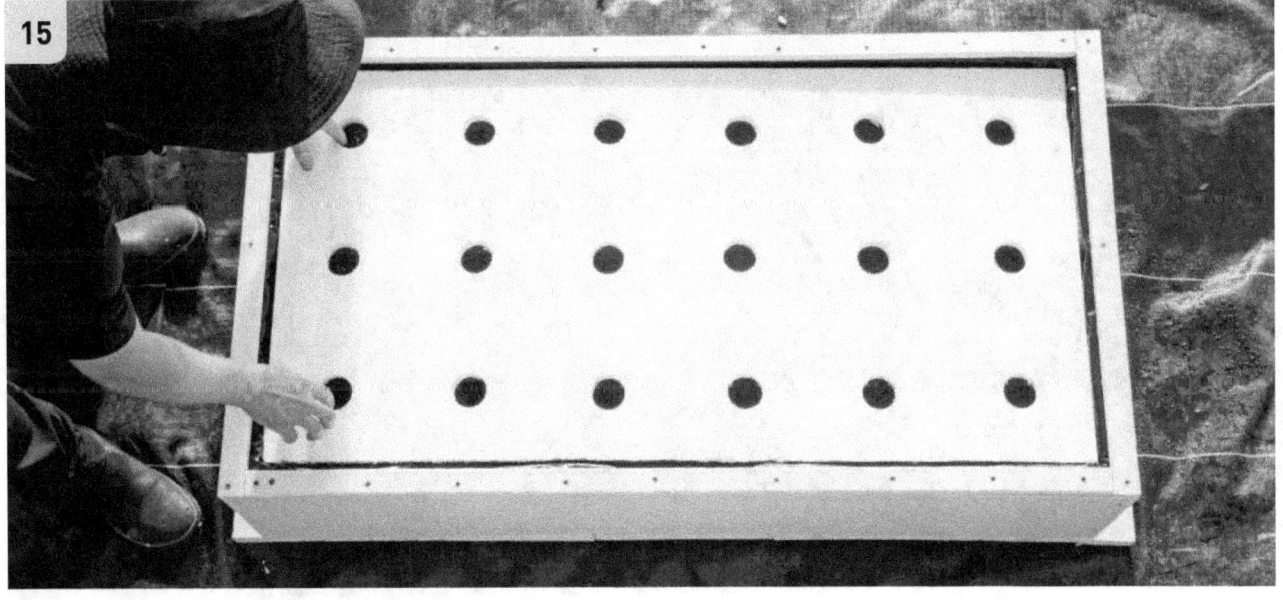

Adding Nutrient Solution, Aeration, and Transplanting

Fill the reservoir with water to 1¼-inch below the start of the furring strip. This will be about 10-inch deep of water, approximately 50 gallons.

Use a hydroponic fertilizer at the recommended rate on the fertilizer bottle or bag. Mix the fertilizer into the water thoroughly until fully dissolved. See the System Maintenance chapter for nutrient solution management strategies, including target EC and pH ranges.

Optional: Adding an air pump can improve plant growth and reduce the risk of root rot. The air pump to the right of the reservoir is a four-outlet 15 liter/minute pump that is connected to four 4-inch round air stones spaced evenly in the reservoir. This air pump provides great aeration. The smaller air pump placed on the top rim of the reservoir is connected to a small solar panel. This small pump has one outlet and provides at most one-fourth the output of the larger air pump, and only in optimal conditions with full sun. A solar-powered air pump is more expensive but it has the ability to provide the benefits of aeration without an electric bill, and the system can be placed anywhere with sunlight.

Float the raft in the reservoir and transplant your seedlings. Stone wool seedlings work great in this system but nearly any hydroponic substrate will work in a floating raft garden. Substrates that hold a lot of water like coco or peat plugs will require more attention because they may have overwatering issues when the plant is young

Adding aeration to a floating raft system is not essential for leafy greens but it generally improves crop health and increases potential yield.

with a small root system. Some growers even use seedlings started in soil in their floating rafts. Soil-started seedlings can be messy and may require more frequent cleaning of the garden, but they are an option.

Maintenance

Most leafy greens can be grown in this system from transplant to harvest without any maintenance of the system. For longer-term crops, see the nutrient solution management strategies detailed in the System Maintenance chapter.

Additional Options

This floating raft garden is used as a reservoir in the DIY nutrient film technique (NFT) system later in this chapter. For this NFT add-on, a frame was constructed to hold PVC pipes above the raft garden. This frame also supports a 4-foot six-tube T5 grow light that acts as a supplemental light source in additional to natural sunlight present in the greenhouse. If this system were placed indoors, this same 4-foot six-tube T5 grow light would be capable of providing all the light required by these crops.

See the DIY nutrient film technique (NFT) for a step-by-step guide to adding a second level of production to the floating raft garden.

58 DIY HYDROPONIC GARDENS

Troubleshooting

Roots are growing poorly or are brown and mushy
- Water may be too warm.
- The pH may be out of target range. Test and adjust based on target pH for your crop (see the appendix for target pHs).
- May have root diseases present and susceptible crops. Flush and completely sanitize reservoir, raft, and net pots before replanting garden.

Plants are growing slowly
- Check EC to make sure it is in target range.
- Garden may not be receiving enough light.
- Water may be too cold. Temperatures less than 65°F can slow growth on some crops. Try painting the reservoir black, adding a water heater, and/or selecting different crops that are more tolerant of cold conditions.

Water level is dropping fast
- May have a leak in the liner. Check for water around the reservoir. If the reservoir is leaking, remove existing liner, check for any objects that may have caused a puncture in the liner, and insert a new liner. If leaks persist, try adding foam boards on side walls and the bottom of the reservoir before adding new liner.

GROWING SYSTEM

WICKING BED

WICKING BED GARDENS ARE VERY versatile and can be modified for a variety of substrates, fertilizers, and crops. Similar to the previous hydroponic gardens in this chapter, the wicking bed garden requires no electricity. The design is incredibly simple.

Wicking beds take advantage of capillary action, a natural phenomenon by which water can flow upward against gravity by using its surface tension and adhesion. A common example is a paper towel wicking water upward from a cup. In a wicking bed garden, the "cup" is the frame of a raised bed garden and the "paper towel" is a fine-textured substrate like coco, peat, or soil.

- **Suitable Locations:** Outdoors or greenhouse; can be modified for indoors
- **Size:** Small to large
- **Growing Media:** Expanded clay pellets and coco coir chips
- **Electrical:** Not required
- **Crops:** Leafy greens, herbs, strawberries, and short flowering crops

The frame of a wicking bed is lined with a waterproof layer, like 6 mil. painter's plastic, to prevent leaks and to protect the wood frame from rotting. The bottom of the bed is filled with a quick-draining substrate like clay pellets, river rock, or washed gravel. The bottom of the bed holds water or a nutrient solution that is wicked up to the fine-textured substrate above. A fabric barrier like burlap or cloth prevents the substrate from dropping into the water reservoir space. An inlet pipe makes filling the reservoir easy and an overflow pipe prevents overwatering.

CROPS

Crops that are tolerant of wet conditions are great for wicking bed gardens. This system may not be appropriate for cacti. It is possible to design wicking beds with several layers of different-textured substrate to create drier conditions while maintaining enough moisture for roots, but it may involve some tinkering to figure out the best mix for your specific environment, crop selection, and garden size.

Often it is the size of a wicking bed garden that limits crop selection. A wicking bed garden like the one described in the step-by-step guide could grow a large flowering crop like a tomato or cucumber, but the limited size of the garden would likely restrict it to just one plant.

LOCATIONS

Wicking bed gardens are typically used outdoors or in greenhouses. By adding a collection bottle to capture overflow water or directing overflow to a sink drain, a wicking bed garden could be used indoors without creating a huge mess. The design that follows does not direct the overflow into a container and would not be appropriate indoors unless modified.

WICKING SYSTEM VARIATIONS

The wicking bed design is very versatile and is seen in both hydroponic and traditional gardens. The design in the step-by-step guide can be modified to use traditional potting mixes and fertilizers that would not be suitable in other hydroponic garden designs. Below are a few optional modifications you can make to the wicking bed design to make it your own.

Optional Modifications
- The inlet and overflow pipe can be made from PVC instead of vinyl tubing.
- The frame could be a metal trough or plastic tote instead of wood with a liner.
- A pond liner could be used instead of painter's plastic.
- The outside could be painted instead of using decorative wood.
- A wood trellis could be built on to support larger crops.
- A raised crossbeam could be installed above the growing bed to support a grow light.

HOW TO BUILD A HYDROPONIC WICKING BED

The wicking bed shown in this chapter is purely hydroponic but do not feel limited to these substrates. Try your own modifications; worst-case scenario, you take out the substrate and try again.

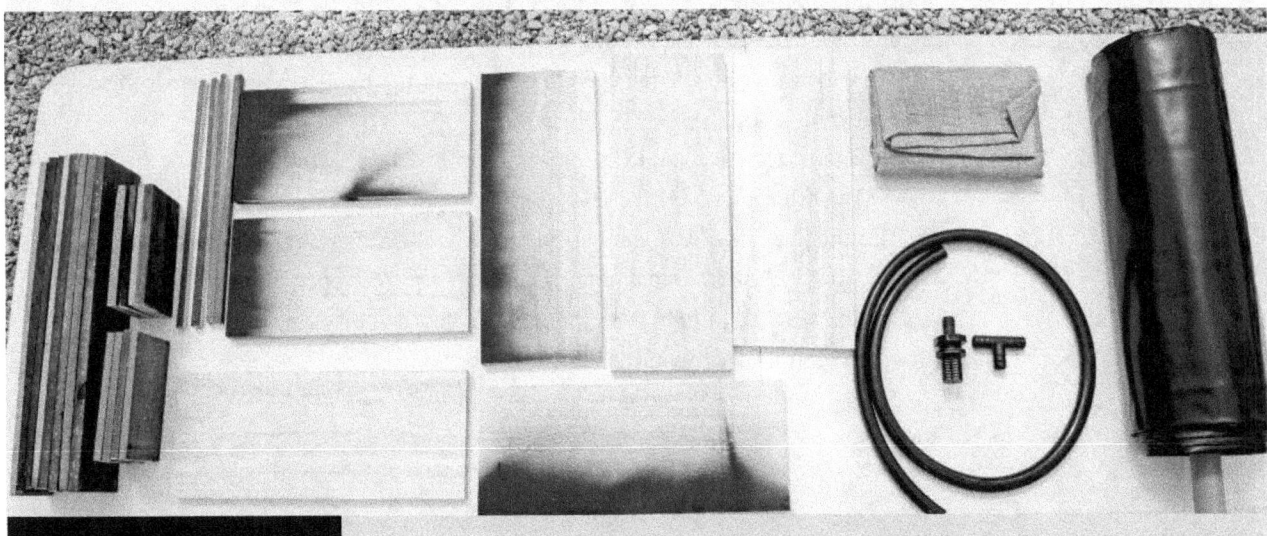

MATERIALS & TOOLS

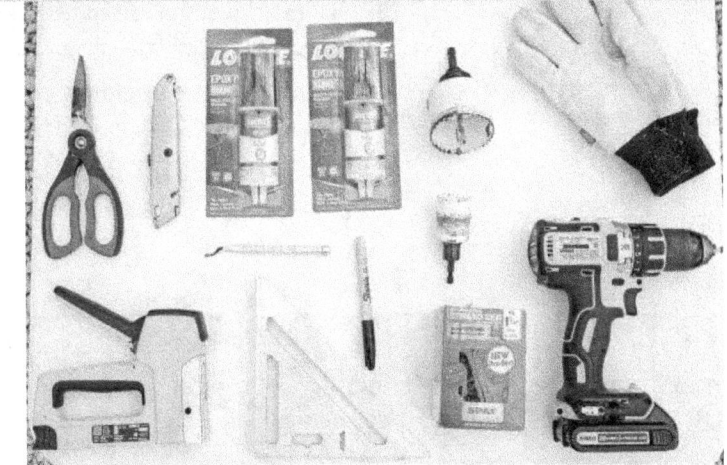

Frame
2	1 × 8" × 8' pine whitewood board (actual dimensions ¾" × 7¼" × 96")
5	½ × 4" × 4' weathered hardwood board
1 lb.	#8 × 1¼" exterior screws
1 lb.	#8 × ¾" wood screws
1	6 × 100' black 6 mil. plastic sheeting
2'	¾" black vinyl tube
1	¾" fill/drain fitting with screen
1	¾" tee
1	2 × 6' burlap

Safety Equipment
Work gloves
Eye protection

Substrate
10 L Expanded clay pellets
2 cu. ft. Coco coir chips

Optional
Chalkboard paint
Paintbrush
Quick-set clear epoxy
Chalk

Tools
Circular saw
Rafter square
Level
Drill
Drill bit matching screws
Tape measure
Permanent marker
1⅜" hole saw drill bit

Step drill bit with ⅛" increments from ¼" to 1⅜"
2" hole saw drill bit
Staple gun and staples
Heavy-duty scissors
Sawhorses with clamps
Razor blade knife

Assemble the Frame

There are several ways to make frame assembly easier. Most stores that sell lumber offer to cut lumber to specific dimensions if requested. Request the dimensions listed in the steps below to skip the work of cutting the lumber and reduce the number of tools required. The weathered hardwood is used purely for aesthetics and could be skipped to make assembly easier.

1. Wearing work gloves and eye protection, cut the two 1 × 8" × 8' boards into the following lengths:
   - One board into four 18" segments and one 14½" segment
   - The other board into one 14½" segment and one 19½" segment
2. Cut the five ½ × 4" × 4' weathered hardwood boards into the following lengths:
   - Two 19½" segments and one 8¼" segment from each of four 4' boards
   - Four 8¼" segments from the other 4' board

   Final lengths and quantities of cut lumber:

4	1 × 8" × 18" boards
2	1 × 8" × 14½" boards
1	1 × 8" × 19½" board
8	½ × 4" × 19½" weathered hardwood boards
8	½ × 4" × 8¼" weathered hardwood boards

3. The top rim of the raised bed frame can be painted before or after assembly with chalkboard paint. This is purely an aesthetic addition and this step is not necessary for the functionality of the garden. If painting the rim before assembly, paint the wide edge of two 1 × 8" × 18" boards and the end of both 1 × 8" × 14½" boards.
4. Making sure the boards are square and level, fasten the end of one 1 × 8" × 14½" board to the 1 × 8" × 19½" board using two 1¼" screws. The 19½" board is the base of the frame.

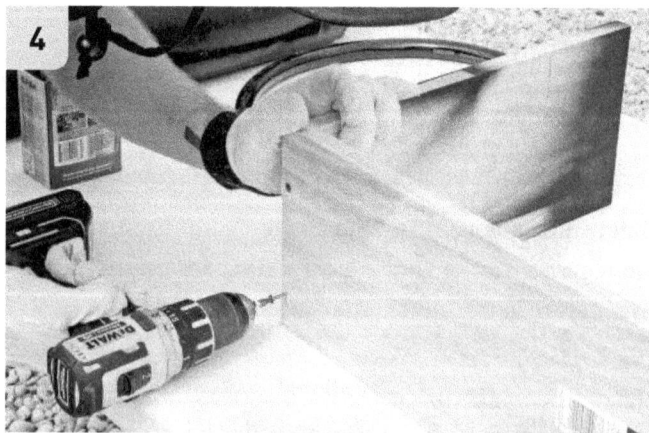

5. Fasten a 1 × 8" × 18" board to the 1 × 8" × 14½" board using two 1¼" screws.
6. Fasten another 1 × 8" × 18" board to the 1 × 8" × 14½" board to complete another side wall.
7. Repeat steps 5 and 6 to assemble the other side wall.
8. Fasten the remaining 1 × 8" × 14½" board to complete the last wall of the frame.

Install the Liner and Drainage Assembly

9. Measure and mark a hole with a center 6" above the bottom of the frame and 3" from the side wall. Use the 1⅜" hole saw drill bit to create the hole.
10. Use the step drill bit to create a slope around the hole on the outside of the frame. This slope is necessary to securely attach the fill/drain fitting.
11. Line the inside of the frame with 6 mil. plastic. Fold the plastic sheet at the corners to shape it to the frame.

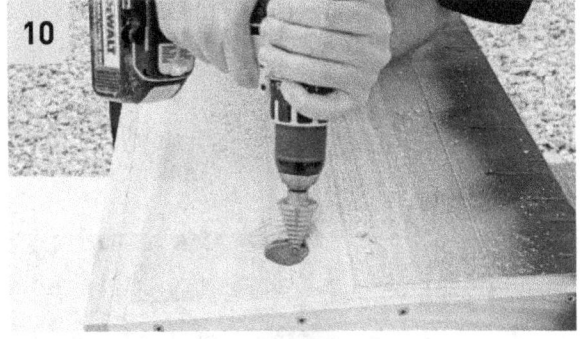
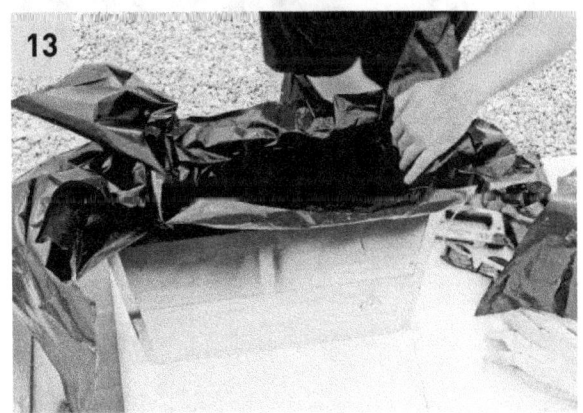

64 DIY HYDROPONIC GARDENS

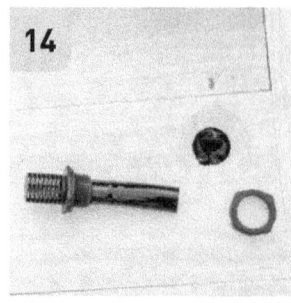

12. Staple the plastic liner along the inside upper rim of the frame to hold it in place.
13. Cut away the excess plastic sheeting with scissors.
14. Assemble the drainage pipe. Attach a 3" piece of ¾" vinyl tubing to the fill/drain fitting. Unscrew the fastener but keep the rubber gasket on the fitting.
15. Create a small hole in the plastic liner in the middle of the drainage hole. The hole in the liner should fit tight around the fitting.
16. Attach the drainage pipe to the frame. Tightly screw on the fastener to make the fitting watertight.
17. Test the drainage pipe before proceeding! Make sure there are no leaks. If leaks are found around the fitting, adjust the liner and tighten the fasten. If leaks are found elsewhere, remove and replace the liner. Do not proceed with leaks; water should only drain from the drain pipe.

Make the Decorative Weathered Hardwood Exterior

Adding the weathered hardwood exterior is optional. This system would also look great painted. During the assembly of the hardwood exterior I accidentally cut the side panels 1 inch short. I improvised a solution by adding long skinny pieces of hardwood to patch in the corners. The dimensions used in these instructions have been corrected so you won't make the same mistake . . . or creative flair . . . lots of ways to looks at mistakes in DIY!

18. Use the 2" hole saw drill bit to create a hole in one of the 19½" segments of weathered wood. The center of the hole should be 3" from the end of the board.
19. Attach the weathered hardwood to the frame.
    Option 1: Use quick-set clear epoxy and hold boards in place with clamps while epoxy dries.
    Option 2: Use ¾" wood screws to secure boards to frame.

HYDROPONIC GROWING SYSTEMS 65

Install the Inlet Pipe and Substrate

20 Assemble the inlet pipe. Attach an 18" piece of ¾" vinyl tubing to the ¾" tee.
21 Prepare the substrate.
22 Rinse the expanded clay to wash off fine clay particles.
23 Soak the coco chip block to expand it.
24 Position the tee end of the inlet pipe on the side opposite the drainage pipe. The irrigation water will enter the inlet pipe and then flow across the bottom of the bed and drain from the drain pipe at the opposite end. Fill the bottom of the bed with clay pellets while positioning the inlet pipe to hold it in place.
25 Fill the bed with clay pellets until the drainage pipe is partially covered. Do not bury the drainage pipe too deep or the system will drain before the upper level of substrate has access to water.

26 Cut a section of burlap large enough to cover the growing bed. This will be the fabric divider between the lower reservoir and the upper substrate. With very porous fabrics like burlap it is helpful to use multiple layers to prevent the upper substrate from entering the lower reservoir.

27 Push the burlap divider into the growing bed so it makes contact with the clay pellets.

28 Fill the growing bed with expanded coco chips. Fill to ¼" from the top of the liner.

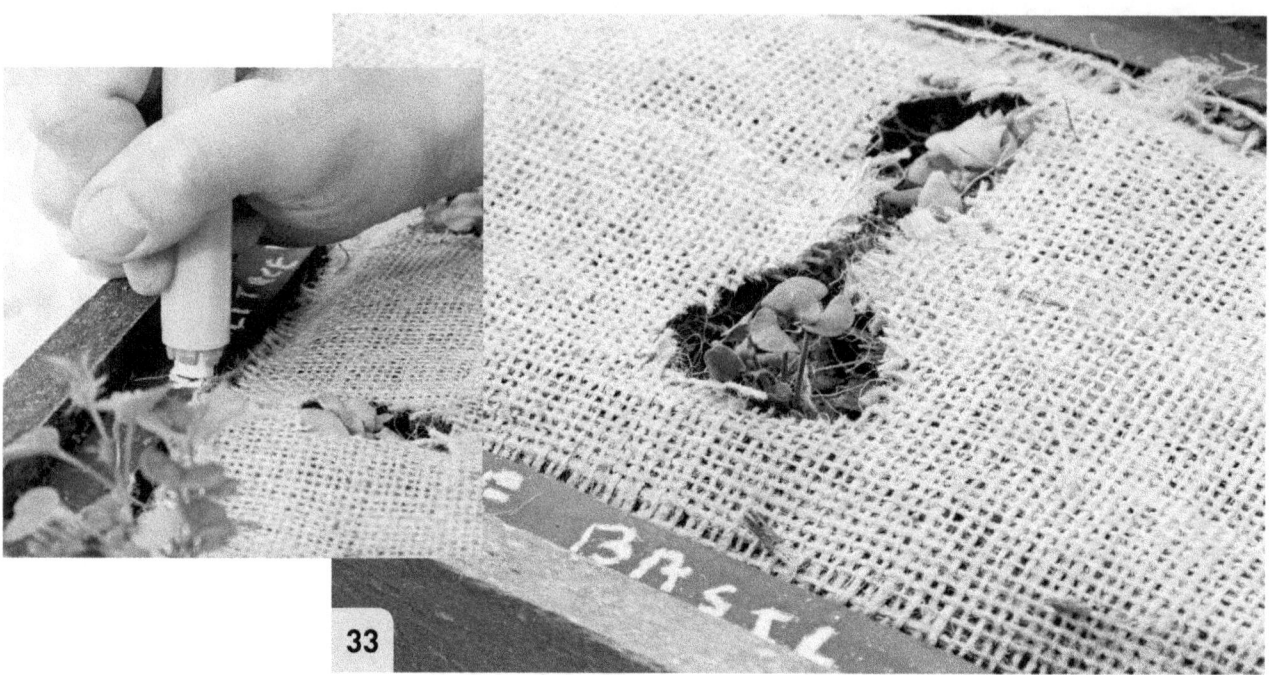
33

Planting and Decoration

29 Cut a section of burlap that covers the growing bed.

30 Use a couple staples to hold the burlap in place.

31 Cut an opening for the inlet pipe and cut away any excess burlap covering the rim of the bed.

32 Cut openings for transplants.

33 Transplant and label seedlings using chalk.

34 Immediately water the garden from above after transplanting to make sure seedling roots make contact with the substrate.

35 For the first 2 weeks, water the garden from above every couple of days. Do not use the inlet pipe until the plants have the chance to send roots deep into the substrate to access water on their own. After a couple of weeks, the plants should be able to access the reservoir below and may not require waterings for a week or more depending on the environment.

36 This garden does not use a substrate that has an initial fertilizer charge, so all nutrients will need to be provided through water-soluble fertilizers during waterings. Watering with a hydroponic nutrient solution once a week is often sufficient to meet nutrient requirements of crops in this system. When adding water to this system, do not stop watering until the system is visibly draining.

The burlap mulch in this wicking bed was added primarily for decoration, but in very warm climates it can help retain moisture in the growing bed.

GROWING SYSTEM

NUTRIENT FILM TECHNIQUE (NFT)

NFT systems are very popular for indoor growing because they are lightweight and water-efficient.

Nutrient film technique (NFT) is a circulating hydroponic growing style that irrigates plants with a shallow stream of nutrient solution in growing channels. NFT is one of the most popular techniques for commercially growing leafy greens. One of the biggest advantages is the ability to grow a lot of plants on a small reservoir. NFT is very popular with rooftop growers because they can cover the entire roof in NFT channels using a small reservoir that won't exceed the load-carrying capacity of the roof. A gallon of water weighs 8.34 pounds . . . that means 240 gallons weighs over a ton! The weight of water can quickly add up. Many home gardeners may also be worried about heavy reservoirs, especially indoors.

- **Suitable Locations:** Indoors, outdoors, or greenhouse
- **Size:** Medium to large
- **Growing Media:** Stone wool
- **Electrical:** Required
- **Crops:** Leafy greens, herbs, and strawberries

NFT is a very popular DIY hydroponic technique because it can be customized in so many ways. I've seen NFT channels arranged in cascading patterns on walls, in A-frame pyramids, and in spiraling coils. Some DIY NFT systems are more successful than others—it can be easy to let creative design take over and forget about the fundamentals that make an NFT garden successful. I encourage everyone to experiment, but first learn the potential limitations and nuances of NFT gardens so you can avoid costly mistakes. The success of your NFT garden will depend on crop selection, growing environment, channel length, channel slope, channel shape, and flow rate.

CROPS

The most popular crops for NFT are leafy greens, herbs, and strawberries. At maturity, these crops have a decent root system but generally not enough roots to restrict flow in the NFT channel. Roots clogging the channels can be an issue when growing larger crops like tomatoes, peppers, and cucumbers. Some DIY gardeners use large PVC pipes (4 inches or more) or very wide gutters to accommodate the roots of these larger crops. Feel free to experiment but, in general, NFT is not the ideal system for growing large crops.

LOCATIONS

The ability to irrigate many channels on a small reservoir, without the weight of hundreds of gallons, makes NFT popular for indoor gardens. NFT is a great choice for rooftops, classrooms, balconies, and apartments. NFT gardens generally have a nice flat canopy, which is great for grow lights. It is sometimes tricky to grow plants of various heights under a grow light because some may receive a lot of light while blocking the light for other crops, but this is rarely an issue with indoor NFT gardens.

NFT CHANNELS

The channels in this build are made from 2-inch PVC pipe with 2-inch net pots. Other popular DIY options are 3-inch PVC pipe, rain gutters, and vinyl fence posts. If using gutters, it is best to create a gutter cover to avoid algae growth in the channel. Flat-bottom channels like gutters and fence posts sometimes direct water to the sides of the channel instead of directly down the middle. This diversion of the water to the sides makes it difficult to get good contact between the seedling and the irrigation stream. Gutters with grooves on the bottom sometimes mitigate this issue by spreading the stream evenly along the bottom of the channel.

The length of the channel is a very important consideration. Most commercial NFT channels range from 4 to 15 feet. Longer channels sometimes have issues with sagging and must be supported at several points. A sagging channel creates areas of stagnant water flow, which can lead to decreased oxygen available to the roots, a rise in water temperature, and an increase in the chance of root diseases.

Long channels are not recommended in warm climates because they often have issues with heat buildup. The water will spend a long time in a long channel before returning to the reservoir, and this increased time in the channel leads to increased temperatures in the nutrient solution. Gardeners in warm climates should focus on channels 8 feet and shorter, unless using a water chiller or another method for cooling the nutrient solution.

The slope of an NFT channel is also important for limiting heat buildup in the nutrient solution and avoiding stagnation of the nutrient solution within channels. A slope of 1 to 4 percent is acceptable; 2 to 3 percent is generally the slope used in commercial systems. The system built in this chapter targets a 1-inch drop over a 4-foot (48-inch) channel to create a 2-percent slope.

Pump Failure and Power Outages

The biggest issue with NFT is its vulnerability to quick crop death in the event of a power outage. Plants in an NFT channel depend on constant or very frequent irrigation. In the event of a pump failure or power outage, there is no substrate to retain water and keep the root zone hydrated. In a warm, sunny environment, all the crops in an NFT channel can die in less than 30 minutes with no irrigation. In five years of working commercially with NFT systems, I've seen far more massive crop failures than I wish to remember, almost all due to pump failure or power outages. Large commercial NFT farms will have backup generators in the event of a power outage to avoid complete crop loss, but this is usually not an option for home gardeners. All the DIY systems previously detailed in this chapter have the capability of living for a several days up to several weeks without electricity, but the rest of the systems in this chapter involve pumps and circulating systems that are very dependent on electricity. The following systems enter the realm of increasing complexity and increasing risk. Now that that disclaimer is out of the way, let's build some really exciting circulating hydroponic systems.

FLOW RATE

Most NFT gardens target a flow rate of ½ to 1 liter per channel per minute. I've found improvements in plant growth with flow rates up to 2½ liters per channel per minute. To measure the flow rate per channel, remove the irrigation line to that channel and redirect it to a measuring cup. Either measure exactly how much water flows from that line in one minute or find how long it takes to fill 1 liter and use that number to calculate the flow rate per minute. The Irrigation section in the Equipment chapter details the process for calculating minimum pump output to meet the flow rate requirements in a hydroponic garden. But because it is such important information, I am repeating it here.

The major factors to consider when selecting a water pump are delivery height, target flow rate, and output tube size. Most systems simply need a pump powerful enough to deliver water to a specific height. For example, a grower selecting a pump for a flood and drain system can primarily focus on whether that pump has a maximum delivery height greater than the distance from pump outlet to flood tray. Some systems perform best when water is delivered at a target flow rate. A couple systems that depend on target flow rates are NFT and aeroponics. For these systems, it is important to consider how delivery height will impact flow rate. A pump that delivers 600 gallons per hour (GPH) at 4 feet high only delivers 200 GPH at 10 feet high. The number of emitters will also impact flow rate. It is generally better to select a pump that may be slightly overpowered than a pump that could be underpowered. It is possible to reduce flow using valves, but it is not possible to increase flow.

Example: An NFT system has a target flow rate of 15 GPH per channel. The system has 20 channels. This means the pump must be able to deliver 15 GPH to 20 channels, so 15 GPH × 20 channels for a total of 300 GPH. Additionally, the channels are 2 feet above the pump outlet.

HOW TO BUILD AN NFT GARDEN

Note: This system uses the floating raft garden detailed earlier in this chapter as a reservoir (see pages 50 to 59).

It is not necessary to build the floating raft garden to build this NFT garden. A prefabricated reservoir can be purchased or a reservoir can be made from a variety of repurposed materials, such as an opaque plastic tote. If growing in a warm environment, it is often advantageous to bury the reservoir to keep the nutrient solution cool.

MATERIALS

Frame

2	2 × 6" × 8' lumber
2	2 × 4" × 8' lumber
1 gal.	White water-based latex primer, sealer, and stain-blocker (KILZ 2 LATEX)
1 lb.	#10 × 2½" exterior screws
1 lb.	#8 × 1¼" exterior screws

Channels

3	2" PVC, 10'
22	2" net pots

Irrigation

4	2" PVC tee
6	2" PVC end cap
4	¾" elbow
11'	¾" black vinyl tubing
3'	¼" black vinyl tubing
1	Zip tie
9	¾" EMT straps
1	¾" gasket
4	¼" straight double barbed connectors
1	Submersible water pump, 550 GPH

Optional Lighting for Lower Level

1	4' six-tube T5 grow light
1	Light hanger

TOOLS

Paint roller and/or paintbrush
Circular saw
Deburring tool
Drill
Hacksaw
Step drill bit with ⅛" increments from ¼" to 1⅜"
Tape measure
Permanent marker
2¾" hole saw drill bit
Rafter square (also called a speed square)
Level
Drill bit matching screws
Sawhorses with clamps
2" hole saw drill bit
Irrigation line hole punch
Heavy-duty scissors

Safety Equipment
Work gloves
Eye protection

Lumber and PVC Preparation

Most stores that sell lumber offer to cut the lumber to specific dimensions if requested. Some home improvement stores will cut PVC too. Request the dimensions listed in the steps below to skip the work of cutting the lumber and/or PVC to reduce the amount of labor and tools required.

1. Wearing work gloves and eye protection, cut the two 2 × 6" × 8' boards into the following lengths:
   - One board into two 4' segments
   - One board into two 2'6¾" segments
2. Cut the two 2 × 4" × 8' boards into four 4' segments.
   Final lengths and quantities of cut lumber:

   2 2 × 6" × 4' boards
   2 2 × 6" × 2'6¾" boards
   4 2 × 4" × 4' boards
3. Paint the lumber before assembly.
4. Cut the 2" PVC to make the following lengths. Clean the edges of the cuts with a deburring tool.

   4 3'7" segments
   3 2¼" segments
   1 4" segment
   1 3" segment
      ¾" grommets

Assemble the Manifold

The manifold will collect the drainage from the NFT channels. Before gluing any of the components together, check that the total length of the manifold is less than 27½ inches. If it is longer, the 3-inch PVC segment can be trimmed down to 2¼ inches. The center of the tees should be 5 inches apart. Channels can be spaced closer or further than 5 inches apart, but this spacing works great for lettuce and basil. The end of the manifold with the 4-inch PVC segment will be used for a ¾-inch drainage line. A ¾-inch elbow will be inserted into the PVC and another ¾-inch elbow will direct the flow to the reservoir. Check that there is enough space to fit elbows before gluing.

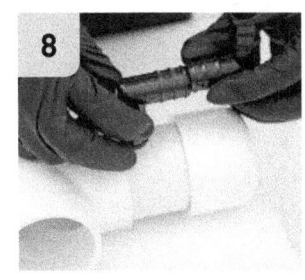

Some PVC tees and caps are longer or shorter than others, so there may be some adjustments specific to your materials. Only proceed once the manifold assembled without glue is less than 27½ inches long, the tees have 5-inch spacing at their centers, and there is sufficient space on the 4-inch PVC segment to fit the ¾-inch elbows.

5 The four 2" PVC tees are connected by the 2¼" PVC segments. Glue the tees so they all lay flat on a surface.

6 One end cap connects to the tees using the 4" PVC segment and the other cap connects using the 3" PVC segment.

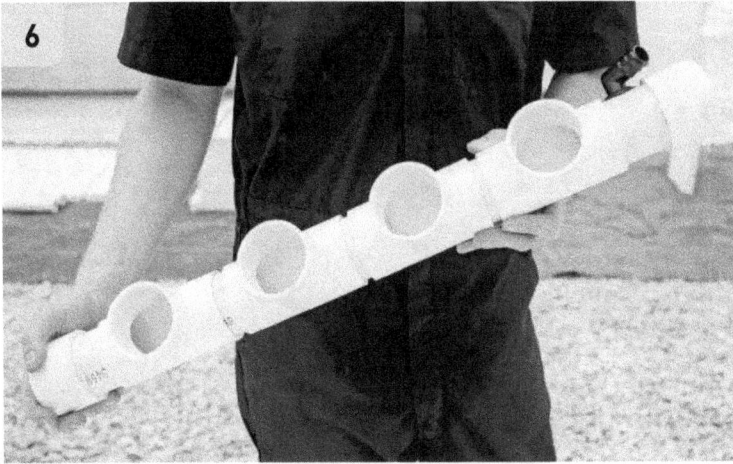
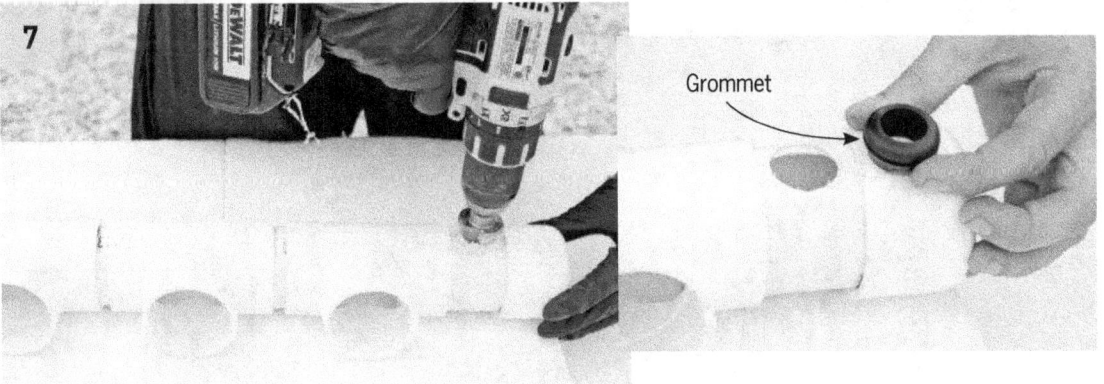

7 The end of the manifold with the 4" PVC segment will be used for the ¾" drainage line. A ¾" elbow will be inserted into the PVC and another ¾" elbow will direct the flow to the reservoir. Check that there is enough space to fit these before drilling. Slowly drill the PVC and check periodically to see if the hole is large enough to hold the grommet. Most ¾" grommets fit in a ¹⁵⁄₁₆" to 1" hole.

8 Fit the grommet snugly into the hole in the PVC manifold and insert one of the ¾" elbows.

Assemble the Frame

9 Place the manifold on one of the 2 × 6" × 2'6¾" boards. There should be at least 1½" of space from the end caps to the 6" edges of the board. The manifold should be ½" from one of the 2'6¾" edges and 2½" from the other 2'6¾" edge. With a marker, trace the ends of the 2" tees.

10 Repeat step 9 on the other 2 × 6" × 2'6¾" board. Be sure to trace the 2" tees near the 2'6¾" edge of the board. It is the positioning of these circles that will determine the slope of the NFT channels.

11 Use the 2¾" hole drill bit to create holes at the traced locations in the 2'6¾" boards. Clean off any sawdust from the boards.

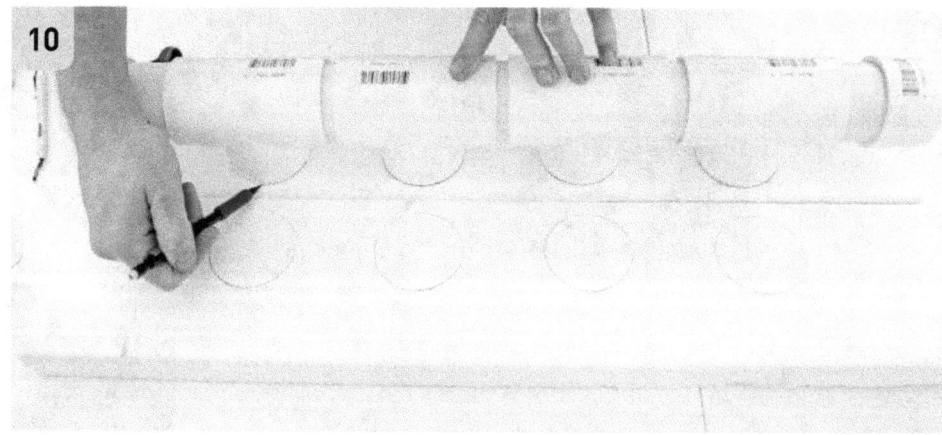

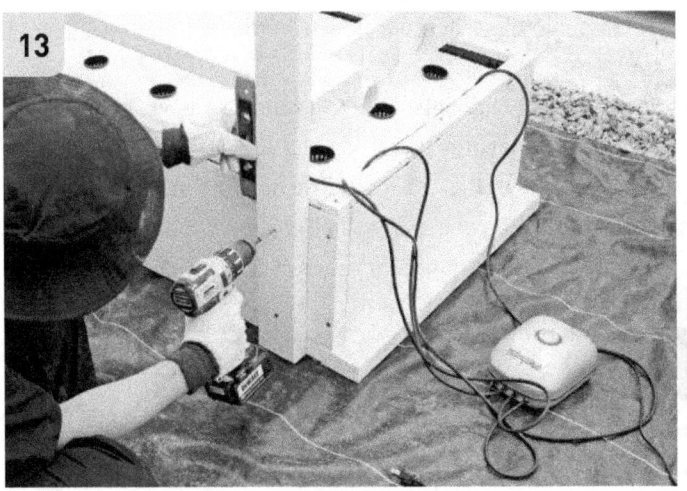

12. Position these 2'6¾" boards on top of the reservoir. Position the 2 × 6" × 4' boards on top of these, running the length of the reservoir. These will be used to guide the positioning of the support legs.
13. Use the square and level when fastening the support legs to the reservoir. It is very important that these legs are straight upright and not leaning. Use two 2½" screws to secure the legs into position.
14. Fasten the 2 × 6" × 4' boards to the support legs. The top edge of the 4' boards should be flush with the top of the legs.
15. Mark the position for the 2'6¾" crossbeams. The high end of the NFT channels will go through a crossbeam 5¼" from the end of the 4' boards and the low end of the NFT channels will go through a crossbeam 6¼" from the other end of the 4' boards.
16. Arrange the 2'6¾" crossbeams so one side has the drilled holes toward the bottom and the other side has the drilled holes toward the top. Fasten the crossbeams with only one screw near the top of the frame. It will be important to have the ability to adjust the angle of this board when inserting the PVC channels. Later they will be secured into place with a second screw.

Crossbeam with drilled holes near the bottom   Crossbeam with drilled holes near the top

17. Insert the 3'7" PVC segments into the crossbeams. These will be the growing channels.
18. Attach the manifold to the 3'7" PVC channels. The ¾" drainage elbow should be on the lower side of the manifold. Do not glue it yet.
19. Mark the placement of the net pots in the channels. The net pots in this design are 6" apart within the channel and are arranged in a checkerboard pattern to create additional space between plants from neighboring channels.

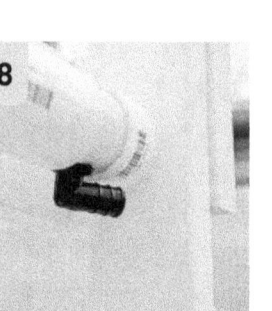

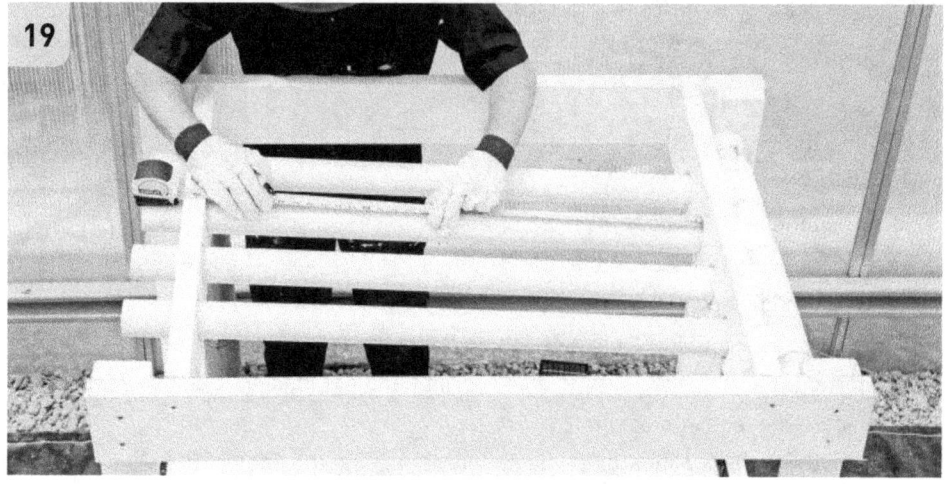

DRILLING REFERENCE

HYDROPONIC GROWING SYSTEMS 77

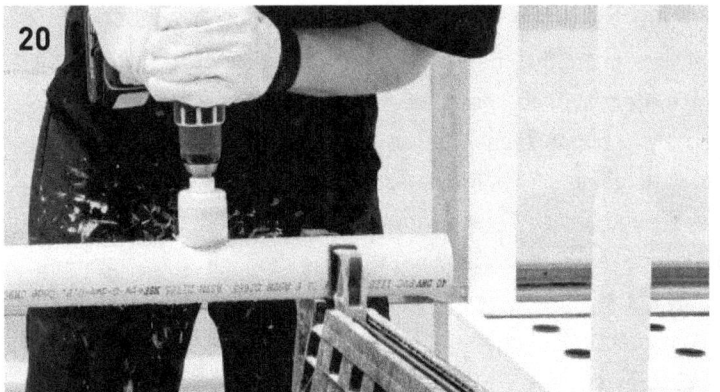
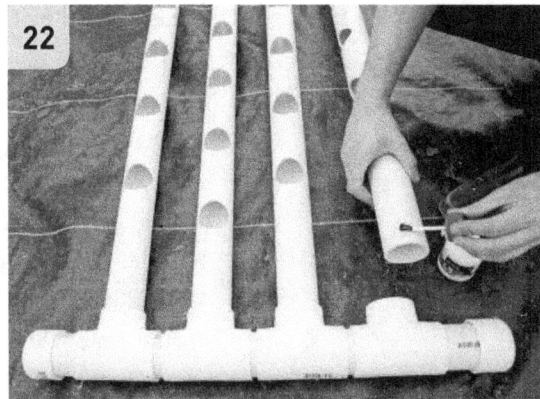

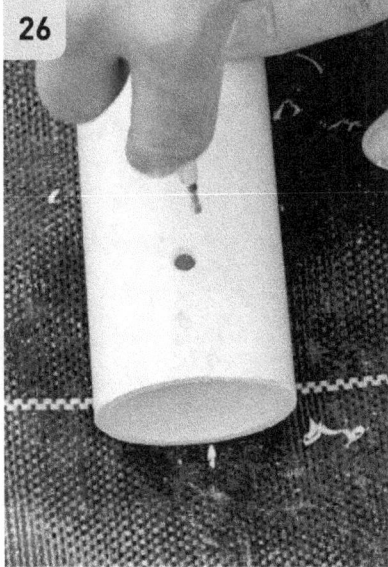

20 Take down the channels from the frame. Use a sawhorse with clamps to hold the channels in place while drilling holes for the net pots. Use the 2" hole drill bit. Be sure to keep the drill straight and position the bit in the middle of the PVC pipe. If the drill is off center or at an angle it can cut into the side wall of the PVC pipe.

21 Use the deburring tool to clean the drilled holes.

22 Glue the drilled channels to the manifold. Keep the holes upright!

23 Insert the channels with attached manifold back into the crossbeams.

24 Position the end caps on the channels but do not glue them into place.

25 Mark positions for the ¼" water delivery lines.

26 Drill a small hole in the marked positions and use the deburring tool to open up the hole until it is wide enough for a ¼" vinyl tube. The ¼" tube should be held tightly in place when inserted. It may be easier to remove the channels and manifold from the frame to drill the holes.

Assemble the Irrigation System

27 The main water delivery line to the channels is a ¾" vinyl tube attached to a submersible pump in the reservoir. The ¾" delivery line can be run up to the channels along one of the support legs. Use an elbow to direct the tube across the crossbeam. End the line going across the crossbeam with a ¾" elbow. This elbow attaches to a short 4" segment of ¾" tube that is held tightly folded in half with a zip tie. This zip tie can be removed to clean out the irrigation line during system cleanouts. The elbow at the end allows the gardener to direct the water away from the system during a cleanout. Fasten the ¾" water delivery line in place with ¾" EMT straps and 1¼" screws.

28 Use the irrigation line hole punch to create four holes in the top of the horizontal ¾" tube. Insert the ¼" double barbed connectors into these holes.

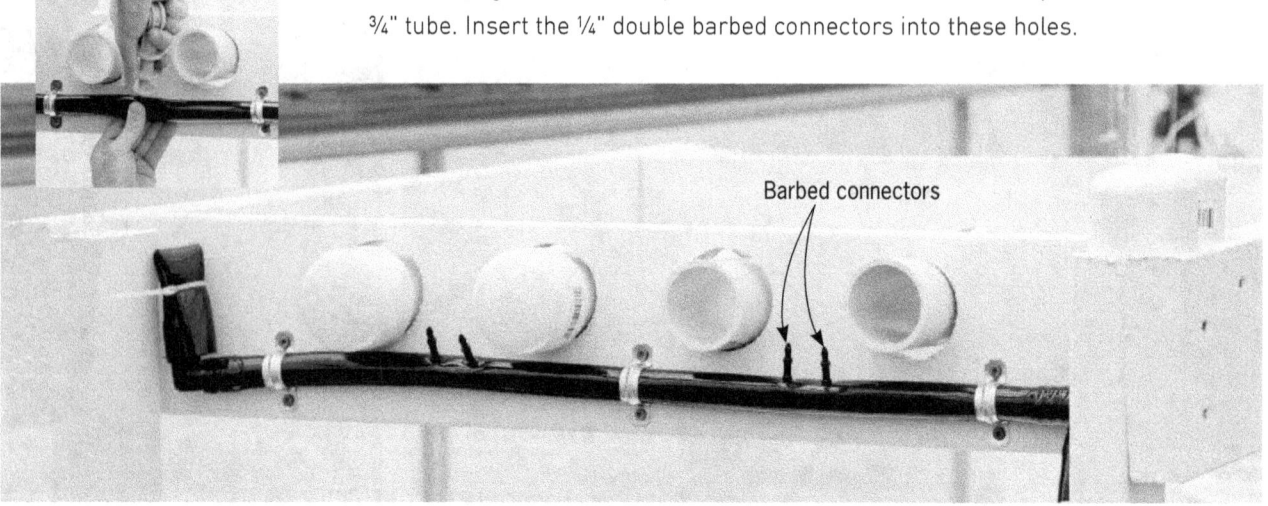

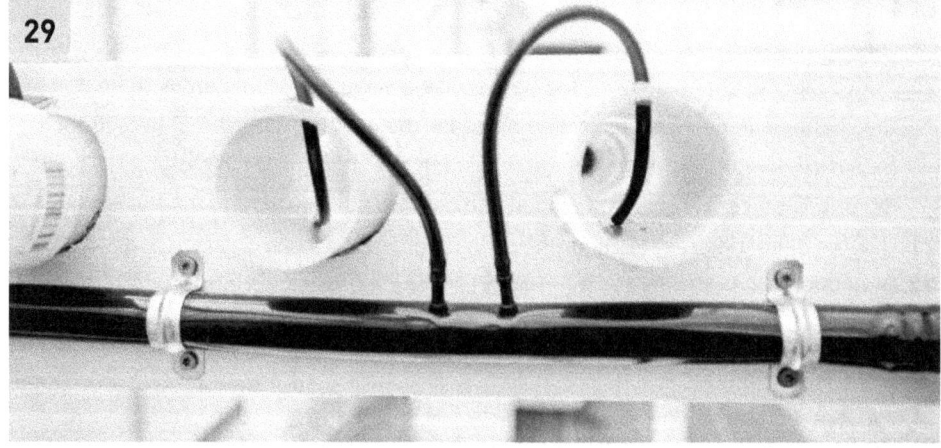

29 With scissors, cut four 8" segments of ¼" black vinyl tubing. Attach one end of the tubes to the ¼" double barbed connectors and insert the other end into the PVC channel. The tube should be positioned in the channel so the flow is directed down the channel.

HYDROPONIC GROWING SYSTEMS

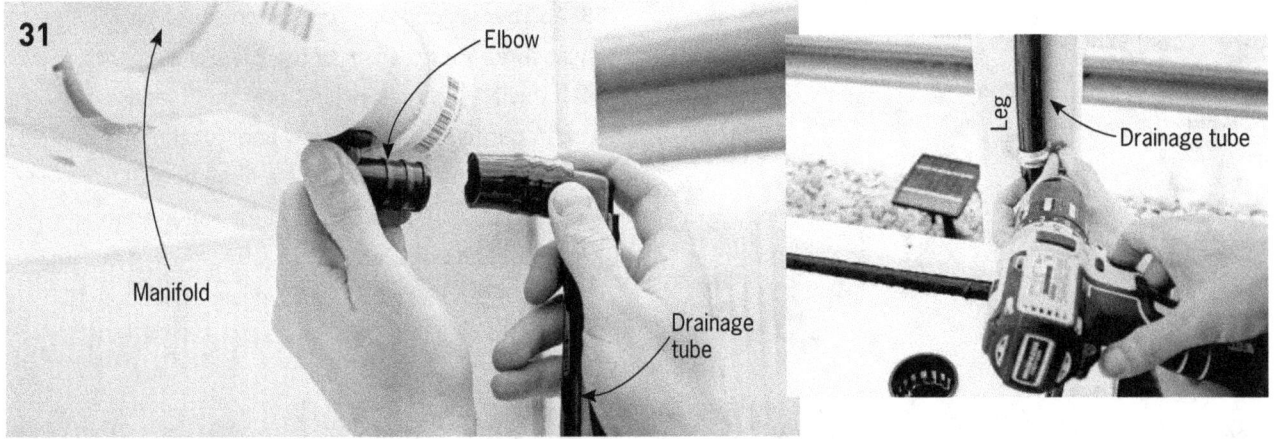

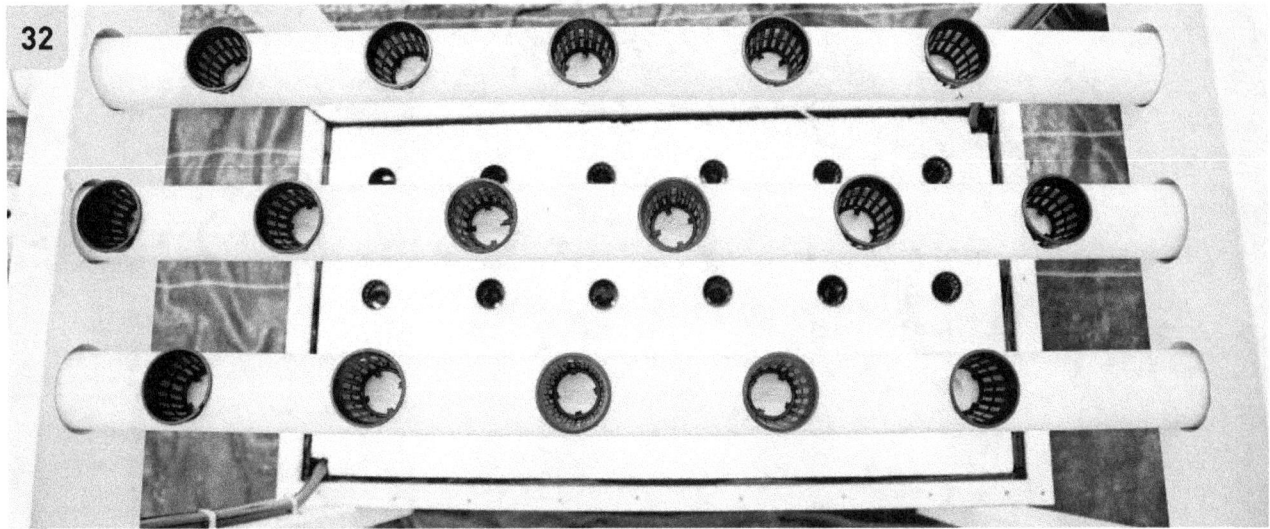

30 Place the end caps on the channels. These end caps should not be glued into place; it is best to have the ability to remove them in the future to facilitate cleaning and make troubleshooting potential problems easier.

31 Create the ¾" drainage line by connecting the elbow in the manifold to another ¾" elbow using a small section of ¾" tubing. This will direct the drainage downward. It also makes it easy to run the ¾" drainage line along one of the support legs. The drainage line should reach the bottom of the reservoir. The submersible pump and drainage line are positioned at corners diagonal to each other so the water will flow across the reservoir when water circulates through the channels.

32 Modify the 2" net pots by cutting out the bottom. This will ensure the seedlings have contact with the nutrient solution and it makes removing the plants from the pots easier during harvest. Insert the net pots into the channels.

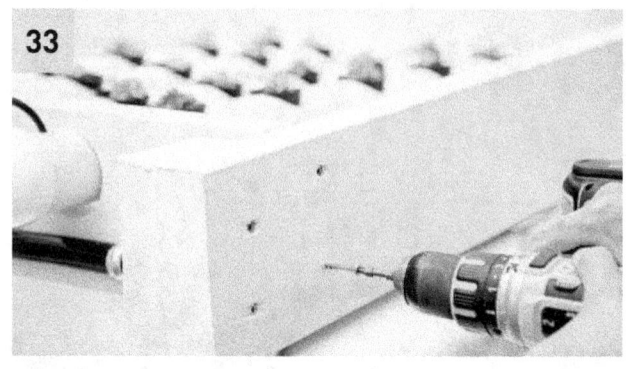

33 Add the second screw to the crossbeams to securely fasten them to the 2 × 6" × 4' boards.

34 If this NFT garden is built over the floating raft garden, adding a grow light for the floating raft garden can be a huge help. It is possible to grow plants in the raft system without adding a grow light, but growth may be slow and stretched. This design uses a 4' six-tube T5 light.

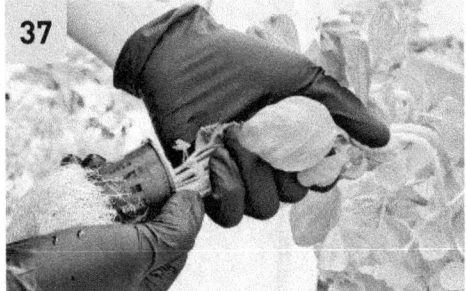

Planting and Harvesting

35 Seedlings should have roots visibly emerging from the bottom of the plug before being transplanted into an NFT channel.

36 Some crops, like basil and other herbs, can be harvested multiple times. This is great and generally not a problem, but sometimes the roots of these plants can grow so massive that they will start to restrict the flow within the channels.

37 Many NFT gardeners like to harvest living plants. The whole plant with roots attached can be stored indoors in a cup of water and the leaves are pulled off as needed. This is a great way to share your harvest with friends while keeping the produce fresh.

38 Net pots can be reused. Remove roots to be composted and save the pots. The pots can washed, rinsed, and reused.

Troubleshooting

Clogged channel
- Check to see if roots are clogging channel. Harvest crops if needed to open up channel.
- Check to see if an expanded clay pellet or other substrate is clogging drainage line.

Clogged irrigation lines
- If using ball valves (shutoff valves), close off flow to all ¼" irrigation lines except the clogged line. If pressure does not remove clog, unfold a paper clip and push it down irrigation line to loosen any debris clogging line. If line is still clogged, replace the line with new ¼" tube. If line is still clogged, replace the ¼" double barbed connector.

GROWING SYSTEM

TOP DRIP SYSTEM

TOP DRIP IS A HYDROPONIC technique that includes a wide range of garden designs, all with one similar feature: Irrigation lines deliver water to the top of the substrate. Sometimes the irrigation lines are attached to flow rate regulators that create a slow drip, thus top drip. One of the more popular variations of top drip is Dutch buckets. Dutch buckets are closed-bottom pots with a single drainage site. This drainage site is slightly raised from the bottom of the bucket so it can be set up to drain into a collection pipe that directs the used nutrient solution back to the reservoir to be recirculated.

- **Suitable Locations:** Indoors, outdoors, or greenhouse
- **Size:** Medium to large
- **Growing Media:** Perlite or clay pellets
- **Electrical:** Required
- **Crops:** Leafy greens and large flowering crops, including tomatoes, cucumbers, and peppers

Top drip systems supply nutrient solutions to the top surface of the substrate.

Single vs. Double Bucket

Traditional Dutch buckets use a single bucket full of substrate. Single bucket systems have a couple limitations: it is difficult to check the health of the plant roots and they can be tricky to unclog if the drainage site gets clogged. These limitations can be removed by using a double-bucket system. A double-bucket design, like the one in this chapter's build, uses a bucket inside a bucket.

The top bucket holds the substrate and has a lot of drainage sites. The bottom bucket has the single drainage site that connects to the collecting pipe leading back to the reservoir. It is possible to pull out the top bucket from the bottom bucket to inspect the root health in a double-bucket system. Temporarily removing the top bucket also makes it easy to fix clogs that are preventing the drainage of nutrient solution into the collecting pipe. Most commercial hydroponic farms using Dutch buckets employ a single-bucket system because it is cheaper than double buckets and still very capable of growing great plants. I think it is important for new hydroponic gardeners to have the ability to check root health, so this chapter shows a double-bucket system.

CROPS

Dutch buckets are commonly used for large flowering crops like hops, tomatoes, peppers, cucumbers, and eggplant. Many of these large crops can be grown for a year or more in a Dutch bucket. Leafy greens and herbs can be grown in Dutch buckets, but most hydroponic gardeners prefer to take full advantage of their buckets by growing large flowering crops.

LOCATIONS

Dutch bucket gardens are typically outdoors or in greenhouses because the crops can get huge. Many gardeners using Dutch buckets install a trellis system next to the buckets so plant growth can be directed upward and managed in a space-efficient manner. Using Dutch buckets indoors is an option, but the growth needs to be managed in a way that makes efficient use of grow lights. Some grow lights can be installed vertically to light a vertically trellised crop. Most indoor gardeners set up a horizontal trellis and weave the plant growth horizontally to create an even height canopy. A nice level canopy is great for grow lights because it creates minimal shading of other plants and maximizes the use of light.

HOW TO BUILD A RECIRCULATING TOP DRIP BUCKET SYSTEM

This build guide only shows one top drip bucket, but this bucket design, irrigation delivery system, and drainage setup could be expanded to accommodate many buckets.

MATERIALS & TOOLS

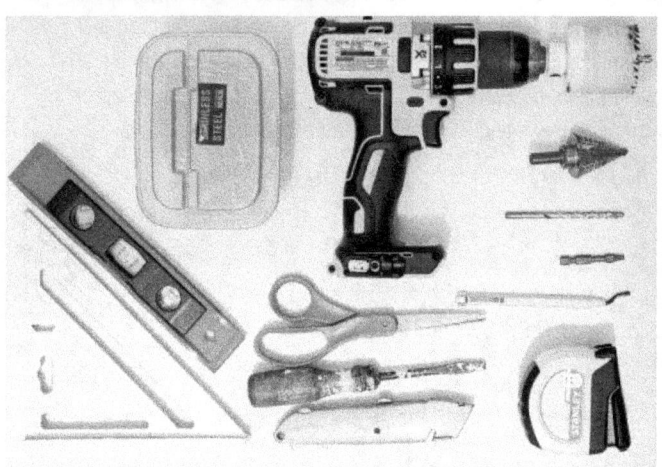
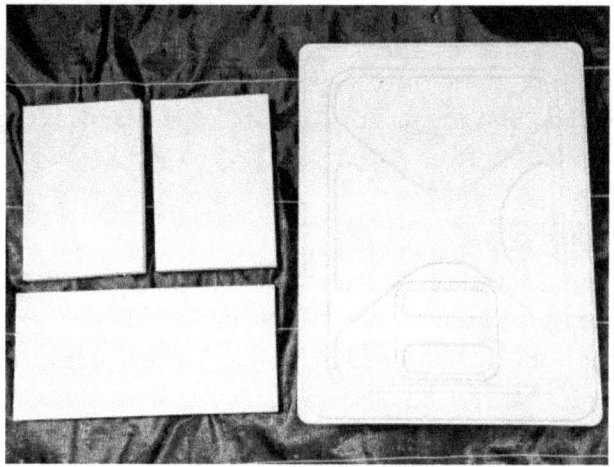

Frame
- 1 — 2 × 12" × 8' lumber
- 1 gal. — White water-based latex primer, sealer, and stain blocker (KILZ 2 LATEX)
- 1 lb. — #10 × 2½" exterior screws

Buckets
- 2 — Square bucket
- 1 — ¾" elbow
- 1 — ¾" gasket

Substrate
- Expanded clay pellets

Irrigation
- 4' — 1½" PVC
- 1 — 1½" rubber cap with clamp
- 1 — 1½" rubber elbow with clamps
- 2 — 1½" EMT 2-hole strap
- 20 gal. — Reservoir
- 5' — ¾" black vinyl tubing
- 1 — Submersible water pump, 550 GPH
- 3 — ¾" EMT 2-hole strap
- 1 — Zip tie
- 2 — ¼" double barbed connectors
- 4' — ¼" black vinyl tubing
- 1 — Outlet timer

Tools
- Circular saw
- Hacksaw
- Paint roller and/or paintbrush
- Level
- Rafter square
- Tape measure
- Permanent marker
- Drill
- 3/16" drill bit
- Drill bit matching screws
- Step drill bit with ⅛" increments from ¼" to 1⅜"
- Deburring tool
- 2" hole drill bit
- Heavy-duty scissors
- Irrigation line hole punch

Optional
- Trellis netting, 5 × 30', 3½" mesh
- 2 — Ball valves (shut off valves)
- 2 — Irrigation stakes

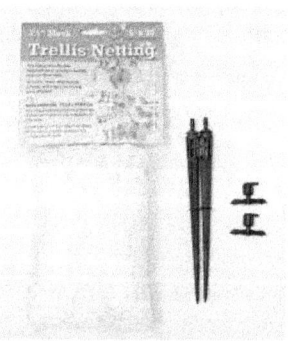

Safety Equipment
- Work gloves
- Eye protection

HYDROPONIC GROWING SYSTEMS **85**

Frame Assembly and Bucket Preparation

Bucket selection is very important. The ideal bucket is square and there should be at least a 2-inch gap between the buckets when stacked into each other. The buckets in this garden were obtained for free from the bakery section of a grocery store. Many bakeries receive their raw ingredients in large square buckets.

There are many ways to make frame assembly easier. Most stores that sell lumber offer to cut the lumber to specific dimensions if requested. Request the dimensions listed in the steps below to skip the work of cutting the lumber and to reduce the number of tools required.

The frame should slope toward the reservoir. Some growers prefer to use cinder blocks as supports for the buckets, or a mix of cinder blocks and wood. Top drip buckets can get heavy, so make sure the frame is capable of supporting a lot of weight.

1. Wearing work gloves and eye protection, cut the 2 × 12" × 8' board into the following lengths:
   - 2 × 12" × 16"
   - 2 × 12" × 16¼"
   - 2 × 12" × 2'
2. Remove any labels from the buckets.
3. Paint the lumber before assembly. The outer buckets can be painted too, if desired. The inner bucket in the double Dutch bucket does not need to be painted.
4. Measure and mark drainage holes in the inner bucket and drill the holes using the $^3/_{16}$" drill bit. The top bucket should be quick draining.
5. Build the frame using the 16" and 16¼" boards as legs. The shorter support leg is closest to the reservoir to create a slope toward the reservoir and is positioned 7½" from the edge of the 2 × 12" × 2' board to create an overhang. Use the level and square to assemble the frame with the 2½" screws.

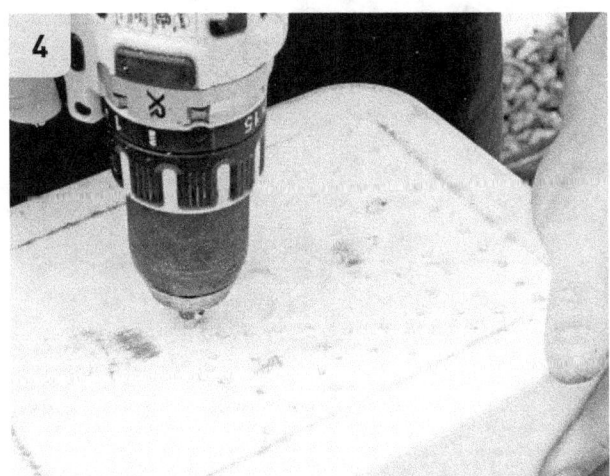

6 Keeping the lid of the top bucket is optional. A lid on the top bucket can help reduce algae buildup. Create holes in the lid larger than the size of the transplants. Most Dutch buckets are capable of growing at least two plants.

Assemble the Irrigation System

This irrigation design can be modified to add more buckets to the garden. To expand this garden, increase the length of the frame, the 1½" PVC line, and the ¾" vinyl tubing, and add additional ¼" lines coming off the ¾" vinyl tubing for the additional buckets.

7 Cut the PVC into a 25" segment and a 10" segment.

8 Check the positioning of the bucket and PVC pipe. There should be enough space on either side of the PVC pipe to fasten an EMT strap.

9 Cap the end of the 25" PVC pipe with the 1½" rubber cap. Tighten the clamp on the cap.

10 Attach the 1½" rubber elbow to the other end of the 2'1" PVC pipe.

11 Fasten the 25" PVC pipe to the frame with the two 1½" EMT straps.

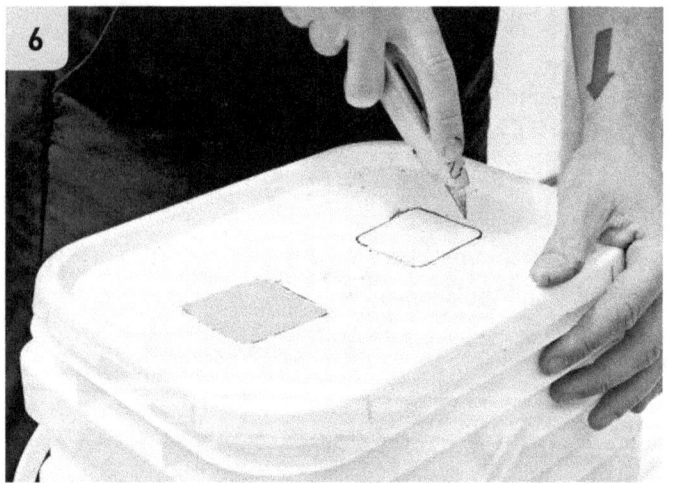
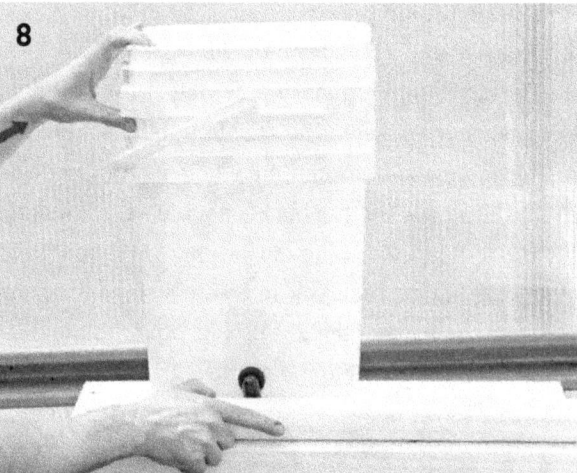
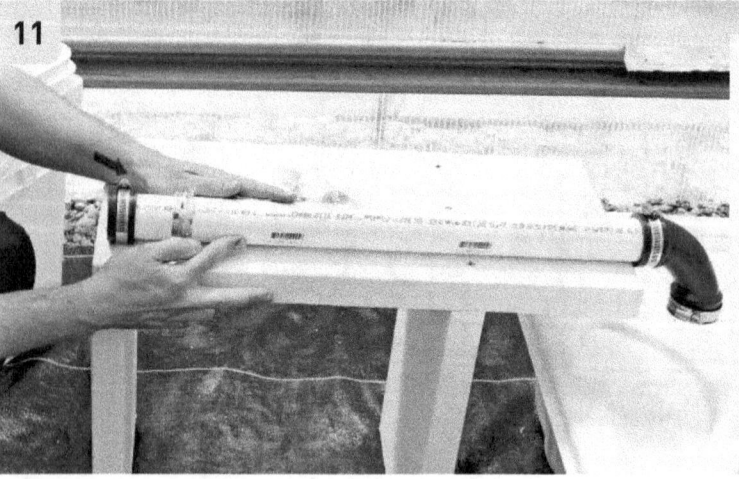
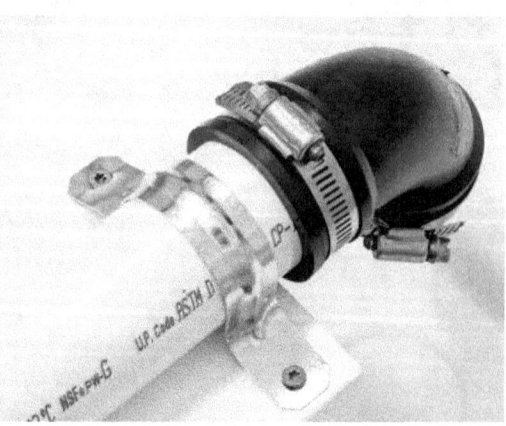

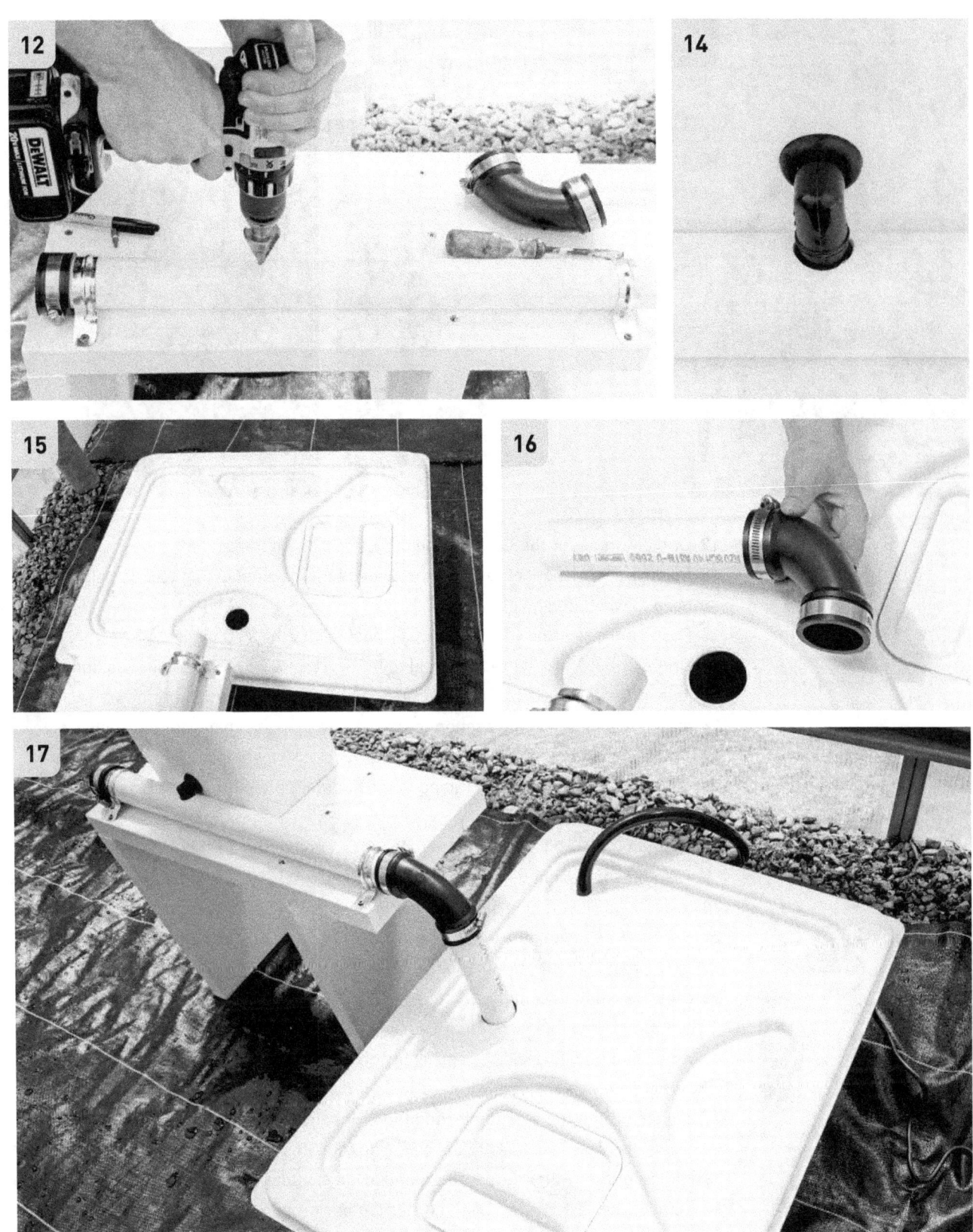

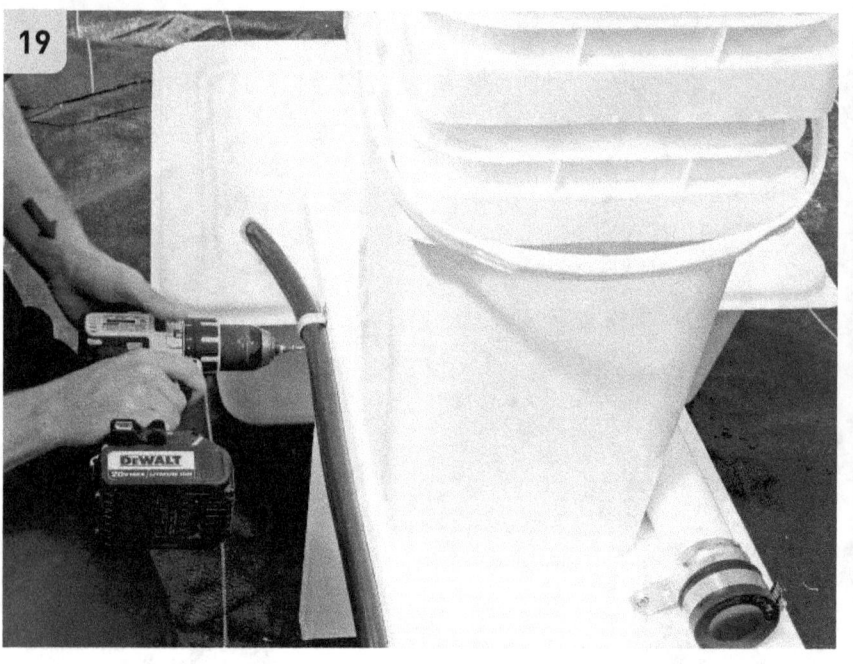

12. Drill a 1" hole for the ¾" drainage elbow from the bucket.
13. Use the deburring tool to clean the drilled hole. The deburring tool can also be used to widen the hole.
14. Position the ¾" elbow from the lower bucket into the PVC pipe.
15. Drill a 2" hole into the reservoir lid to fit the 1½" PVC drainage line. Position the hole in the reservoir so there will be minimal bend in the rubber elbow.
16. Attach the 10" PVC pipe section to the 2'1" PVC pipe section with the rubber elbow.
17. Drill a 1" hole in the reservoir lid for the ¾" black vinyl tubing.
18. Connect the ¾" black vinyl tubing to the submersible pump placed inside the reservoir.
19. Position the ¾" black vinyl tubing along the edge of the 2 × 12" × 2' board. Fasten into position using the ¾" EMT straps.
20. Leave 6" of vinyl tubing after the last EMT strap. Cut off the excess.
21. Use a zip tie to kink the end of the ¾" tube. This zip tie can be removed to rinse out the irrigation line or to expand the system.
22. Create a small hole in the ¾" tube for the ¼" double barbed connector. The hole can be made with an irrigation line hole punch or the tip of a screw. Start with a very small hole to avoid the possibility of making the hole too large. If the hole is too large, the ¾" tube will need to be replaced. Insert the ¼" double barbed connector into the small hole, and then repeat to add a second ¼" double barbed connector. This is similar to the NFT irrigation design, starting on page 69.
23. Fill the bucket with pre-rinsed expanded clay pellets.
24. Remove the reservoir and hand water the bucket to rinse out any plastic shavings or remaining clay dust on the pellets.

25 Place the reservoir back in place and partially fill with water.

26 Cut two 2' segments of ¼" black vinyl tubing. Connect these ¼" tubes to the ¼" double barbed connectors in the ¾" black vinyl tubing.

27 Plug in the pump to test the irrigation. Check for leaks in the ¾" tube. If leaks are detected at the ¼" double barbed connectors, replace the ¾" tube. If leaks are detected at the end of the ¾" tube, tighten and/or replace the zip tie.

28 In this top drip design, I used ball valves (shutoff valves) and irrigation stakes. This is not required, but it is helpful. Ball valves are great for controlling flow when connecting many buckets to one pump. The flow can be restricted at buckets near the pump to even out the flow among all the buckets.

29 Fully fill the reservoir, amend with fertilizer, and adjust the pH if needed. Attach the pump to a timer. This system has operated great with 15 minutes on and then 30 minutes off, cycling 24 hours a day. This irrigation frequency works in my specific environment, which is very sunny and hot. Indoors or in cooler environments it may be beneficial to increase the off time between irrigation cycles. This system uses clay pellets that drain very quickly, so fortunately it is difficult to overwater plants in this top drip design.

When transplanting seedlings, check to see that the seedlings receive water when the pump turns on. Adjust the ¼" lines and/or irrigation stakes if necessary.

A trellis is very helpful with large, sprawling crops like cucumbers. It can help manage and contain the growth to a small footprint by directing the growth vertically.

GROWING SYSTEM

MEDIA BEDS

Media beds are a fairly simple hydroponic garden design. A grow bed is periodically flooded and drained using nutrient solution from a reservoir that is generally placed directly under the grow bed. This setup is very similar to the flood and drain garden design covered in the next section, the major difference being the placement of the substrate. Media bed gardens simply load the substrate into the grow bed, eliminating the need for pots.

Pros
- Easy to grow a wide range of crops
- Great for aquaponics, provides a lot of surface area for beneficial bacteria

Cons
- Limited to just a few substrate options for filling the grow bed, difficult to use fine-textured substrates
- Difficult to clean

A fun approach to hydroponics that lets you use your imagination.

- **Suitable Locations:** Indoors, outdoors, or greenhouse
- **Size:** Small to large
- **Growing Media:** Expanded clay pellets
- **Electrical:** Required
- **Crops:** Leafy greens, herbs, strawberries, and other short crops

CROPS

Media beds are great for long-term crops. When a plant is removed from a media bed it is very difficult to completely remove the roots. Often some of these roots will break off and these can quickly accumulate in a media bed if using fast-growing crops like lettuce. Herbs that can be cut and regrow are great options because they can be harvested without removing the plant and damaging the root system. The media bed in the following guide is too small for flowering crops like tomatoes

> **Aquaponic Media Beds**
>
> Media beds are very popular in aquaponics. The bed acts as both a physical and a biological filter for the fish waste. The coarse substrate in the grow bed provides plenty of surface area for beneficial bacteria that are capable of breaking down and converting fish waste into plant-available nutrients. The grow bed can also catch the solid fish waste, helping keep the fish tank clean.
>
> Media beds often function well for the first couple of crops but eventually they need to be cleaned. The root systems of harvest crops start to break down and organic matter begins to accumulate in the grow bed. Some of this organic matter is broken down into nutrients that are available to the plants, but eventually there will be too much organic matter and the substrate in the bed will need to be removed to do a deep clean of the grow bed. Most of the substrates used in media beds can be sterilized, rinsed, and reused.

and cucumbers, but some aquaponics media beds are much larger and can easily handle large flowering crops.

LOCATIONS

Media beds can be designed for any location. The media bed in the following guide is great for indoors but could also be placed outdoors or in a greenhouse. Media beds placed outdoors may have some issues if there is a lot of rain—the reservoir may flood and the nutrients washed away—but the reservoir can easily be amended with fertilizer to return the EC to a target range.

SUBSTRATE OPTIONS

Expanded clay pellets, expanded shale, river stone, lava rock, aquarium gravel, and drainage gravel are just some of the substrate options in a media bed. Be sure to use substrate made from large particles that are pH neutral (avoid limestone). Always prewash any substrate used in a media bed. It is possible to use a very coarse coco coir (coco croutons), but it is not ideal. Coco holds more water than traditional media bed substrates, so the irrigation frequency will likely need to be reduced. Coco will trap more roots from harvest plants and cleanings may need to be more frequent. Coco also decomposes, so eventually it will need to be completely replaced.

IRRIGATION METHODS

The traditional method for irrigating a media bed is with fill and drain fittings. Both of the fittings are secured in the bottom of the grow bed. The fill fitting is flush, or nearly flush, with the bottom of the grow bed and the drain fitting is elevated to just slightly below the surface of the grow bed. During an irrigation cycle the water enters the grow bed through the fill fitting and nutrient solution drains back into the reservoir through the drain fitting. The drain fitting prevents the grow bed from overflowing. When the irrigation cycle ends, the nutrient solution drains from the media bed by flowing back into the reservoir through the fill fitting. There are a couple of other popular ways to irrigate a media bed, including bell siphons and U-siphons, but for beginners I'd recommend sticking to traditional fill and drain fittings.

HOW TO BUILD A MEDIA BED FAIRY GARDEN

TOOLS

Drill
Step drill bit with ⅛"
  increments from ¼"
  to 1⅜"
Deburring tool
Heavy-duty scissors
Irrigation line hole punch
  (optional)

Safety Equipment
Work gloves
Eye protection

MATERIALS

Reservoir and Grow Bed
1	14" L × 11" W × 3¼" H plastic tote
1	14.7" L × 10.6" W × 9.1" H plastic tote (4 gal.)
	Scotch tape
	Chalkboard spray paint

Irrigation
1	Fill/drain fitting combo kit:
	¾" fill/drain fitting with screen
	½" fill/drain fitting with screen
14"	½" black vinyl tubing
1	Submersible water pump, 160 GPH
1	Timer

Substrate
10 L	Expanded clay pebbles

Optional Waterwheel Addition
1	¼" double barbed connector
3'	¼" black vinyl tubing
1	Waterwheel
1	¼" shutoff valve
1	Zip tie

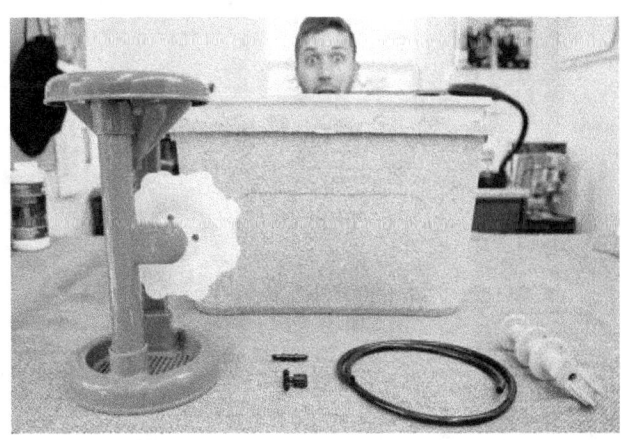

94 DIY HYDROPONIC GARDENS

 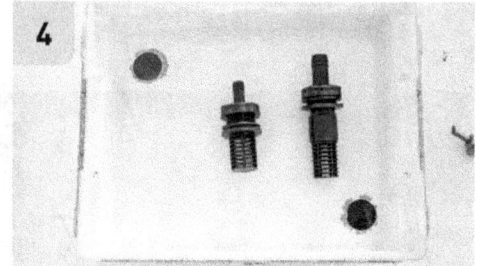

Prepare the Reservoir and Grow Bed

Picking a grow bed and reservoir that fit well together is critical. The bottom of the grow bed should fit inside the reservoir and the lip of the grow bed should hang over the edge of the reservoir.

1. Add a strip of tape on the side of the reservoir. Fold the end of the tape under the bottom. This tape will be removed after painting to create a viewing window into the reservoir to check water height.
2. Spray paint the grow bed and reservoir. Make sure they are fully opaque so light does not enter the reservoir, leading to algae growth. I used two layers of spray paint on this garden.
3. Remove the tape once the spray paint dries to create a viewing window.
4. Wearing work gloves and eye protection, drill 1⅜" holes in opposite corners of the grow bed.
5. Use a deburring tool to smooth the holes.

Assemble the Irrigation System

6. Connect the fill and drain fittings to the grow bed. The drain fitting has a ¾" connector. Use one riser on the drain fitting.
7. Cut a piece of ½" black vinyl tubing long enough to reach the fill fitting while connected to the pump positioned at the bottom of the reservoir. It is better to have this tube be a little too long rather than too short.
8. Connect one end of ½" vinyl tubing to the fill fitting and the other to the submersible pump.

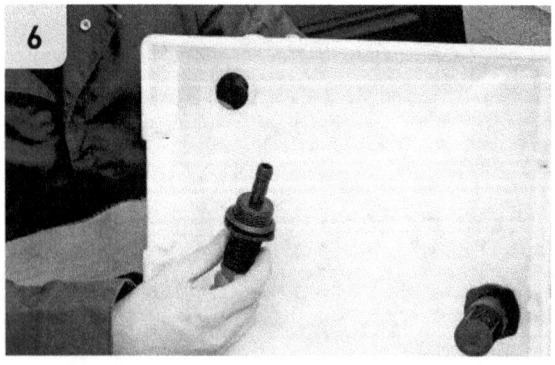 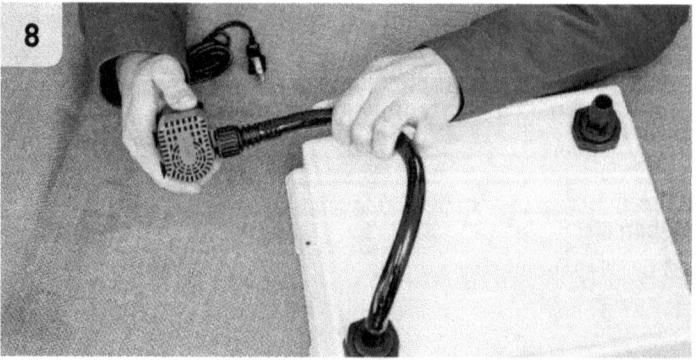

HYDROPONIC GROWING SYSTEMS

9. Fill the reservoir with water.
10. Position the pump at the bottom of the reservoir and place the grow bed over the reservoir.
11. Plug in the pump to test the irrigation system. Check that the grow bed does not overflow and the drain fitting is working properly.
12. Fill the grow bed with pre-rinsed expanded clay pellets. The water should not flood higher than the surface of the grow bed, so the clay pellets should cover the screen of the drain fitting. This grow bed was shallower than I originally thought, so I ended up removing the riser on the drain fitting so the drain fitting would be submerged under the clay pellets.
13. At this point the media bed is operational. Simply amend the reservoir with fertilizer and plant. The following additions are purely for aesthetics and are not required for this garden to function properly.

TIP

Expanded clay pellets can be reused. Remove old plant roots after harvesting, and then sterilize the pellets with a mild bleach solution, hydrogen peroxide, isopropyl alcohol, or heat. Boiling clay pellets is a great way to sanitize them without using chemicals.

Waterwheel Addition (Optional)

Most of the decorations in this fairy garden are Legos and small toys. The only decoration that involved any major adjustment to the garden was the waterwheel. The following steps detail how to add a water line from the main irrigation line to power a waterwheel.

14. Use the irrigation hole punch to create a small hole in the ½" vinyl tubing.
15. Insert a ¼" double barbed connector into the ½" vinyl tubing.
16. Connect the ¼" black vinyl tubing to the ¼" double barbed connector.
17. Drill a ¼" hole in the funnel of the waterwheel using the step drill bit.
18. Remove the clay pellets from the grow bed so the base of the waterwheel is set on the bottom of the grow bed. Place the waterwheel in the middle of the grow bed.
19. String the ¼" black vinyl tubing to the waterwheel. Insert the shutoff valve.
20. Secure the ¼" black vinyl tubing to the legs of the waterwheel with a zip tie.

21 Connect the remaining ¼" vinyl tubing to the shutoff valve and string it through the ¼" hole in the waterwheel funnel. Cut off the excess tubing.

22 Turn on the pump to test the waterwheel. Adjust the shutoff valve until water flows to the waterwheel. Make sure the pump intake is set to fully open for maximum flow.

Above: The crops planted in this garden include rainbow swiss chard, nasturtium, dill, chervil, purslane, and Thai basil. These crops can be harvested multiple times. A 2' four-tube T5 grow light fits perfectly over this garden.

Left: Fairy gardens don't need to house only fairies! This garden has dump trucks, dinosaurs, and Legos.

GROWING SYSTEM

FLOOD AND DRAIN

- **Suitable Locations:** Indoors, outdoors, or greenhouse
- **Size:** Small to large
- **Growing Media:** Perlite, expanded clay pellets, stone wool, or coco coir
- **Electrical:** Required
- **Crops:** Any crop depending on pot size

THE FLOOD AND DRAIN TECHNIQUE goes by many names, including "ebb and flow" and "ebb and flood." These names all describe the irrigation method used in this garden design. A nutrient solution is pumped to flood a grow tray and then it drains. This is similar to the media bed design covered in the previous section, but flood and drain gardens do not fill the grow bed with substrate. Flood and drain gardens generally use pots filled with a hydroponic substrate or stone wool blocks.

CROPS

The flood and drain garden shown in the guide below can easily be modified for anything from microgreens to large flowering crops. A flood and drain garden can grow nearly any crop with a few adjustments to irrigation frequency, pot size, substrate selection, and flood height (drain height).

LOCATIONS

Suitable for any location. This garden will have similar issues as other garden designs if placed outdoors and exposed to heavy rain, the primary issue being the washing away and dilution of the nutrient solution.

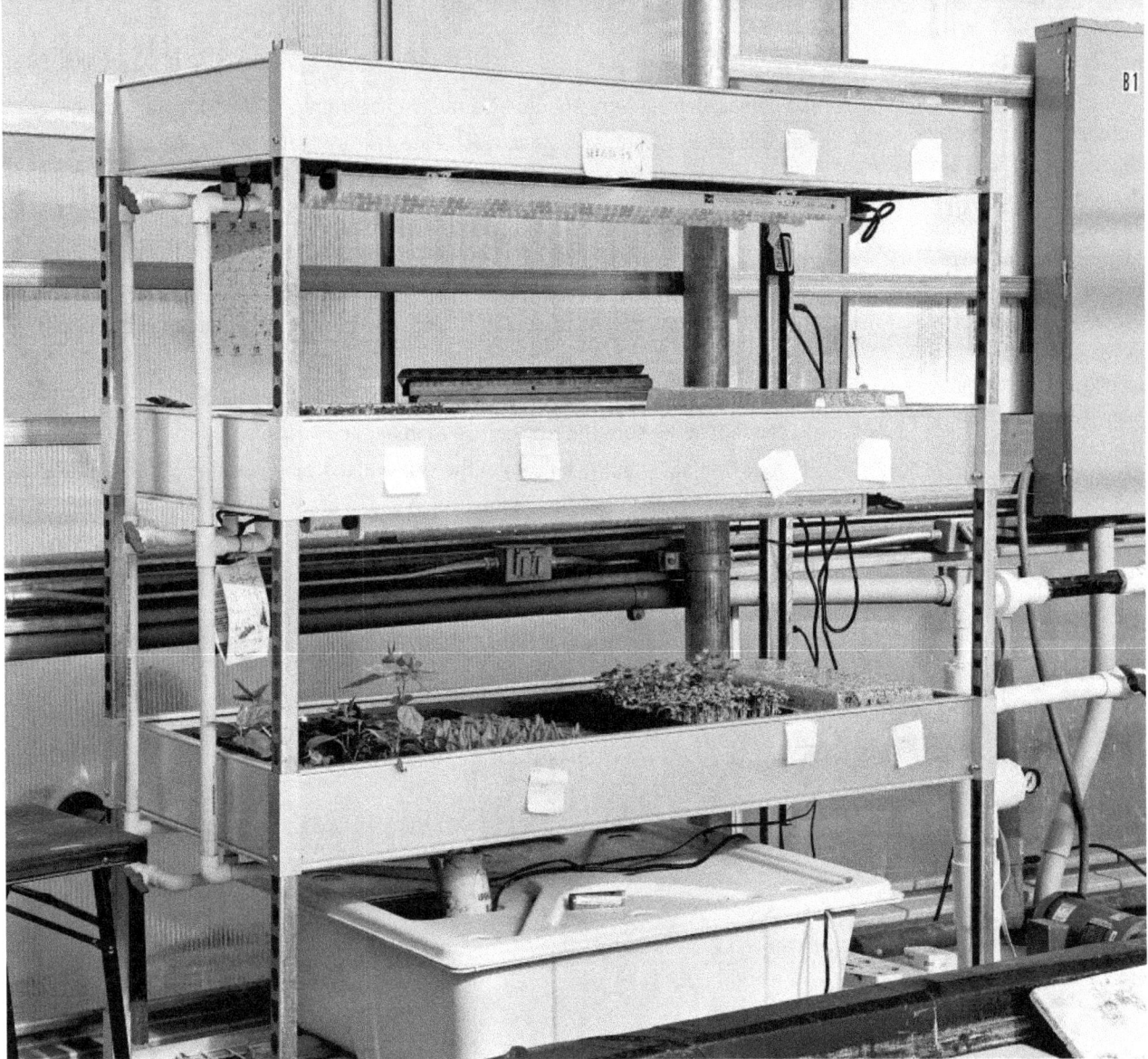

VARIATIONS

The build guide shows several flood and drain variations. Here are just a few ways to modify this garden design:

- Change pot size. Larger pots are great for large flowering crops. Many small pots might be more manageable for leafy greens and herbs.
- Change pot material. Plastic pots are great but they can sometimes lose substrate through drainage holes. This loose substrate can then clog irrigation lines. Fabric pots are perfect for flood and drain gardens because they make it nearly impossible to lose substrate. The fabric allows the nutrient solution to quickly reach the plant, and then it drains quickly, giving the roots access to air and preventing overwatering.
- Change substrate. Expanded clay pellets are great because they are difficult to overwater and are reusable. Coco is another great option; it holds more water,

Flood and drain is a popular design for vertical gardens because the grow beds can be stacked on a rack with one reservoir at the bottom for all the levels.

Coco root rugs create a hybrid between flood and drain and media bed systems. The root rugs allow roots to grow along the entire tray, similar to a media bed, yet the plants are kept in individual pots (or blocks) like a flood and drain. Root rugs keep the surface of the grow tray clean and reduce the potential for algae growth. The primary drawback of root rugs is the price.

so irrigation frequency should be adjusted accordingly. Other popular options include perlite, peat, and stone wool. Fine-textured substrates like coco, peat, and small perlite are often best in fabric pots to avoid losing substrate from the pots' drainage holes.

- Change grow bed size. Prefabricated flood and drain trays come in many sizes, generally ranging from 1 to 4 feet wide and 2 to 12 feet long. DIY grow beds can be as big or as small as you want. A grow bed can be constructed from concrete mixing trays, intermediate bulk containers (IBC totes), plastic storage totes, dish tubs, or even wood with a plastic liner (similar to the wicking bed design). Whatever is chosen, make sure the tray can be modified to include a fill fitting that is flush, or nearly flush, with the bottom of the tray and a drainage fitting that is elevated above the surface. Most flood and drain designs place the drainage fitting about one-third the height of the selected pots.

HOW TO BUILD A FLOOD AND DRAIN SYSTEM

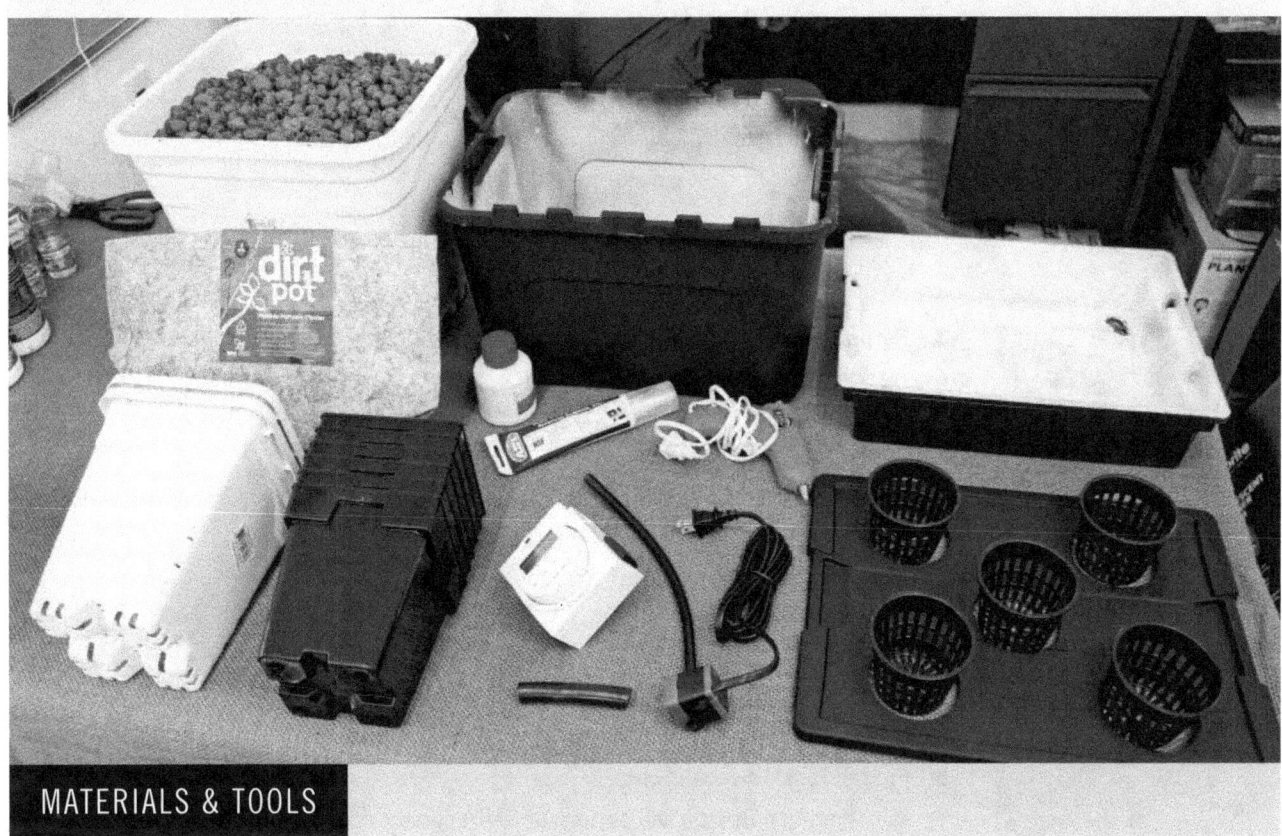

MATERIALS & TOOLS

Reservoir and Grow Bed
- 1   14" L × 11" W × 3¼" H plastic tote
- 1   14.7" L × 10.6" W × 9.1" H plastic tote (4 gal.)
- Scotch tape
- Spray paint

Irrigation
- 11"   5/16" black vinyl tubing
- 4"   ½" black vinyl tubing
- 1   Submersible water pump, 40 GPH
- 1   Outlet timer

Substrate and Pots*
- 2   6" square pot
- or
- 4   5" square pot
- or
- 1   2-gal. fabric pot
- or
- 5   3" net pot
- or
- Grodan A-OK 36/40 cubes (for microgreens)

This garden can be modified to fit a wide variety of pots. See the planting options before deciding on pot selection.

Tools
- Drill
- Step drill bit with ⅛" increments from ¼" to 1⅜"
- Hot glue gun
- Heavy-duty scissors
- 2¾" hole saw drill bit

Safety Equipment
- Work gloves
- Eye protection

Prepare the Reservoir and Grow Bed

Picking a grow bed and reservoir that fit well together is critical. The bottom of the grow bed should fit inside the reservoir and the lip of the grow bed should hang over the edge of the reservoir.

1 Add a strip of tape on the side of the reservoir. Fold the end of the tape under the bottom. This tape will be removed after painting to create a viewing window into the reservoir to check water height.
2 Spray paint the grow bed, grow bed lid, and reservoir. Make sure they are fully opaque so light does not enter the reservoir. If light enters the reservoir it can lead to algae growth. I used two layers of chalkboard spray paint on this garden.
3 Remove the tape once the spray paint dries to create a viewing window.
4 Wearing work gloves and eye protection, drill a ⅝" and a ⅜" hole in the grow bed.

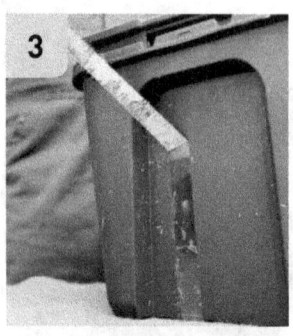

Assemble the Irrigation System

5 Insert the 11" segment of the ⁵⁄₁₆" black vinyl tubing into the ⅜" hole in the grow bed. Use the hot glue gun to fasten the ⁵⁄₁₆" tube in place. The ⁵⁄₁₆" tube should be flush with the surface of the grow bed.
6 Insert the 4" segment of ½" black vinyl tubing into the ⅝" hole in the grow bed. It does not need to be glued into position. The height of the ½" tube will be adjusted based on substrate and pot selection.
7 Connect the ⁵⁄₁₆" tube to the submersible pump.
8 Fill the reservoir with water.
9 Position the pump on the bottom of the reservoir and place the grow bed on top of the reservoir.
10 Turn on the pump. Water should fill the grow bed and drain from the ½" tube.
11 Turn the pump off and water should drain back into the reservoir through the pump.

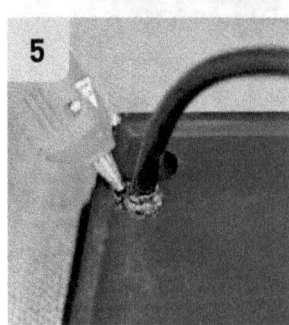

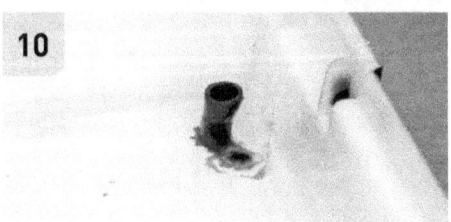

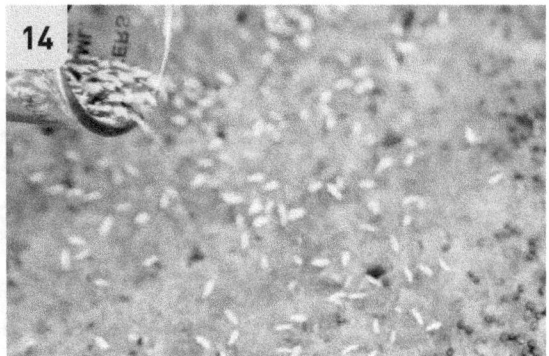

Planting and Harvesting Microgreens

12 Prepare the stone wool by rinsing it in nutrient solution.
13 Remove plugs as needed for the stone wool sheet to fit the grow bed.
14 See the Microgreen Crop Chart in the appendix for recommended seeding rates. Some microgreen seed packets will provide a recommended seeding density.
15 Gently mist the microgreen seeds. Misting the seeds twice daily for the first 3 to 5 days will help germination.
16 Most microgreens are ready to harvest after 10 to 15 days. Some varieties are slower growing and require 3 to 4 weeks before they are ready to harvest.
17 Many microgreen varieties can be harvested multiple times. Cut the young plants above their lowermost leaves to give them an opportunity to regrow.

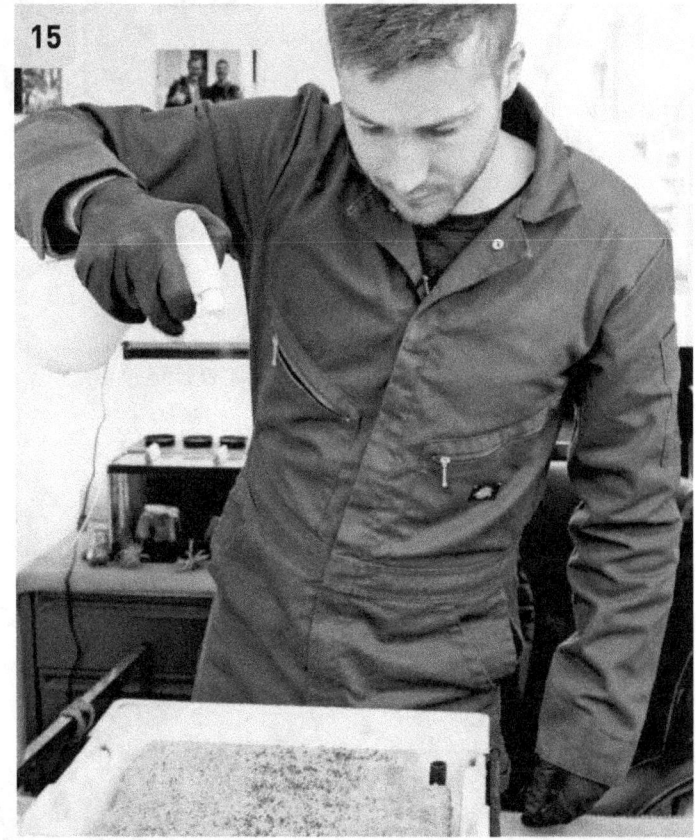

Planting Options

Option 1 This garden can fit two 6" square pots. These pots are a little tall for this flood tray. The height of the drain should be about one-third of the height of the pots in the tray. It may be possible to use taller pots, or it may be necessary to water the plants from the top for the first few weeks until the roots reach the bottom of the pot.

Option 2 This garden can fit four 5" square pots. These are a great fit for this flood tray.

Option 3 This garden can fit one 2-gallon fabric pot. Fabric pots are great for holding loose substrates like coco, peat, and perlite.

Option 4 This garden can fit five 3" net pots. Drill five 2¾" holes in the lid of the flood tray to fit the net pots. This setup is great for herbs and leafy greens. The lid will reduce the potential for algae development in the flood tray. This garden can grow microgreens too.

GROWING SYSTEM

AEROPONICS

Aeroponics is a very exciting hydroponic technique. It offers the potential for very fast growth and huge yields while using very little water. There are two major categories within aeroponics: high pressure and low pressure.

High Pressure The build guide below shows how to build a high-pressure aeroponic garden. Most hydroponic growers think of high-pressure designs when they hear the term *aeroponics*. A pump is attached to a main irrigation line, often PVC, and misters are inserted into the PVC line. The pump creates pressure in the PVC pipe, which helps generate a fine mist. High-pressure aeroponic designs are very popular for rooting cuttings or "clones." The fine nutrient solution mist creates a great environment for new root growth.

Low Pressure Low-pressure aeroponic gardens do not use misters. The aeroponic "mist" is often created by passing the nutrient solution through perforated disks and/or creating splashes near the plant roots. Low-pressure aeroponic systems generally have fewer moving parts and are less prone to clogging.

CROPS

Nearly any crop can be grown aeroponically. I've seen papayas grown in aeroponic systems! The most common crops for aeroponic systems are leafy greens and herbs, but do not feel limited to these options. If growing larger flowering crops, be sure to consider how the plant will be supported. Plants grown in pots can support themselves (to a certain extent) by securing their roots to the substrate. Without a substrate, the plant roots do not have much physical support and a top-heavy plant could lean or fall over if not provided with support, such as a vertical or horizontal

In an aeroponic system, plants are suspended in air, not water. Moisture is provided by emitters that deliver mist under pressure.

- **Suitable Locations:** Indoors, outdoors, or greenhouse
- **Size:** Small to large
- **Growing Media:** Perlite or clay pellets
- **Electrical:** Required
- **Crops:** Leafy greens, herbs, strawberries, and other short crops

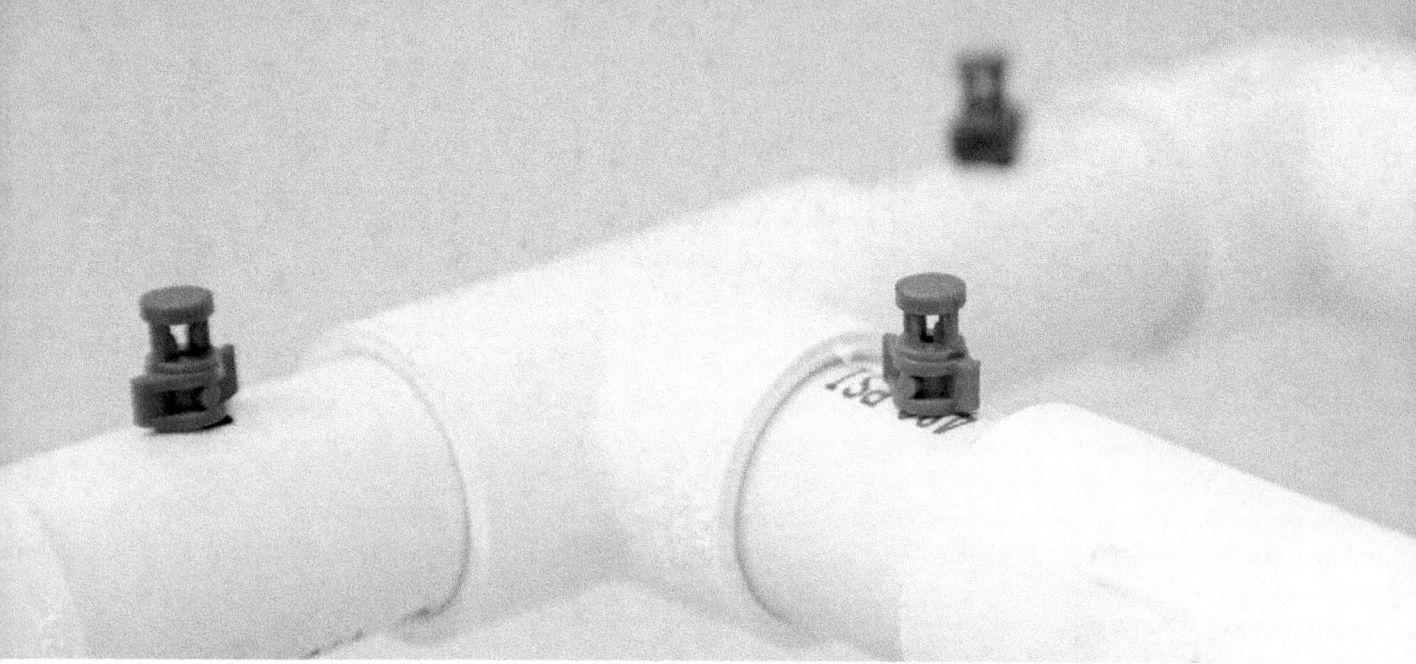

Caution

Many first-time hydroponic gardeners get very excited about aeroponics: it looks futuristic and promises the fastest growth, but it also comes with the most risk. Plants grown in aeroponics are very sensitive to grower mistakes or equipment failures. The roots are hanging in air, and if they are not watered frequently they will dry out. It does not take long for the roots to dry out to the point of being permanently damaged. Disruptions to waterings can occur for a variety of reasons, including pump failure, irrigation line clogging, mister clogging, and power outages. Other hydroponic methods are sensitive to these disruptions in watering too, but aeroponics is especially susceptible because of its fine misters and lack of substrate protecting the roots. I would never recommend a first-time hydroponic gardener start with an aeroponic garden. Some aeroponic gardens, like the low-pressure Tower Gardens, are more beginner friendly than others, but these prefabricated aeroponic systems can be very expensive. Start with a hydroponic garden that is cheap and robust, like a mini floating raft garden, and then start to experiment with more advanced techniques like aeroponics.

trellis. Long-term crops also have a greater chance of facing a power outage or an equipment failure that could quickly damage roots or kill plants that may have required many months of care.

LOCATIONS

Aeroponics is suitable for any location. Aeroponic gardens can be small and fit on kitchen counters or be massive vertical towers stretching over 15 feet tall. DIY aeroponic gardens can sometimes have issues with leaks and they should be tested before being placed in a leak-sensitive location.

HOW TO BUILD A HIGH-PRESSURE AEROPONIC SYSTEM

MATERIALS & TOOLS

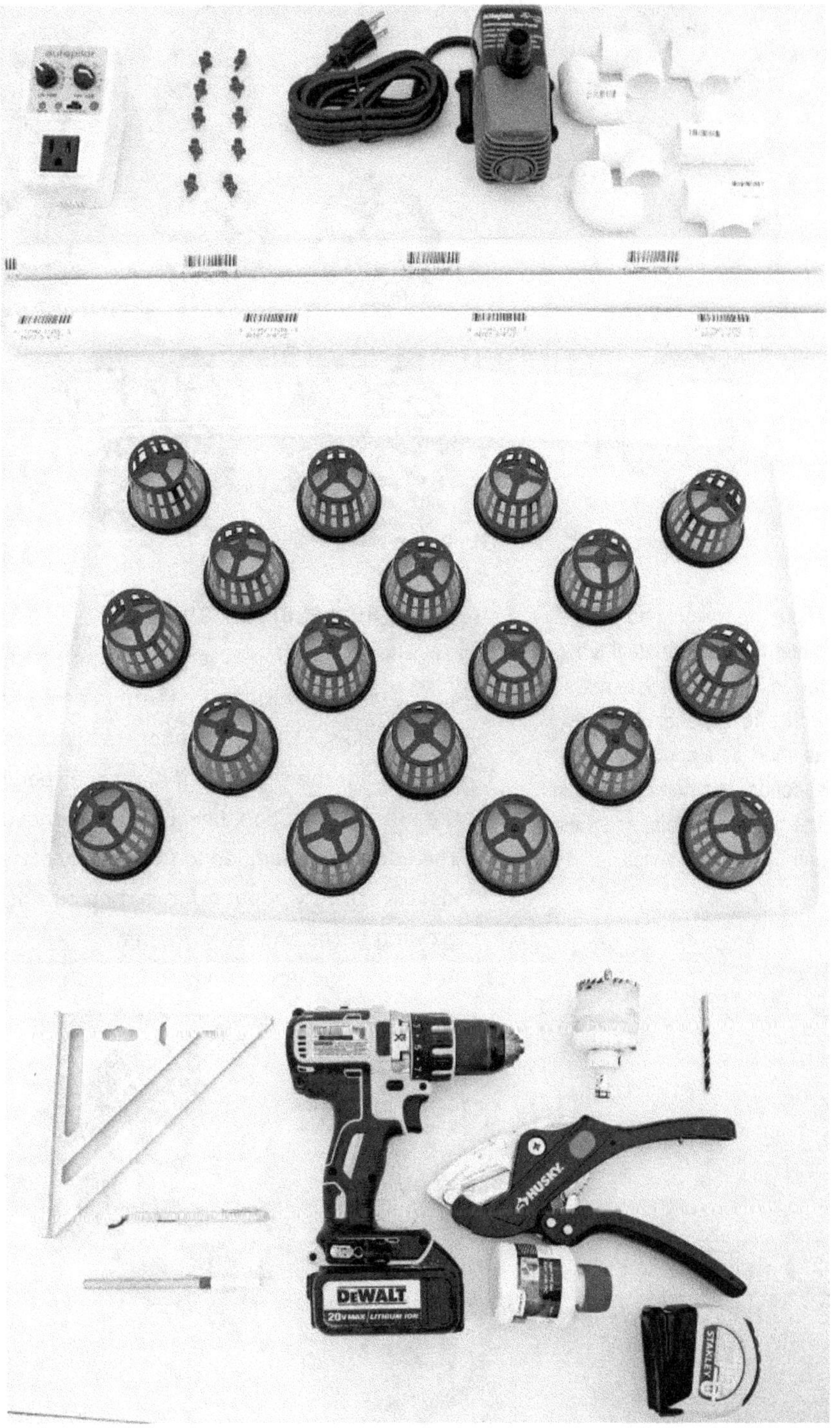

Frame

1	23½" L × 16⅞" W × 12¼" H storage tote with lid
18	2" net pot

Irrigation

6'	¾" PVC pipe
4	¾" PVC elbow
3	¾" PVC tee
1	Submersible water pump, 400 GPH
	PVC glue
10	360° mister, flow rate 31.4 GPH at 20 PSI
1	Outlet timer

Tools

Permanent marker
Drill
2" hole drill bit
Deburring tool
11/64" brad point drill bit
Titanium step drill bit with ⅛" increments from ¼" to 1⅜"
Ratcheting PVC cutter (or hacksaw)
Spray paint (if not using an opaque tote)

Safety Equipment

Work gloves
Eye protection

108 DIY HYDROPONIC GARDENS

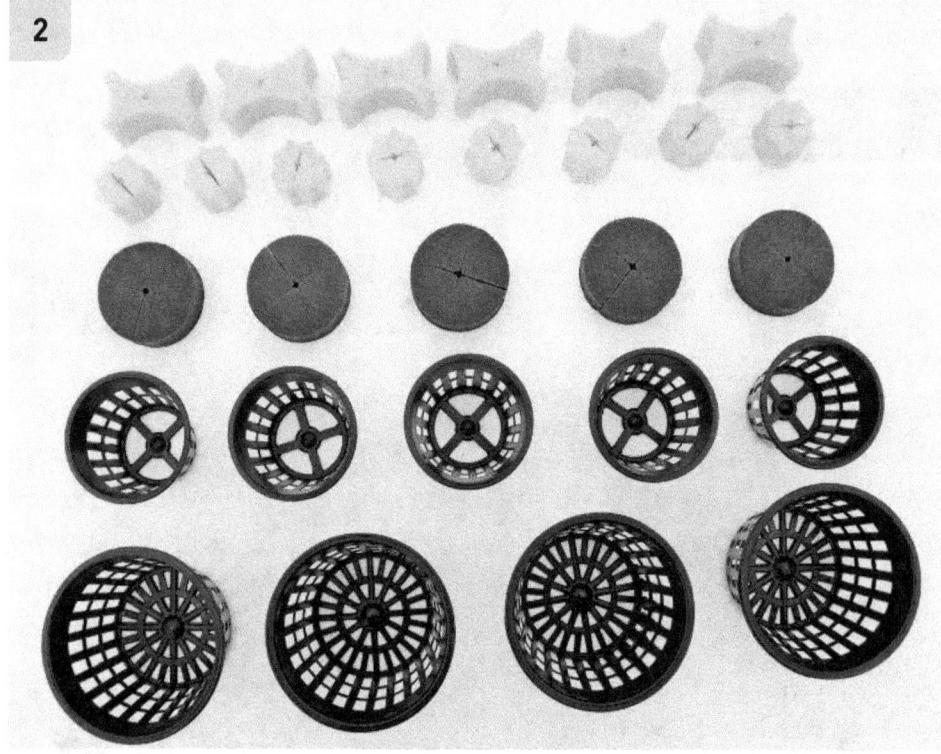

There are many options for outlet timers. The ideal timer for an aeroponic system works in very short intervals, as short as a couple of seconds. Most timers work in 15-minute intervals, and these can do the job as well.

Prepare the Reservoir and Lid

The reservoir selection is very important! It should have a tight-sealing lid. When the aeroponic irrigation turns on, there is a lot of spraying, so make sure the lid fits tightly to prevent leaks. Five-gallon buckets also work great and come with a tight-fitting lid.

1. Spray paint the reservoir if it is not already opaque. Make sure light does not reach the nutrient solution, because it can encourage algae development.
2. The lid can be modified to fit a variety of net pot sizes or foam inserts. Foam inserts are very popular for rooting cuttings, and 2" or 3" net pots are great for growing herbs and leafy greens.
3. Aeroponic systems designed for rooting cuttings can fit many sites for foam inserts. These sites are sometimes spaced 2½" apart. This aeroponic system will be using net pots spaced 3" apart, which is suitable for a variety of herbs, baby green mixes, and some miniature romaine lettuce varieties. Space the net pots 6" apart to grow full-size lettuce. Mark the lid with the location of the plant sites.

HYDROPONIC GROWING SYSTEMS

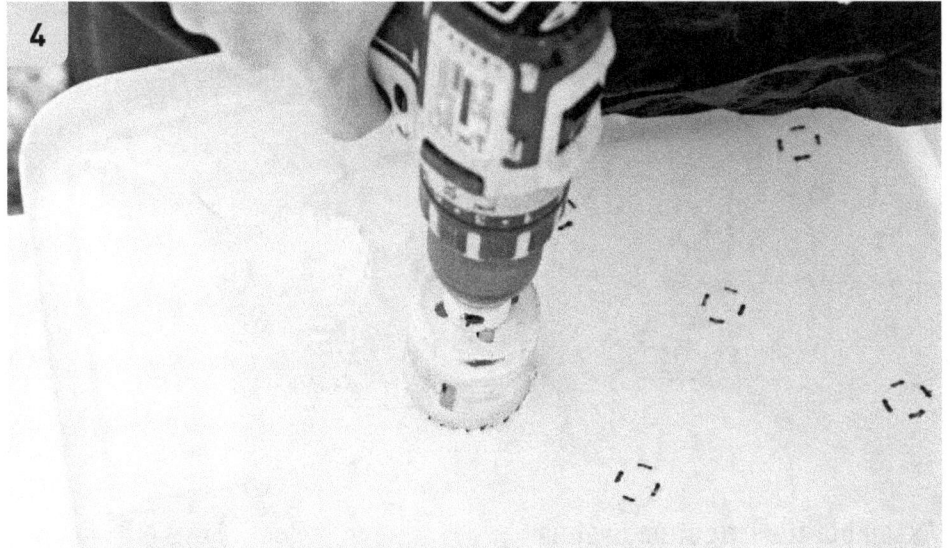

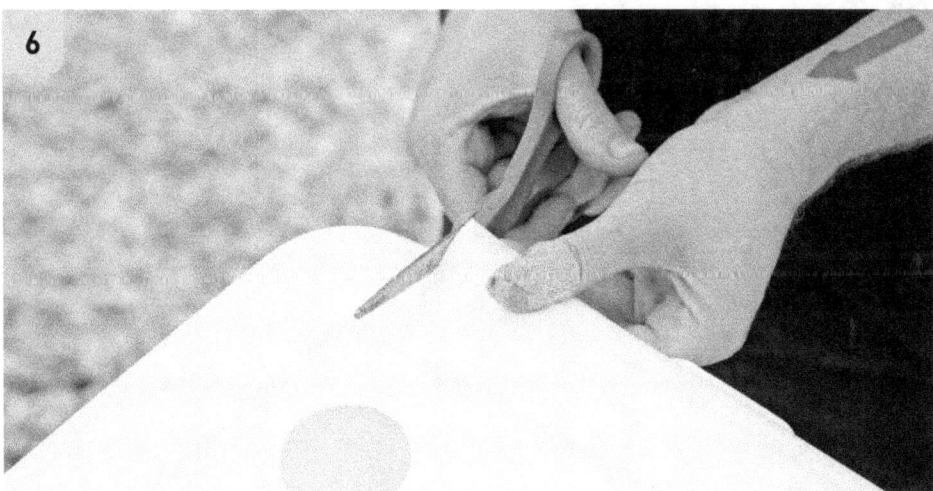

4. Wearing work gloves and eye protection, use a 2" hole drill bit to create holes for the net pots.
5. Clean the edges of the drilled holes with the deburring tool.
6. Create a very small flap on the side of the lid. This will be used for the pump's power cord. Sometimes this flap can be a source of leaks, so another option is drilling a hole in the lid for the cord to pass through and using a foam insert around the cord to cork the drilled hole.

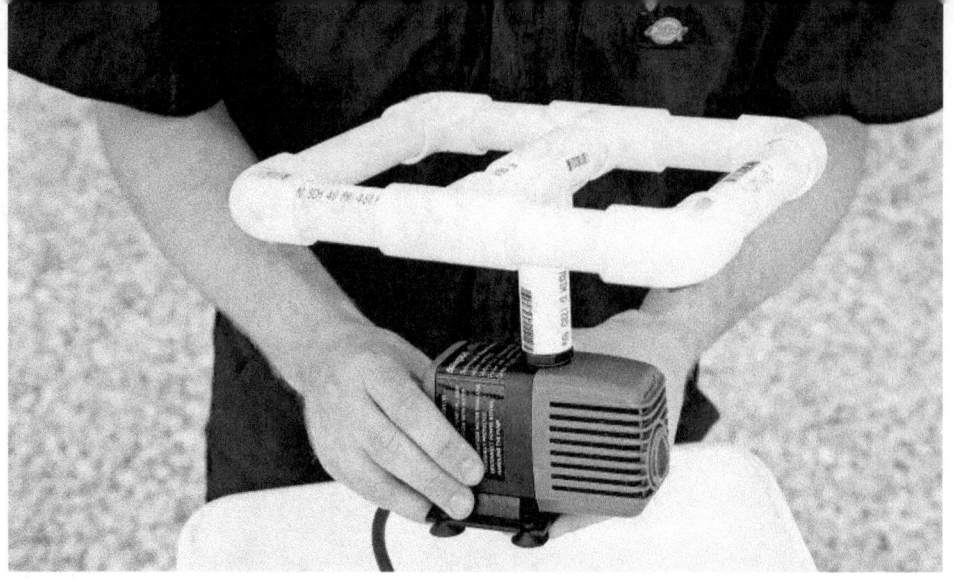

Assemble the Irrigation System

This irrigation design (pictured above) can be modified for a variety of reservoir sizes by adjusting the length of the PVC segments and moving the placement of the 360-degree misters.

7 The exact lengths of the PVC segments will depend on the reservoir and specific ¾" elbows and tees used. Do not glue any of the components together until the entire irrigation system has been test-fitted. Only glue the components together once they fit well without glue.

8 Build the center part of the irrigation manifold first. It will need to be compact enough to fit within the width of the reservoir but there should be enough space between the tees so an aeroponic mister can be installed.

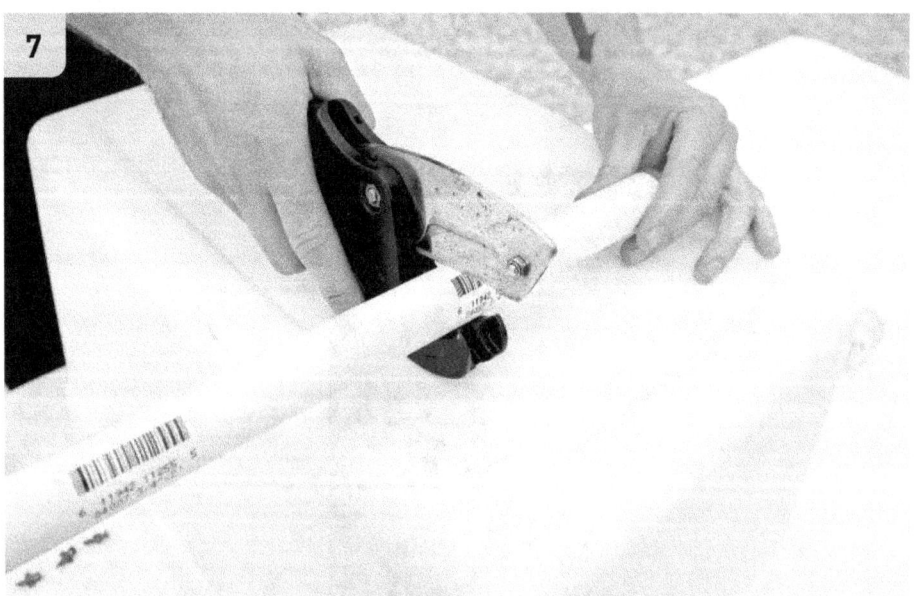

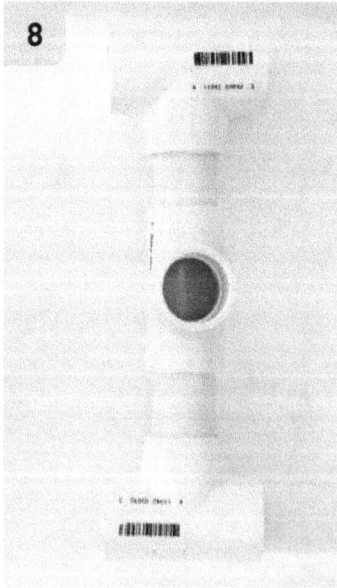

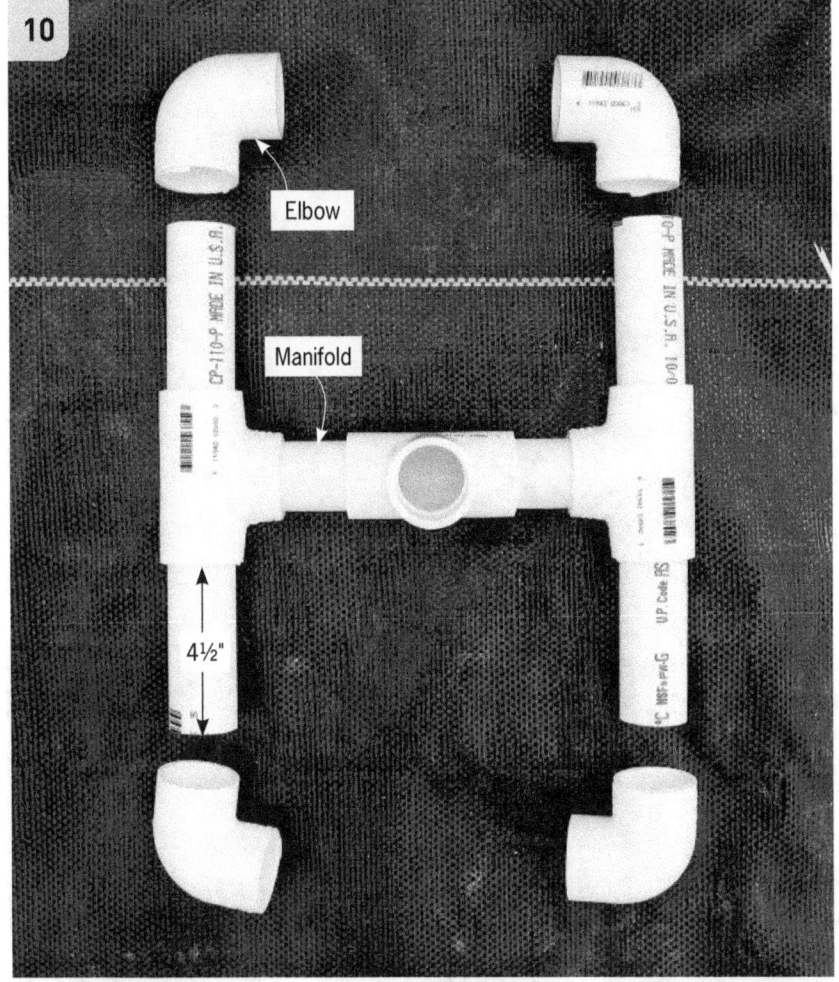

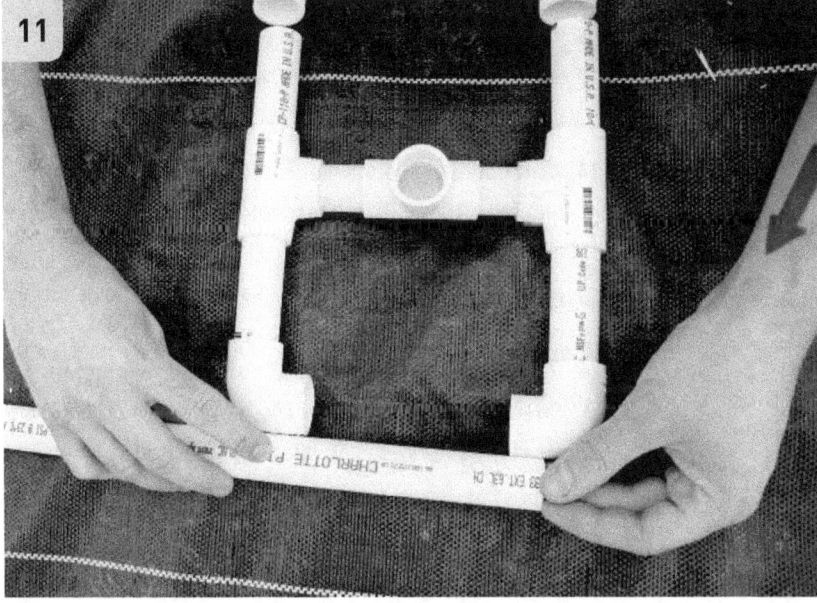

9. Cut four PVC segments of equal length and attach them to the center manifold. The segments in this design are 4½" long.
10. Connect the four elbows to the manifold.
11. Place a PVC pipe between the elbows and mark the pipe at the appropriate length for it to connect the elbows. Cut two segments of this length to connect both sides.
12. The length of the final PVC segment that will connect the manifold to the pump will depend on the height of the reservoir. It should be long enough to place the top of the manifold within 5" to 7" of the lid once it is attached to the pump. The PVC manifold should fit snugly to the ¾" fitting of the pump. If it does not fit snugly, try another fitting that came with the pump or use PVC glue to fasten PVC pipe to the fitting on the pump.
13. Mark the placement of the 360° misters. This system uses a 400 GPH pump. The misters each have a flow rate of 31.4 GPH. So, 400 GPH divided by 31.4 GPH equals 12.73. To ensure good pressure, I only used 10 misters in this system. This pump has a valve to adjust flow rate, so I added fewer misters than its maximum to ensure good flow. The flow rate can always be reduced on the pump if there is too much pressure.

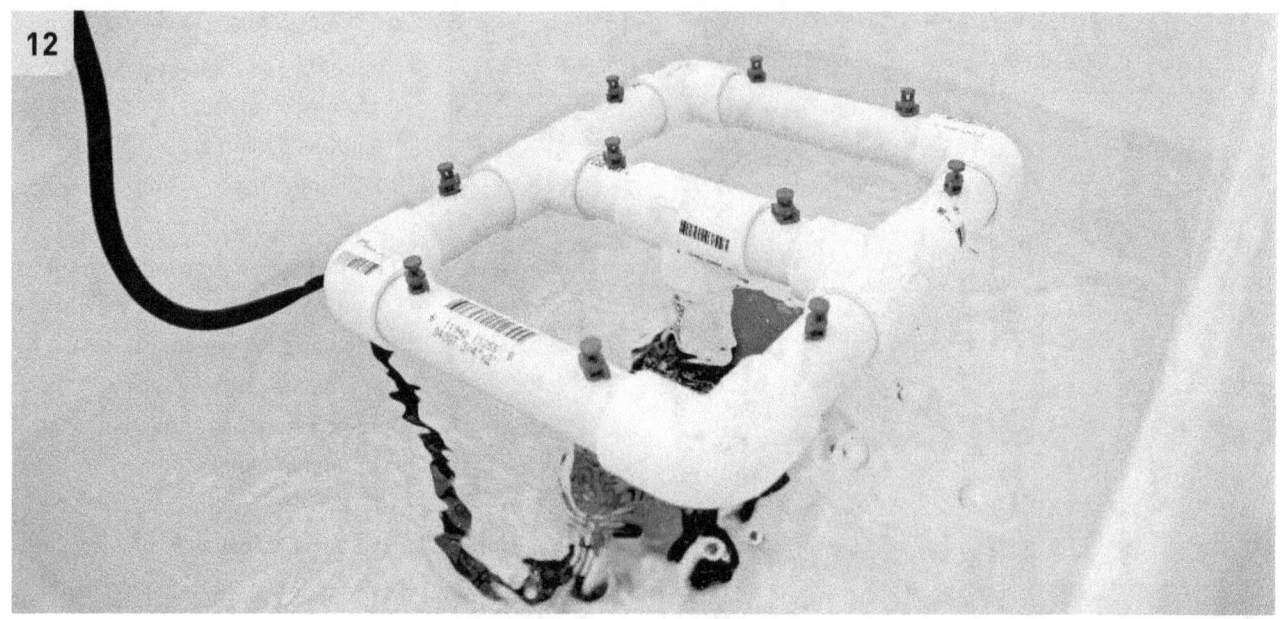

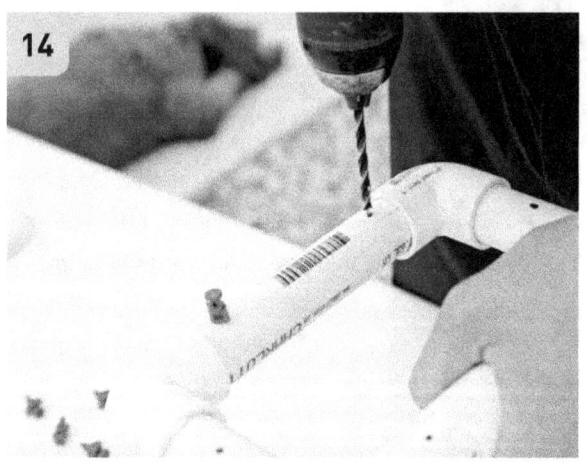

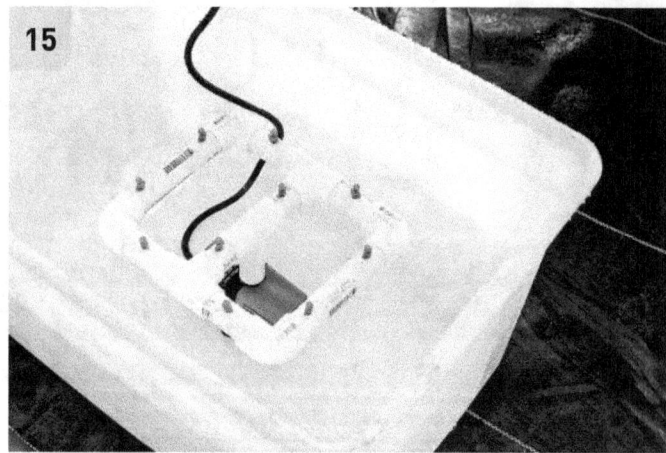

14 Drill holes at the marked spots with the ¹¹/₆₄" drill bit. Twist the 360° misters into the drilled holes.

15 Place the fully assembled irrigation manifold and pump in the center of the reservoir. Fill the reservoir with water. Do not fill over the height of the misters.

16 Place the lid on the reservoir and plug in the pump. Check the distribution of the misters to make sure all plant sites receive water.

17 Plug the pump into a timer. This garden was set to water for 10 seconds every 5 minutes. The irrigation frequency will depend on the age of the crop, the environment, the size of the pots, and the timer selection. Many aeroponic systems operate well when on for 15 minutes and then off for 15 to 45 minutes.

Plant

18 Add the net pots.

19 Amend the reservoir with a hydroponic fertilizer (do not use an organic hydroponic fertilizer). Transplant!

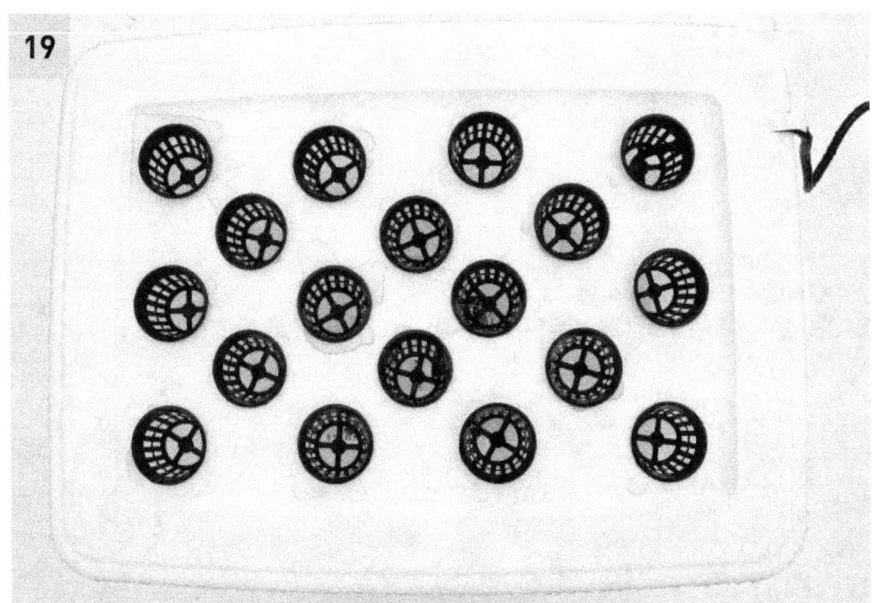

GROWING SYSTEM

VERTICAL GARDENS

VERTICAL GARDENS COME IN ALL shapes and sizes using both soil and hydroponic growing techniques. Vertical gardens are popular for gardeners with limited space because they can maximize the available growing area in a given footprint. Vertical gardens are also popular as living art installments. It is increasingly common to go to a bar, restaurant, office, or school and see a vertical garden used as an edible art installation.

There are a few considerations to keep in mind when choosing a vertical garden. First, not all crops are well suited for this production method. Large, top-heavy crops like tomatoes, eggplant, and peppers may not have the support they require if grown in a vertical garden. Most vertical hydroponic systems are best suited for leafy greens, herbs, and strawberries. The second major consideration is the light requirement of the chosen crop. Vertical gardens are notorious for having light issues if poorly designed or positioned. Sometimes vertical systems cast shade on lower crops. Insufficient light for lower crops may not be an issue during summer when there is a lot of light, but in lower light conditions this can be a problem.

Although this book focuses on hydroponics, hydroponics is not the only option when selecting a vertical garden design. The garden shown in the following project could easily be modified to use a potting mix and receive hand waterings. I personally find that putting in the initial effort of building a hydroponic system pays off in the long run because I don't have to remember to water my plants, but to each his or her own—this is DIY! Here are some of the common vertical hydroponic garden setups.

AEROPONIC TOWERS

Aeroponic systems can be either low or high pressure. A high-pressure aeroponic vertical garden will generally have a main irrigation line in the middle of a large tube or square. This main irrigation line will have evenly spaced foggers or misters that emit a fine mist for the plant roots positioned on the inside of the outer tube or square. These systems require a decent amount of pressure and can be prone to clogging. An irrigation system that uses misters or foggers requires the use of a high-quality fertilizer that will not precipitate. The grower must also be cautious of leaves and roots falling into the system, because these may break down and clog emitters.

A low-pressure aeroponic vertical garden will also have a main irrigation in the middle of a large tube or square but it will only release the nutrient solution at the top

Aeroponic towers feature a tubular tower with evenly spaced planting pockets on the outside of the tower. A central irrigation line runs vertically up the length of the tower and provides pressurized water that is dispersed to the plants through foggers or emitters inside the tower.

of the garden. The nutrient solution then falls through a series of disks that disperse the water. Tower Garden is a very popular low-pressure vertical aeroponic system. DIY versions of this system are possible, but it sometimes is advantageous to simply purchase a complete system.

DRIP TOWERS

Drip towers also come in many shapes and sizes. They almost all consist of either a vertical post or bag full of an inert substrate like perlite, coco, or stone wool. The ZipGrow tower is a vertical drip tower that has gained a lot of popularity in the past few years. It uses a plastic matrix and a capillary mat in the middle of a square post.

FLOOD AND DRAIN GROW RACKS (see pages 99 to 105)

Flood and drain grow racks are a common vertical system in commercial farms. Shown below is an image of a vertical flood and drain system by Growtainer. Many growers create their own versions of these systems. Most of these are constructed out of metal storage shelves, flood tables, and lights. When designing your own flood and drain grow rack, it is important to include shutoff valves for each level. These valves will help you adjust the flow to each level so they all fill in roughly the same amount

A drip tower circulates water into horizontal tubes at the top of the system. The water seeps down into the tops of a series of vertical growing towers that are filled with growing mats to absorb and hold the water and provide rooting material for the plants. The water runoff is captured in troughs and is recirculated to the feeder tubes on top.

Flood and drain racks are relatively simple hydroponic growing systems. Metal shelving supports plastic tubs and provides mounting surfaces for lighting. Water *floods* the tubs to irrigate the plants, then the water *drains* back to the reservoir on the lowest level.

of time. The height between levels and placement of lights is also important. Most of these grow racks have 18 to 24 inches between levels. I suggest using T5 fluorescent or LED bars for lighting. The most common problems I see with grow racks are insufficient light and poor airflow. One of the best indicators that light levels are low is spindly, stretchy growth in seedlings. The seedlings are reaching out for more light. Often, it is better to remove spindly seedlings and start over. Airflow can also help strengthen seedlings. A small clip-on fan can gently shake the seedlings, encouraging them to develop stronger stems and better-established roots. With crops like head lettuce, poor airflow will sometimes result in tip burn.

ROTATING/FERRIS WHEEL

Rotating hydroponic systems are very cool looking, but generally not practical. Gardens like the Omega Garden are fun to look at but the growers using these systems seem to quickly lose interest. Difficulty viewing and accessing the crop, issues with airflow, water dripping onto leaves, high price, high maintenance . . . these are just a few of the reasons growers abandon rotary hydroponic systems. That said, I've had a lot of fun building Ferris wheel hydroponic systems. These systems are not designed to optimize production, increase yield, or reduce labor; they are designed to simply be aesthetically pleasing. Ferris wheel planters can be found at some garden shops and a search through online vendors will generally result in several options. I've tried building a couple of Ferris wheel systems and have learned a few lessons in the

Ferris wheel systems are largely visual novelties, but they do function when it comes to growing small plants. Nutrient solution is delivered to small, quick-draining grow pots when they reach the peak of the wheel. The increased weight of the grow pot after irrigation encourages it to rotate downward, queuing up the next grow pot for irrigation.

process. First, moving the Ferris wheel with a motor so the plants can be dipped into a nutrient solution can be a headache. Second, gravity and the weight of water are great for moving plants in a Ferris wheel. Third, use pots that drain quickly. Generally, stone wool and/or perlite are good options for these systems.

NFT A-FRAME

An NFT A-frame system consists of NFT channels arranged in an A shape. These systems have pros and cons. The pro is the ability to increase the number of plant sites in a given footprint. The cons are an uneven distribution of light and possible flow rate issues. If you plan on building an A-frame NFT system, follow the same guidelines for slope and flow rate as mentioned in the NFT project. Additionally, use ¼-inch shutoff valves for each channel to balance flow among all levels. The use of ¼-inch shutoff valves is further described in the project for the rain gutter garden.

RAIN GUTTER SYSTEMS

These are one of my favorite and are fun to build and customize. See next page.

HOW TO BUILD A RAIN GUTTER GARDEN

This system is one of the more complicated systems in this book, but that is because I was focused on the aesthetics of the final system. I personally like a system that looks so nice that a visitor to my garden would not immediately think it is a DIY project. To simplify the assembly of this system, you can skip the paint job, use vinyl tubing to connect troughs, and reduce the number of levels. Alternatively, this system can be thought of as a model for a much larger system. I cut my channels to 33 inches wide, but this system could easily be modified to have 10-inch-wide channels. It could be many levels taller too. When adding more vertical levels, it is important to consider pump size. I prefer to oversize a pump and use shutoff valves to control flow for each level. Oversized pumps also help reduce the potential of debris clogging the irrigation lines.

- **Suitable Locations:** Indoors, outdoors, or greenhouse
- **Size:** Medium to large
- **Growing Media:** Perlite, clay pellets, and other fast-draining materials
- **Electrical:** Required
- **Crops:** Leafy greens, herbs, strawberries, and other short crops

MATERIALS

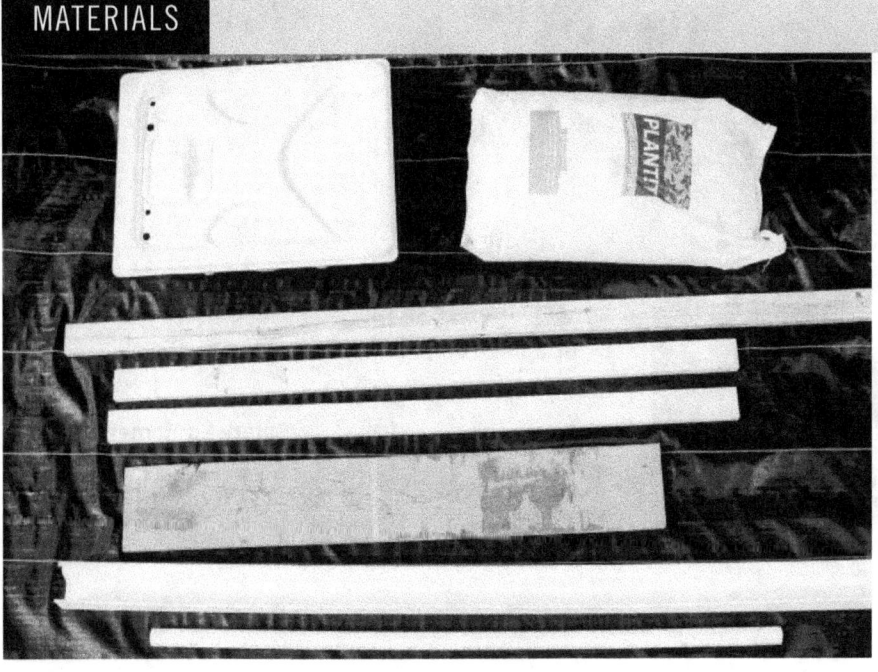

Frame
1	2 × 10" × 8' board
2	2 × 4" × 8' board
1 lb.	#10 x 2½" exterior screws
20 gal.	Reservoir

Troughs
1	10' vinyl rain gutter
6	White vinyl gutter hanger
3	White vinyl K-style end cap set
50 L	Coarse perlite

Irrigation
3	½" rubber grommet
3	½" elbow connectors
10'	½" black vinyl tubing
6'	1½" PVC pipe
3	1½" PVC coupling
4'	¼" black vinyl tubing
1	½" stopper
3	¼" double-barbed connectors
3	¼" shutoff valve
1	Submersible water pump (800 GPH)
3	Active Aqua screen fitting

Optional
3 cans White water-based latex primer, sealer & stain-blocker (KILZ 2 LATEX)

Paint roller and/or paint brush (paint frame before assembly)

TOOLS

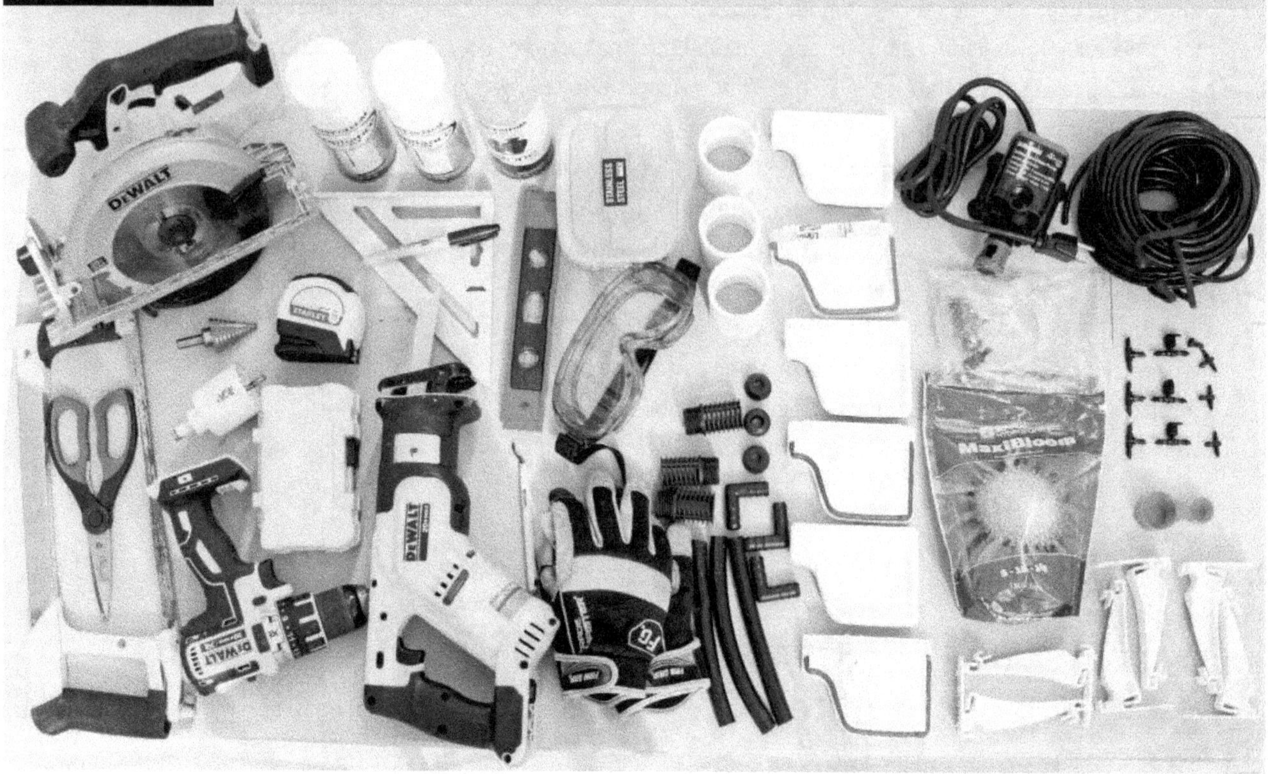

Sawhorses with clamps
Tape measure
Permanent marker
Circular saw
Drill
2" hole saw drill bit (shown at right)

Step drill bit with 1/8" increments from 1/4" to 1 3/8"
1/4" drill bit
Level
Rafter square
Hacksaw
Heavy-duty scissors

Deburring tool
Reciprocating saw
Irrigation line hole punch

Safety Equipment
Work gloves
Eye protection

Build the Frame

Choose a reservoir before building the frame. The width of the frame needs to be wider than the reservoir so the reservoir can easily fit between the vertical supports.

1. Move the 2 × 10" × 8' board onto the sawhorses and fasten with clamps. Measure and mark two 30" segments to be used as the base of the frame.
2. Draw square cutting lines for each segment of the 2 × 10.
3. Wearing work gloves and eye protection, cut the 2 × 10" × 8' board into two 30" segments with the circular saw.
4. Move the two 2 × 4" × 8' boards onto the sawhorses and fasten with clamps.

5. Measure and mark a 5' segment in both boards. Placing the boards on top of each other can help make sure they are cut to the exact same length.
6. Cut the two 2 × 4" × 8' boards along the marked lines to create two 5' segments and two 3' segments.
7. Measure, mark, and cut a 30" segment using one of the 3'2" × 4" segments from step 6.
8. Move the 30" 2 × 4" segment onto the sawhorses, fasten with clamps, and mark the center.
9. Use the 2" hole saw drill bit to create a 2" hole in the marked center of the 30" 2 × 4" segment.

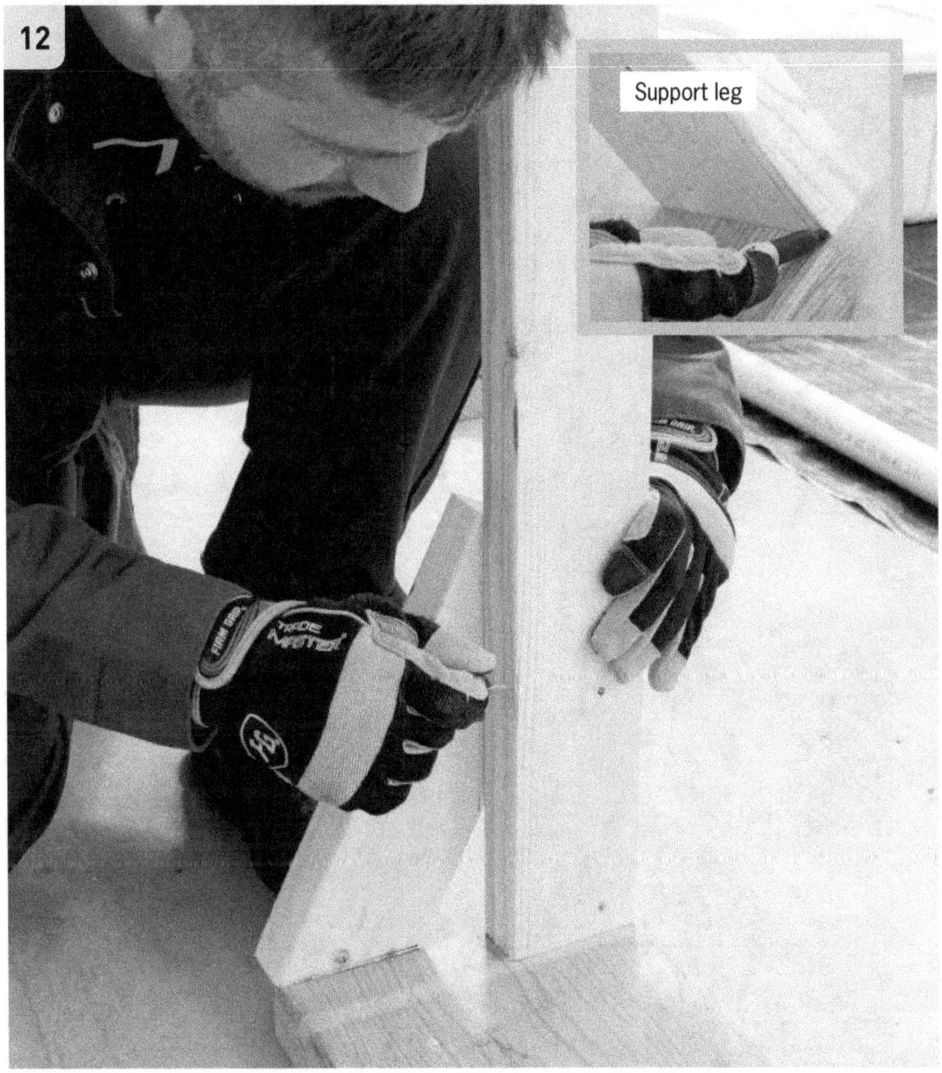

10 Attach the two 5' 2 × 4" segments to one of the 30" 2 × 10" bases. Use two screws on each side.

11 Attach the other side of the two 5' 2 × 4" segments to the 30" 2 × 4" segment. Use two screws on each side.

12 To build the support legs for the frame, cut two small 2 × 4" segments from the remaining 2 × 4" wood. Place the segments in the angles between the base and vertical 2 × 4" supports. Mark the small segments so the cuts will be a perfect match.

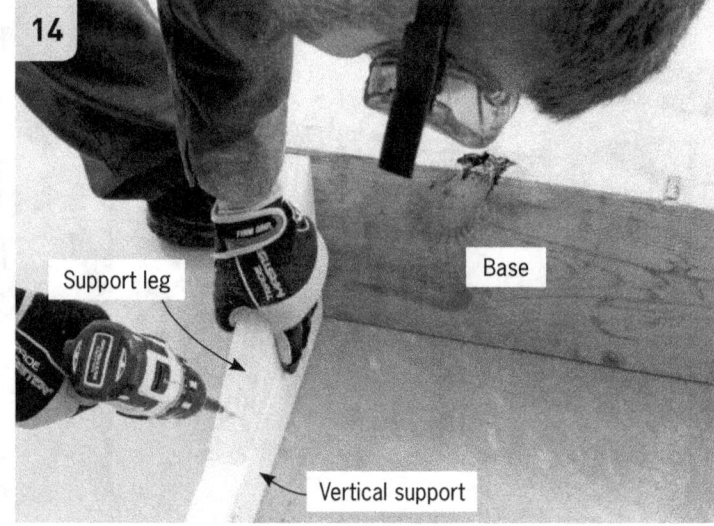

13 Cut the angle support legs.
14 Secure the support legs to the base using two screws. Secure the support legs to the vertical supports with one screw.
15 Set up the frame in a level area. Check that the base and top crossbeam are level and square.
16 Position the reservoir in the frame.
17 Level the reservoir by moving the second 30" 2 × 10" board under the front of the reservoir.

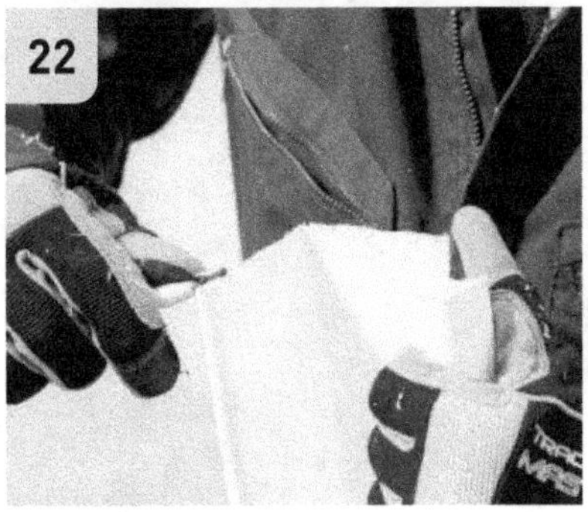

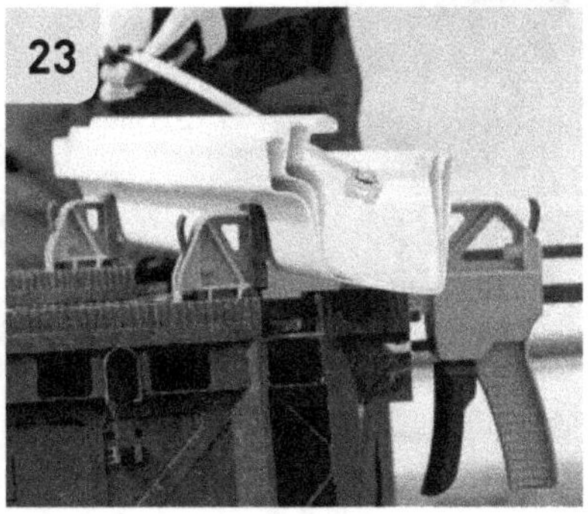

Trough Assembly

Build the frame before assembling the troughs. The troughs need to be at least 3" wider than the frame to allow the gutter end caps to fit securely.

20 Measure and mark three 33" segments in the 10' vinyl gutter.
21 Cut the three 33" segments using a hacksaw and/or heavy-duty scissors.
22 Use the deburring tool to remove any burrs from the ends of the gutters.
23 Stack the three 33" gutter segments and fasten onto sawhorses with clamps. Measure and mark the center of the gutters at 16½".
24 Use a step bit to create a ¾" hole in the marked center of the gutters. The placement of this hole is very important! It should be placed closer to the curved edge of the gutter. The center of the hole is approximately 2" from the flat back of the gutter. Deburr the hole but make sure not to widen the hole too much.

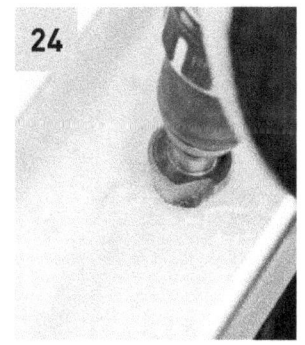

25. Insert the ½" grommet into the hole. If the hole is too small, use the deburring tool to widen the hole.
26. Repeat steps 24–25 for each of the three 33" gutter segments.
27. Insert a ½" elbow into the ½" grommet in each gutter section.
28. Cut three 4" segments of ½" tubing. Attach to the elbows.

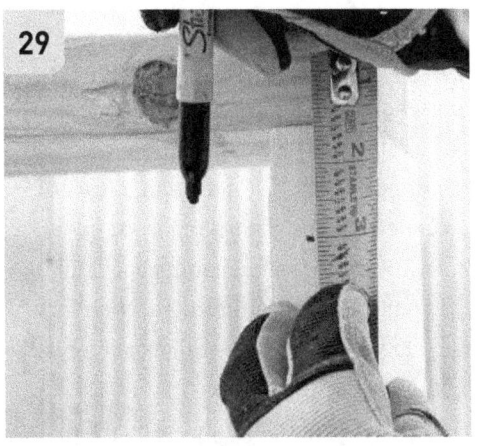

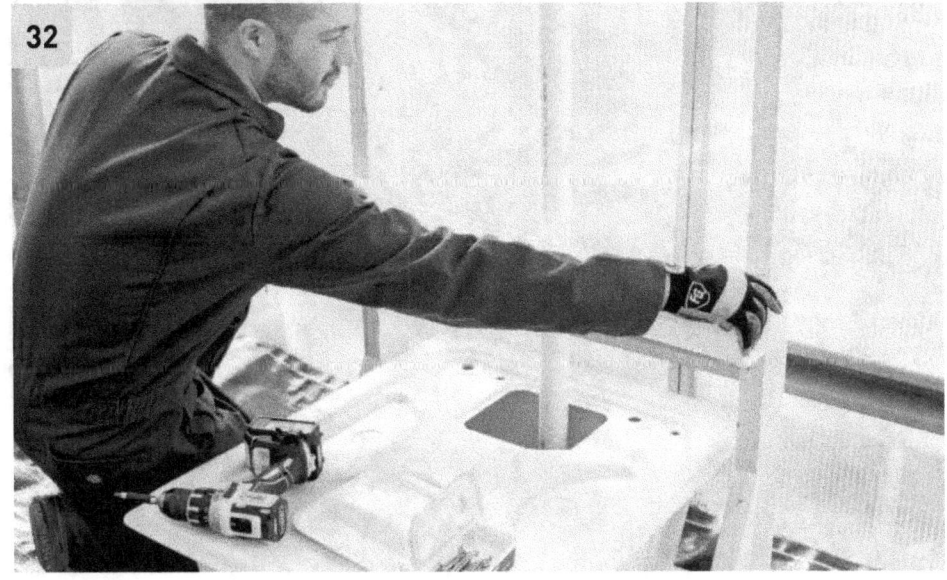

Attaching Troughs to Frame

The troughs in this design are 18" apart starting 3" from the top beam. This gives 18" of space below the lowest trough for the 11"-tall reservoir.

29 On each of the vertical 5' 2 × 4" segments, mark 3", 21", and 39" from the top beam.

30 Screw in the gutter hangers into the marked areas on the vertical 5' 2 × 4" segments.

31 Slide the gutters into the hangers.

32 Add the end caps.

Irrigation Assembly

The irrigation design in this system uses one main PVC pipe both for drainage and to conceal the tubing used for water delivery. The assembly of the irrigation could be simplified by removing the PVC pipe and using 1/2" vinyl tubing to connect all the drains and by running the water delivery tubing in the open (not concealed in a PVC pipe). I chose a more complicated irrigation design because it looks cleaner and avoids a potentially unsightly web of tubing.

33 Insert the 6' 1½" PVC pipe through the guide hole in the top crossbeam. Mark the approximate intersection of the 1½" PVC pipe and the ½" drainage tube coming from each gutter level.

34 Make a second set of marks approximately ½" above each gutter level. It will be important to distinguish between the marks made in the previous step and this step.

35 Remove the 1½" PVC pipe and fasten to the sawhorses using clamps. Using the step bit, drill a ⅝" hole into each of the three marks made in step 33. This will be used for the ½" drainage tube.

36 Using the ¼" drill bit, drill a hole into each of the three marks created in step 34. This will be used for the ¼" water delivery line.

37 On the bottom end of the 1½" PVC pipe (the end closer to the ½" hole), drill four 1⅜" drain holes. This pipe will be resting on the bottom of the reservoir and drainage water will pass through these holes into the reservoir. Use the deburring tool to clean all edges.

38 The 1½" PVC couplings will be placed above the ¼" hole for the lower two levels and between the ¼" and ⅝" hole for the top level. Make a mark 2" above the two ¼" holes for the lower two levels. Make a mark 2" below the ¼" hole for the top level. Make sure the coupling will not cover the ¼" holes when the coupling is put in place.

39 Cut the 1½" PVC pipe at the marks made in step 38.

40 Connect the cut PVC segments with couplings.

41 Move the assembled PVC main line back into the system with the top coming out of the guide hole in the 2 × 4" wood crossbeam.

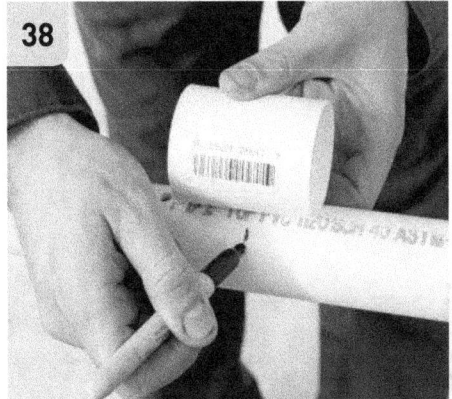

42 Check to see if ½" drainage tubes from all three levels can be inserted into the PVC main line. If not, shorten segments in the main PVC line until all ½" drainage tubes match with their corresponding holes in the PVC main line. The PVC couplings can create gaps (sometimes big ones) that increase the total length of the pipe, throwing off the previous measurements.

43 Mark the top of the 2 × 4" wood crossbeam on the 1½" PVC pipe.

44 Remove the top PVC pipe segment and cut along the mark made in step 43. This is to prevent the PVC pipe from sticking out high above the top wood crossbeam.

45 Move the PVC mainline to a flat service. Gather the ¼" vinyl tubing, ½" vinyl tubing, ½" stopper, ¼" double-barbed connectors, ¼" shutoff valves, irrigation line hole punch, and scissors.

46 Cut three 10" segments and three 2" segments of the ¼" vinyl tubing.

47 Place the ½" vinyl tubing next to the PVC main line. It may be helpful to use clamps to hold the line straight.

48 Insert the ½" stopper into the end of the ½" vinyl tube near the top of the PVC main line.

49 Begin poking holes into the ½" vinyl tubing with the irrigation line hole punch. Place holes adjacent to the ¼" holes drilled into the PVC main line.

50 Insert ¼" double-barbed connectors into the three holes in the ½" vinyl tubing created in step 49.

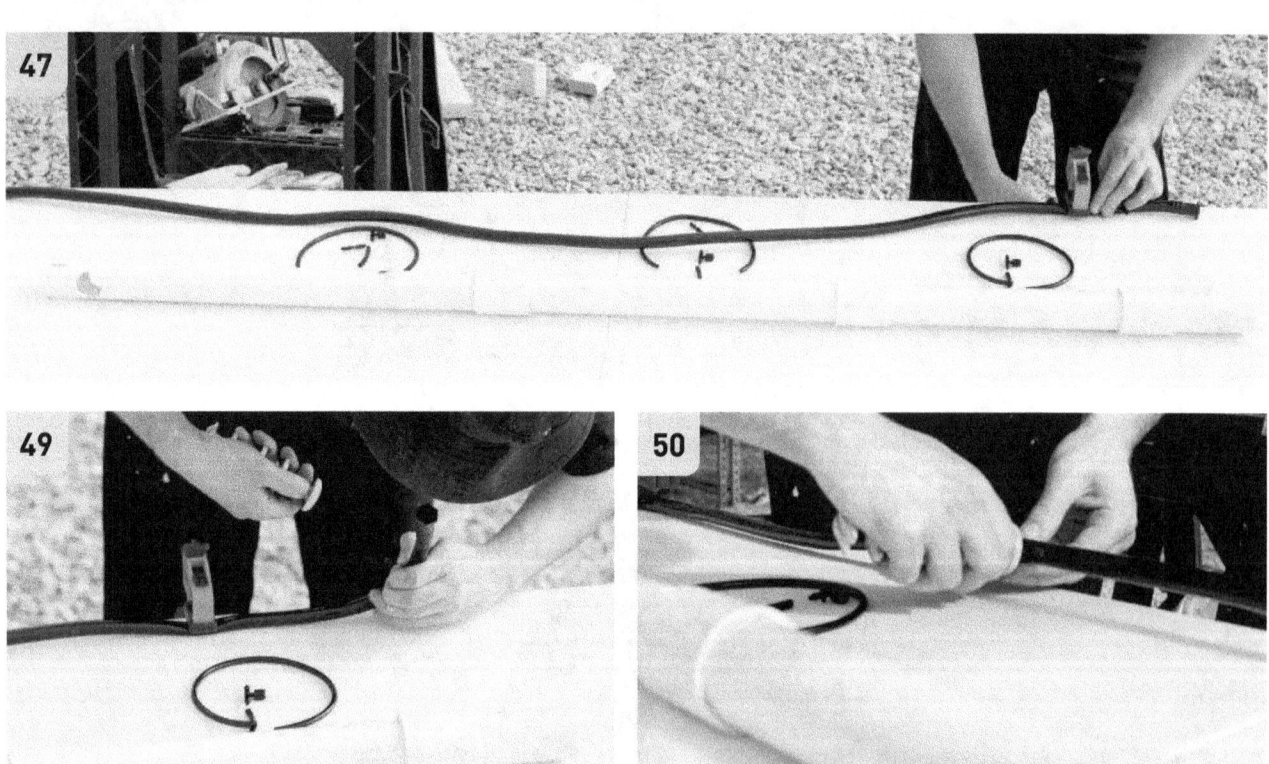

51 Connect the 2" segments and 10" segments of ¼" tubing using the ¼" shutoff valves.

52 Disconnect the PVC mainline at the 1½" couplings.

53 Insert the assembled ¼" tubes from step 51 into the ¼" holes in the PVC main line. Insert the 10" segment into the PVC so the ¼" shutoff valve remains outside of the PVC mainline.

54 Starting from the top of the PVC main line, connect the 10" segment of the ¼" vinyl tubing to the ¼" double-barbed connector in the ½" vinyl tubing.

55 Slide the ½" vinyl tubing down the PVC main line and continue connecting the 10" segments of the ¼" vinyl tubing to the ¼" double-barbed connectors in the ½" vinyl tubing.

56 Reconnect the PVC main line segments.

57 Slide the bottom end of the ½" vinyl tubing through one of the drain holes created in step 37.

58 Place the assembled PVC main line back into the vertical system with the top held in place by the guide hole in the 2 × 4" wood crossbeam.

59 Insert the ½" drain lines coming out of each gutter into their corresponding ⅝" hole in the PVC main line.

60 Connect the bottom end of the ½" vinyl tubing to a pump in the reservoir.

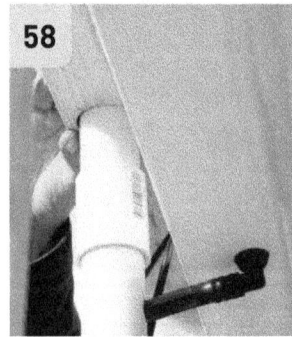

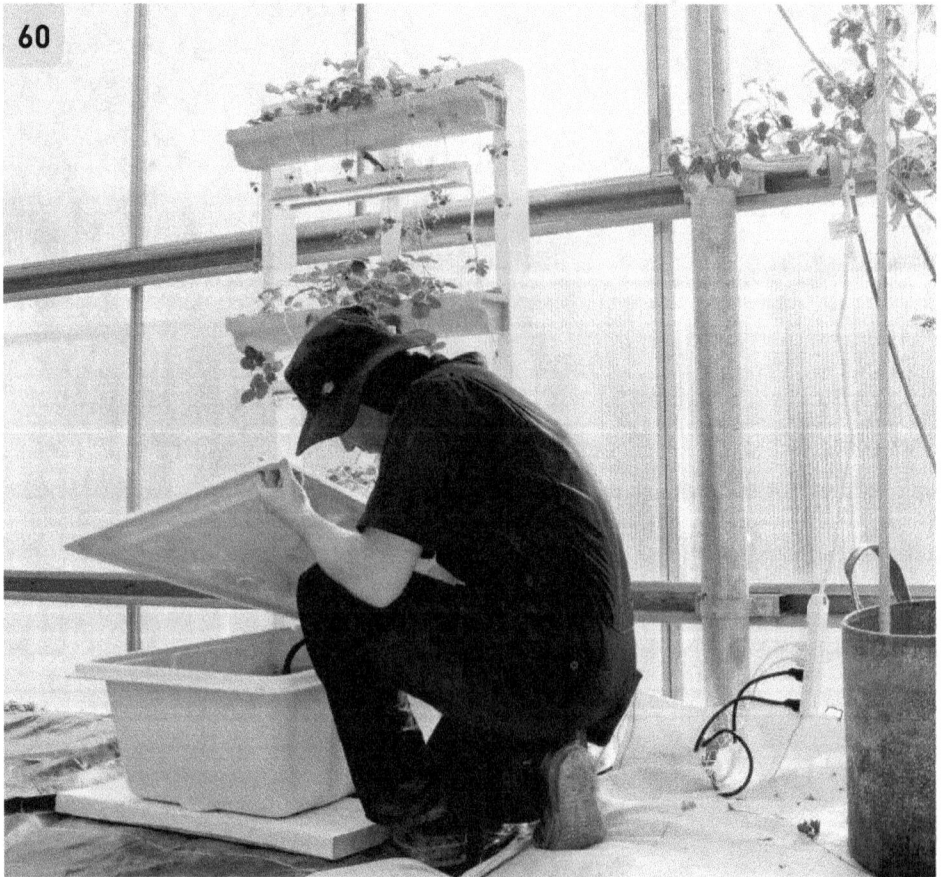

Planting

Test the irrigation system before planting. Fill the reservoir with enough water to cover the pump, turn on the pump, and check that each level is receiving water. Adjust the flow to each level by adjusting the shutoff valves. This irrigation test will also help clean out the irrigation lines and catch any loose plastic particles left over from the assembly. Dump the test water.

61 Place the Active Aqua screen fittings over the ½" drain grommets before filling each trough.

62 Pre-rinse the perlite in a bucket. This will help keep the system clean. Fill each trough with perlite.

63 The amount of space you leave at the top of each trough will depend on the amount of plants you plan to add. The seedling plugs will take up space in the trough, so filling the trough to the top before transplanting is not recommended.

64 Fill the reservoir with clean water and prepare a nutrient solution specific to the crop you plan on planting (see System Maintenance chapter).

65 Turn on the pump and check to see that each level is receiving nutrient solution.

66 Transplant the seedlings.

Additional Options

Reservoirs There are many alternative reservoirs that could be used with this rain gutter system. A nontranslucent plastic storage tote, a 5-gallon bucket, or even a small pond would work as a reservoir. It is important to cover the reservoir to reduce the development of algae, which can attract fungus gnats that can potentially damage plant roots. If growing in a warm climate, it may be beneficial to bury the reservoir to keep the nutrient solution cool.

The framework supporting the rain gutter troughs provides ample opportunity for mounting grow lights.

Lighting This system can be modified for use indoors by adding grow lights. I added two 2-foot fluorescent lights for the lower two levels to supplement light in the greenhouse. LED light bars are another option. LED light bars are often more powerful than fluorescent lights and may be better suited for gardeners planning on using the rain gutter system indoors. If using this system indoors, you may want to build a fourth level to support a grow light for the top trough.

Troubleshooting

Trough is leaking from end caps
- Drain reservoir and let system dry.
- Use PVC cement to attach and seal end caps.

No water coming out of multiple levels
- Check power to pump.
- Check pump for materials clogging intake.
- Make sure pump intake valve is in fully open position.
- Make sure shutoff valves are open for all levels.

No water coming out of one level
- Reduce flow from other levels to direct more pressure to dry level.
- Completely shut off flow to other levels to force out any debris clogging line.
- Loosen any potential debris by pushing an unfolded paper clip down clogged ¼" line.
- Disassemble and reassemble irrigation for that level. It may be helpful to shorten ¼" irrigation line too.

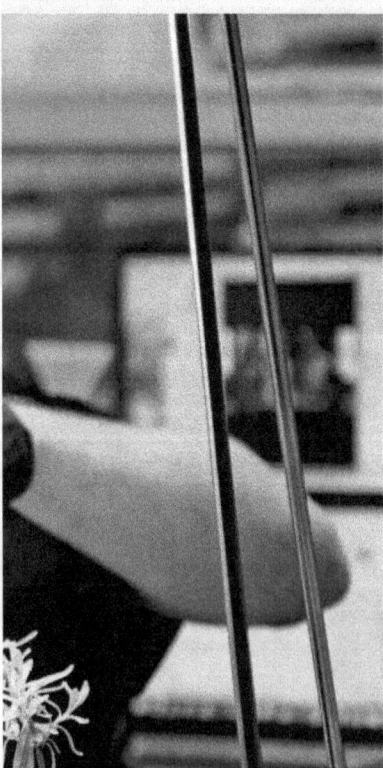

4
STARTING SEEDS and CUTTINGS

GROWING A HEALTHY, ROBUST SEEDLING or root cutting is often one of the biggest challenges for new hydroponic gardeners. The ideal conditions for germination or root establishment are dependent on crop selection. Refer to the crop selection charts in the appendix to find recommended germination temperatures for various crops. Do not be discouraged if you struggle to grow healthy seedlings or rooted cuttings on your first try; it may take a few attempts to understand the proper practices for your environment. Worst case, you can transplant traditional soil seedlings purchased from a garden center into a hydroponic system using the steps listed in the final section of this chapter.

Stone Wool Preparation

It is important to rinse stone wool before seeding. Some stone wool growers prefer to soak their stone wool overnight, but I've found that is generally unnecessary. Technically, stone wool should be rinsed or soaked with water at a pH of 5.5, but I've also found this to be unnecessary. I've had success starting seeds in stone wool with water anywhere in the pH range from 5 to 7. If you don't have a pH meter, don't worry—chances are you will still have success. The initial rinse of stone wool can be with either water or a nutrient solution, but it is important to eventually rinse the stone wool with a nutrient solution so the young seedlings or cuttings have access to nutrients once roots emerge. Most recommendations say to use a nutrient solution at one-fourth to half strength, but I've had success starting seeds in nutrient solutions anywhere from one-fourth up to full strength. The point is, most things in the process of growing plants are slightly flexible, so don't panic if your pH, nutrient solution, root temperatures, or other factors are slightly off from the recommendations.

My preferred method of rinsing stone wool is using a mesh bottom tray, which allows any loose stone wool dust to be easily rinsed away. It is also possible to rinse stone wool in a solid bottom tray by simply soaking the sheet and pouring off the excess nutrient solution.

STARTING SEEDS IN STONE WOOL

Starting seeds in stone wool can be incredibly easy and involve very little effort. The most important factors for success are having the proper amount of light, airflow, heat, and humidity. There are many different techniques for starting seeds in stone wool; the methods I describe have repeatedly worked for me for my hobby hydroponic and commercial hydroponic systems. There are definitely more bare-bones methods for starting seeds in stone wool that involve far less equipment, but my goal is to give you a method that will provide a high likelihood of success with minimal maintenance.

MATERIALS

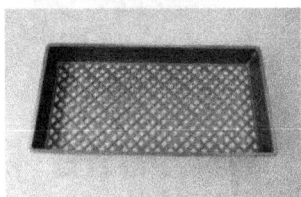

Stone wool starter cubes (Grodan A-OK 36/40)
10 × 20" mesh bottom tray
10 × 20" solid bottom tray
Nutrient solution
Seedling heat mat with controller
Seeds
Labels and marker
Misting bottle
Vented humidity dome
2' 4-bulb T5 fluorescent light
Fan

1. Place the stone wool seedling sheet into the 10 × 20" mesh bottom tray. Rinse and prepare the stone wool with a half-strength nutrient solution.
2. Let any excess nutrient solution run off the seedling sheet through the mesh bottom tray.
3. Place the mesh bottom tray into the solid bottom tray. The stone wool should be damp to the touch but not sitting in water.
4. Place the solid bottom tray on the seedling heat mat.

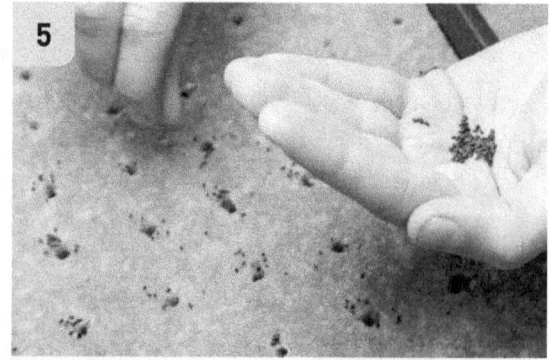

5   Seed that sheet.
6   Pelleted seeds should be seeded one per plug.
7   Basil often yields more when three to eight seeds are used per plug. Basil will often germinate great even when not placed directly in a dibbled hole.
8   Lettuce mixes using raw seed (not pelleted) yield more and look better when three to five seeds are used per plug.
9   Plants like tomatoes, peppers, cucumbers, and eggplant should be seeded two per plug if possible. Once the seedlings emerge, identify the smaller plant in the plug and remove it by pinching and pulling. Using two seeds per plug and removing one later increases the chances of having successful seedlings in every plug. If one seed doesn't germinate, then there is a backup.
10 Label your varieties. Use plant markers or make a note on a sheet of paper; either way, it is important to keep track of what varieties you plant.
11 Misting the seeds can help ensure they have good contact with the stone wool and have enough moisture to germinate. Misting is very helpful with pelleted seeds because sometimes they struggle to absorb enough moisture by simply making contact with the stone wool.

12. Plug in the heat mat to the heat mat controller. Weave the controller's thermometer through one of the humidity dome vents and insert it into the stone wool.
13. Secure the humidity dome on the tray and pull any excess slack on the thermometer cord.
14. Set the heat mat controller to a desired minimum temperature. Various target germination temperatures can be found in the appendix in the Crop Selection Charts.
15. For the first few days, there should be no need to touch the seedling tray. The initial stone wool rinsing/soaking will provide enough moisture for several days.
16. Remove the humidity dome once 50 percent of the seedlings have germinated. For most vegetable crops this will be after 3 to 5 days. Leaving the humidity dome on too long can increase the chance of fungal diseases and seedling death.
17. Stone wool will feel heavy when it is wet and it is noticeably lighter when in need of irrigation. It is best to develop a sense of how much water is in your seedling sheet by lifting up the tray to gauge the weight. Irrigate with a nutrient solution when the tray feels light; often this is every 2 to 4 days indoors depending on air temperature and crop age. Depending on the environment, it may not be necessary to irrigate the seedlings at all, because they may be ready to transplant into your hydroponic garden within 1 to 2 weeks before an irrigation would be necessary.

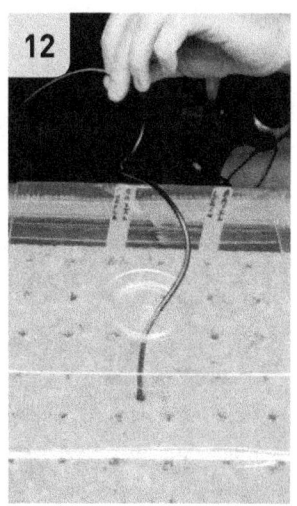

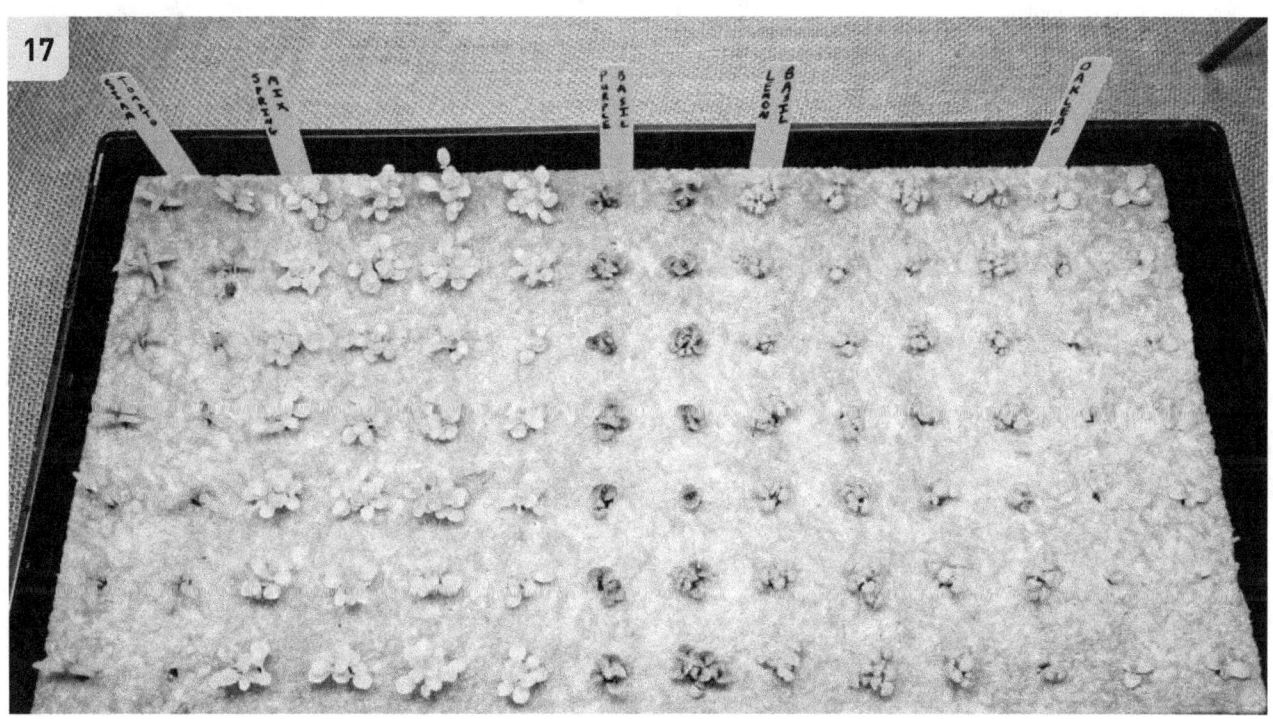

Collecting Cuttings

Collecting cuttings is a skill that many struggle with at first. It is very important to collect cuttings from clean plants using clean tools. The ideal environment to root a cutting is also the ideal environment for various plant diseases that can quickly kill or severely weaken cuttings. Before you collect cuttings it is important to wash your hands, pruners, and any containers used to hold the cuttings. Many gardeners prefer to use gloves to prevent contamination from their hands and use alcohol wipes to sanitize pruners.

The minimum length required to use a cutting will depend on the rooting technique, but it is generally best to collect longer cuttings (6 inches or more) and cut them shorter later if needed. Remove all the side shoots and leaves so only a few leaves remain at the top of the cutting.

Cut just above leaf internodes.

When possible, select cuttings that have thick woody stems (left) over weaker thin stems (right).

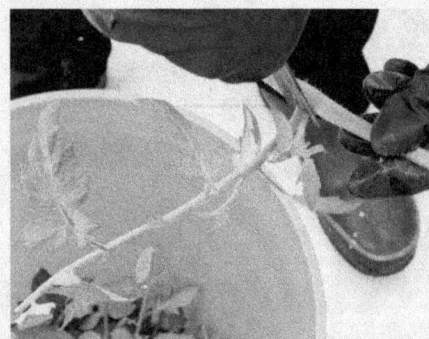

Remove side shoots and leaves.

Cuttings only need a few leaves; too many leaves will increase their chance of drying out and dying before establishing roots. Collect more cuttings than needed to give yourself options later.

Remove any flowers so the cutting can focus its energy on growing roots instead of producing fruit.

Store cuttings in water during the collection process.

- **Suitable Locations:** Indoors or greenhouse with shade
- **Growing Media:** Stone wool
- **Electrical:** Required indoors, not required outdoors
- **Crops:** Basil, mint, sage, rosemary, thyme, lavender, tomatoes, peppers, sweet potato, and many more

ROOTING CUTTINGS IN STONE WOOL

There are many different ways to root a cutting and there are many variations in technique within these methods. This tutorial covers a few of these variations; please experiment and see what works best for you, your crop, and your unique cloning environment.

MATERIALS & TOOLS

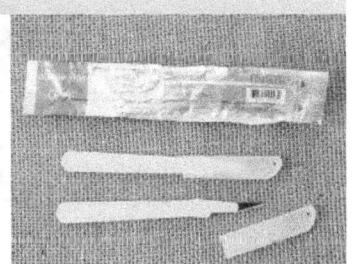

Stone wool starter cubes (Grodan A-OK 36/40)
Nutrient solution
10 × 20" solid bottom tray

Sharp pruners and/or scalpel
Rooting hormone (optional)
Tall vented humidity dome
2' 4-bulb T5 fluorescent light

Seedling heat mat with controller (optional)
Gro-Smart tray (optional)

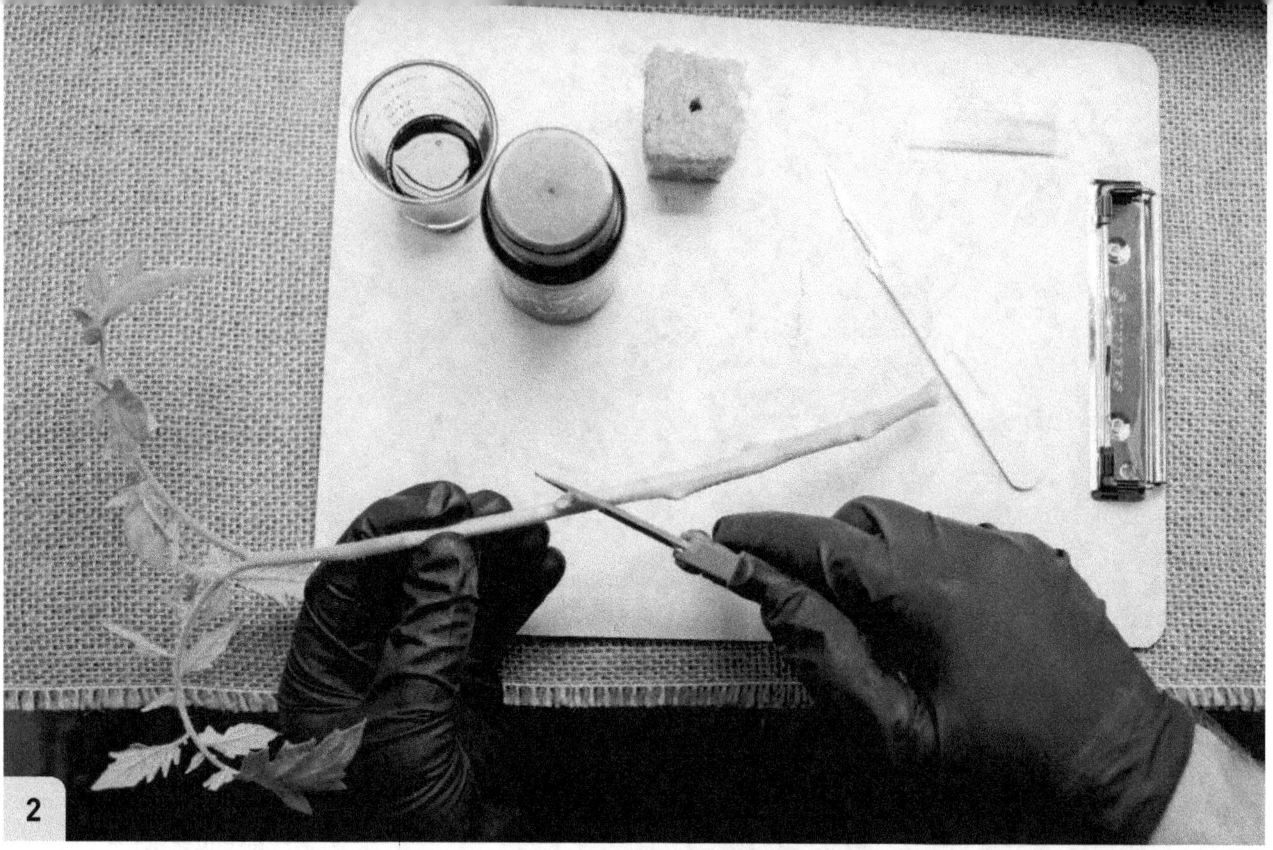

1. Rinse and prepare the stone wool with half-strength nutrient solution. Place it in the solid bottom tray. With sharp pruners, collect cuttings (see the Collecting Cuttings guide on page 141).
2. Shorten the cuttings to 4" to 7", making a 45-degree cut below an internode.

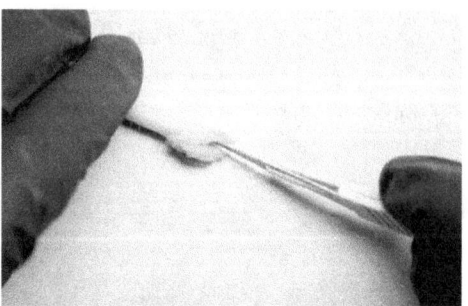 

(Optional) Some growers prefer to make a horizontal cut and then split the bottom of the stem, some growers prefer just a 45-degree cut, and some growers prefer to do both a 45-degree cut and split the stem.

(Optional) Some growers remove a thin layer from one side of the cutting to expose more cambium, a white layer inside the stem from which new roots emerge.

(Optional) Rooting hormone can be very helpful when rooting challenging crops. Some gardeners use honey instead of a rooting gel.

STARTING SEEDS AND CUTTINGS

3. Always wear gloves when working with rooting hormone.
4. Pour some of the rooting solution into a separate container to avoid potentially contaminating the entire bottle.
5. Dip the end of the cutting into the rooting hormone, and let any excess rooting solution drip off before moving the cutting to the cube.
6. The cutting can be positioned in the cube in several ways:
    A. The standard method is to insert the cutting into the cube about 1" deep through the pre-dibbled hole.
    B. Another option is creating a smaller dibble hole so the cutting fits more snugly into the hole. This is beneficial when using thin cuttings because it increases the amount of contact between the stem and the stone wool.
    C. Another option is to insert the cutting into the bottom of the stone wool cube. This has similar benefits to the previous option plus it has a wider bottom, making it possible to place individual cubes in a tray without a holder.

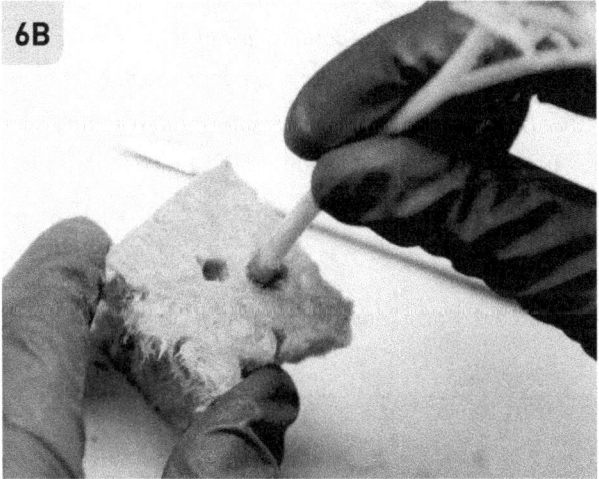

7 Try to avoid leaves touching, which can create areas of excessive moisture and increase risk of fungus.

8 Snugly place the humidity dome onto the tray and place under a low-intensity light. I turned off two bulbs in this four-bulb light to reduce the potential of stressing out my cuttings before they have a chance to establish roots.

9 If your cuttings are drying out before establishing roots, try removing more leaves to reduce transpiration, decreasing light intensity, adding water to the bottom of the tray to increase humidity, adjusting the humidity dome vent to keep in more humidity, or adjusting the heat mat temperature. If adding water to the bottom of the tray, do not add so much that the cubes are sitting in water.

10 A heat mat with a controller is great for speeding up the rooting process. Most gardeners target 70° to 80°F.

11 Cuttings should be slowly acclimated to normal humidity levels by incrementally opening up the dome vents.

12 Some plants root very quickly from cuttings, in less than a week, but most will require a couple of weeks or more until they have enough roots to be transplanted into a hydroponic garden. Cuttings can be transplanted when roots emerge from the stone wool cube.

ROOTING CUTTINGS IN A HYDROPONIC CLONER

Most hydroponic gardeners find rooting cuttings in a hydroponic cloner far easier than rooting cuttings in stone wool. The plants often root faster, appear less stressed during the rooting process, and rarely require a rooting hormone. There are a few variations within hydroponic cloners, including aeroponic and deep-water culture options. This book describes how to build an aeroponic cloner that could be used in the following process. To show another option, this tutorial uses a deep-water culture hydroponic cloner.

Hydroponic cloners do not need to be limited to starting plants. They often can grow plants to full maturity. I've grown strawberry bushes full of berries and monstrous mint plants in hydroponic cloners. A hydroponic cloner is a great addition to a hydroponic garden or it can be the hydroponic garden.

1. With sharp pruners, collect cuttings (see the Collecting Cuttings guide on page 141). The cutting should be long enough to have at least 1" of stem submerged in the nutrient solution. I generally aim for 6" cuttings so I can have a couple of inches of stem submerged in the nutrient solution.
2. Assemble the cloning system and place under the grow light if using indoors.
3. Fill with half-strength nutrient solution or use a hydroponic fertilizer specifically for rooting cuttings (sometimes called a "clone solution").
4. Plug in the air pump and water pump.
5. Use a soft collar to hold the cuttings in place. Make sure no leaves are stuck in the collar.

MATERIALS & TOOLS

Sharp pruners
oxyCLONE 40 Site
   Cloning System
2' 4-bulb T5
   fluorescent light
Nutrient solution

- **Suitable Locations:** Indoors, outdoors, or greenhouse
- **Growing Media:** Just water
- **Electrical:** Required
- **Crops:** Basil, mint, sage, rosemary, thyme, lavender, tomatoes, peppers, sweet potato, strawberries, and any other plant that can be rooted from a cutting

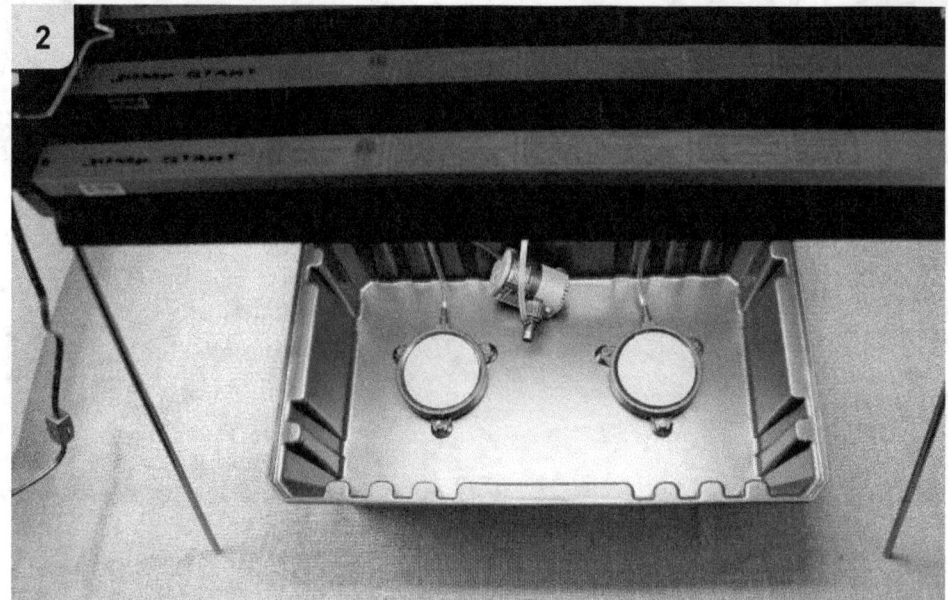

6. Evenly space cuttings in the cloner and cover any unused holes with a collar.
7. After 4 to 7 days, most cuttings show evidence of roots. Some plants root more slowly than others and may need to stay in the system longer.
8. Plants with established roots are ready to be transplanted into a hydroponic garden. Simply remove the collar and your new plant is ready to go.

TRANSPLANTING PLANTS STARTED IN SOIL

The option of using a soil-started plant in a hydroponic garden is often very attractive to new hydroponic gardeners because it makes it possible to purchase plants from a garden center or use plants from their existing soil garden. It is definitely possible to transplant soil-started plants into a hydroponic system, but it is not the best way to source plants for a hydroponic garden. The process of rinsing off the soil from a plant's roots usually involves some root loss and damage, which increases the potential of exposure to root diseases.

If the hydroponic garden uses small irrigation lines (¼ inch or smaller), it is possible that any soil particles not rinsed off from the transplant may clog the irrigation lines. I would not recommend transplanting a soil plant into a hydroponic system if you are not okay with the possibility that the plant may not survive the process. Now that the disclaimers are out of the way, I must personally say that I really enjoy the process of washing off the soil from a plant's roots.

1. If possible, prune off all the fruit and some of the vegetation from the plant. Less fruit and vegetation means less need for water uptake and less demand on the root system. It is important to reduce the demand on the root system because it might be damaged in the rinsing process and unable to deliver the water and nutrients required for the full-size plant.
2. Pour off any loose soil from the top of the transplant.
3. Remove the plant from its pot.
4. Gently dunk the root system into a bucket of water.

TOOLS

Sharp pruners
Bucket

5   Gently shake the plant to wash off soil from the roots.
6   Use your fingers to loosen up the roots to expose soil clumps trapped deep within.
7   It may be necessary to dump and refill the bucket multiple times to get all the soil off the roots. A watering wand with a gentle flow can help speed the process.
8   Pick out as much soil and debris as possible without ripping up the roots.
9   Clear some space for the transplant.
10 Insert the transplant and cover the root system.
11 Water in the new transplant to improve root contact with the substrate.

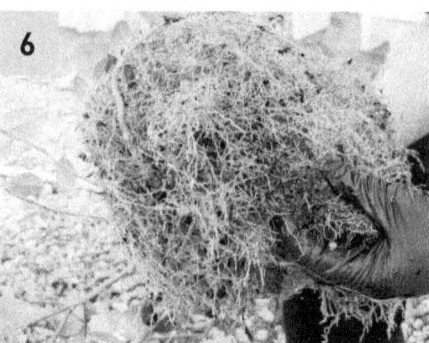

STARTING SEEDS AND CUTTINGS

5
PLANT NUTRITION

PLANT NUTRIENT UPTAKE

PLANTS CANNOT TELL THE DIFFERENCE between natural and synthetic fertilizers. Plants have specialized pathways that only allow them to uptake a very short list of ions and simple molecules. In traditional soil-based gardening, these ions and molecules are often derived from manure or decaying plant matter broken down by a series of biological processes. For example, nitrogen is primarily only available to plants when present as ammonium (NH_4^+) or nitrate (NO_3^-). In manure, nitrogen can be present in a wide variety of forms, including organic nitrogen (Org-N), ammonia (NH_3), ammonium (NH_4^+), hydrazine (N_2H_2), hydroxylamine (NH_2OH), nitrogen gas (N_2), nitrous oxide (N_2O), nitric oxide (NO), nitrous acid (HNO_2), nitrite (NO_2^-), nitrogen dioxide (NO_2), nitric acid (HNO_3), and nitrate (NO_3^-). Bacteria present in the soil can transform these forms of nitrogen into the specific plant-available forms of nitrogen. The process of breaking down a raw nutrient source like manure into simple molecules and ions available to the plant is dependent on many factors, including bacterial populations, soil temperature, and water content. In traditional hydroponic fertilizers, nitrogen is applied in its plant-available forms (ammonium and nitrate) and there is no need for bacteria to process the fertilizer into plant-available forms.

Plants grown in soil are constantly searching for nutrients. Their roots are on a scavenger hunt for nutrients spread through the soil. The roots generally find nutrients dissolved in water in the soil, often called the soil solution, which can then be picked up by the roots. The availability of nutrients in the soil is dependent on not only the presence of nutrients, but also the moisture in the soil, pH of the soil, distribution of nutrients in the soil, the cation exchange capacity of the soil, and more.

On the other hand, plants grown in hydroponic systems can have constant access to nutrients. The nutrients are evenly dissolved in water to create a nutrient solution, similar to a soil solution. Any time the plant needs water or nutrients, they're available. This allows a plant to reach its full potential without needing to expend energy searching for nutrients or being stunted by the inability to find essential nutrients.

FERTILIZERS

Fertilizers can be a very difficult topic. It is one of the most common issues I deal with when working with commercial hydroponic growers. Decades ago, almost all growers had to blend more than ten ingredients to create a hydroponic fertilizer recipe that met all their crop's nutrient requirements. This involved a lot of chemistry, lab tests, and spreadsheets! Today many commercial growers still create custom fertilizer blends using many ingredients but there is an increasing use of pre-blended fertilizers. These pre-blended fertilizer mixes allow growers to simply purchase two or three different fertilizer bags to create a recipe that meets all their crop's nutrient requirements. The manufacturers of hobby hydroponic fertilizers have further simplified the process by creating one-part fertilizer options. One-part fertilizers are as easy as making fruit punch from concentrate. Just add the fertilizer powder or liquid concentrate to a specific volume of water using the rate on the fertilizer bag or bottle.

ORGANIC HYDROPONIC FERTILIZERS

Organic hydroponics is possible, but I would not recommend it for new growers. It is important to have some experience with hydroponics and understand how plants should perform under normal conditions before venturing into organic hydroponics. One of the most beginner-friendly choices for a new hydroponic grower looking to grow organically is aquaponics. Aquaponics is a combination of hydroponics and aquaculture, or fish farming. In an aquaponic system, the fish waste is broken down in a series of biological processes to create nutrients that are available to the plants.

You may be tempted to experiment with an organic fertilizer created for traditional gardening but this often results in a foul-smelling mess. Many organic fertilizers are made from animal manure or byproducts from the meat industry. These fertilizers can quickly turn rancid in a hydroponic system. The nutrient solution will begin to smell foul and the system will get covered in goop, requiring the gardener to frequently flush and clean the system. Most successful organic hydroponic fertilizers use nutrients derived from plant sources like sugarcane. I've managed several successful organic hydroponic systems using a molasses-based fertilizer called Pre-Empt.

> **Nutrition Definitions**
>
> **Nutrient solution**
> Nutrients dissolved in water.
>
> **Stock solution**
> Nutrients dissolved at a highly concentrated rate, often 50x–200x the strength of a nutrient solution. Stock solutions are created because measuring and adding a liquid fertilizer to a reservoir is generally easier than measuring and adding a dry fertilizer.

CONVENTIONAL FERTILIZER SOURCES

Liquid or Dry Fertilizer

Within conventional fertilizers there are several categories. The first decision most hydroponic gardeners make is between liquid or dry fertilizers. Liquid fertilizers are often easier to use because they are easy to measure and don't require much mixing, but liquid fertilizers are often more expensive than dry fertilizers. Most liquid hydroponic fertilizers are simply a dry fertilizer mixed with water and then sold in a bottle. Liquid fertilizers are often less concentrated than dry fertilizers and more expensive due to the increased costs of shipping a liquid.

One-Part, Two-Part, or Many Parts

Many hydroponic fertilizer companies try to create a product line with many add-on products, but these add-ons are often unnecessary for healthy plant growth. Many new hydroponic gardeners get carried away with fertilizer amendments and cause more harm than benefit. It is surprisingly easy to love a plant to death. New hydroponic gardeners want to give their plants every flashy product they see, but too much love will quickly kill your crop.

One-part fertilizers like those listed below are able to grow healthy crops 99 percent of the time without any amendments. Most of the one-part fertilizers are formulated for either vegetative growth, like lettuce and young plants, or reproductive growth, like mature tomato plants developing fruit or any other flowering crop.

Many fertilizers come in two or three parts. These multipart fertilizers are very different from add-on products, and they come in two or three parts because certain nutrients have a tendency to bind to each other when mixed in high concentration. This binding is called precipitation. The usual culprits are calcium with phosphate or calcium with sulfate. When these nutrients bind, they create a precipitate that looks like sand. This sand will fall to the bottom of the reservoir and becomes unavailable to the crop. Many companies sell their fertilizer in two parts: one part containing calcium (along with other nutrients) and the other part containing phosphorus and sulfur (along with other nutrients). Sometimes one-part liquid fertilizers have a poor shelf life because the nutrients begin to create precipitates that gather at the bottom of the bottle. It is always a good idea to shake a one-part liquid fertilizer bottle before purchasing to check if there is a solid chunk of fertilizer precipitate at the bottom.

Another benefit of two- and three-part fertilizers is the ability to adjust the ratio of nutrients. Many of the fertilizers created for the hobby hydroponic gardener have suggested ratios of each of the ingredients for various stages of growth.

Large commercial hydroponic growers and universities create fertilizers from many parts. Each of these additions generally contains one or two of the thirteen essential nutrients for plant growth. These fertilizer recipes often involve ten or more different ingredients. If you get very excited about stoichiometry and want to

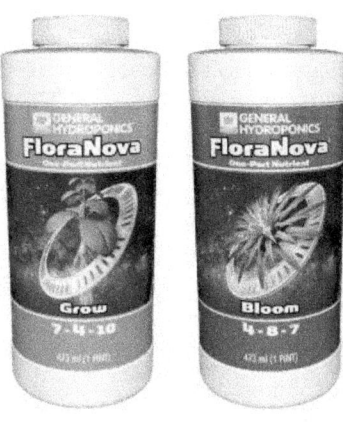
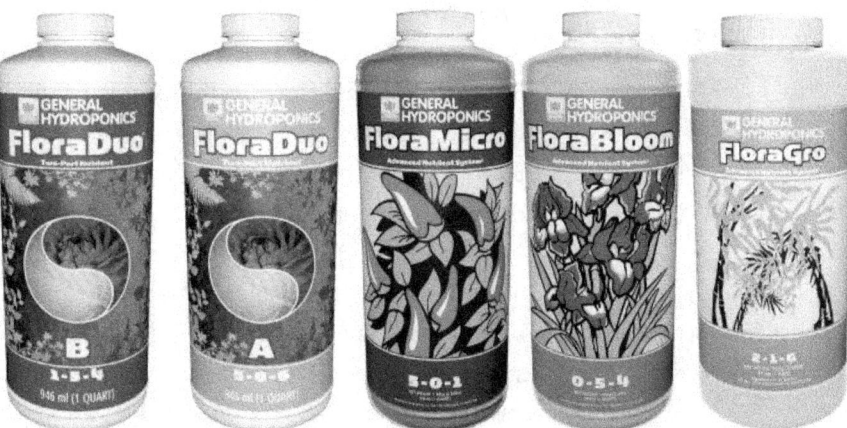

One-part liquid fertilizer is easy to use but more costly. Examples include FloraNova Grow (left), formulated for vegetative growth, and FloraNova Bloom (right), formulated for reproductive growth.

Two-part and three-part liquid fertilizers are also easy to use, have a great shelf life, and offer the ability to adjust the ratio of nutrients. Examples include FloraDuo two-part fertilizer (left) and Flora Series three-part fertilizer (right). Two-part and three-part dry fertilizers have the same benefits as liquid ones but are often cheaper. It is sometimes difficult to find multipart dry hydroponic fertilizers at traditional grow stores. A few of the more popular ones are blended by Hort Americas, Hydro-Gardens (Chem-Gro), JR Peters Inc. (Jack's), and Plant Marvel (Nutriculture).

learn about advanced hydroponic fertilizers, a great place to start is researching the Hoagland solution. The Hoagland solution and the many versions of modified Hoagland solutions are based on the original hydroponic nutrient recipes developed at the University of California in the 1930s.

MEASURING FERTILIZER CONCENTRATION

There are several ways to measure fertilizer concentration in a hydroponic nutrient solution. The preferred unit of measurement varies by country and application.

ELECTRICAL CONDUCTIVITY

Electrical conductivity (EC) is a measure of a material's ability to transport an electrical current. Water's ability to conduct electricity is the reason swimming during a thunderstorm or using an electrical appliance near a bathtub is incredibly dangerous. Surprisingly, pure distilled water with no mineral content is actually a very poor conductor. Pure distilled water is not common, and virtually all water sources have some degree of conductivity due to their mineral content. In hydroponics, growers increase the mineral content of the water by adding fertilizers. These fertilizers increase the water's ability to conduct electricity in a predictable pattern. For this reason, EC is a great way to estimate the fertilizer concentration in a hydroponic nutrient solution. EC is commonly measured in millisiemens per centimeter (mS/cm). Some countries, primarily Australia and New Zealand, may use conductivity factor (CF) instead of EC. The conversion chart on page 155 compares the EC, CF, and ppm.

MaxiBloom is a one-part dry fertilizer formulated for reproductive growth.

Fertilizer Storage

Always store fertilizer in airtight containers. Some of the ingredients in dry fertilizers, like calcium nitrate, are able to absorb moisture from the air. Dry fertilizer not stored properly can turn into a big solid brick once it absorbs moisture from the air. This fertilizer brick may still be usable but it is difficult to get accurate measurements because its weight and volume are affected by the additional moisture.

PARTS PER MILLION

Parts per million (ppm) refers to the mass of a nutrient in a specific volume of water, typically measured in milligrams per liter. Ppm is generally associated with total dissolved solids (TDS) meters. The conversion chart has a couple of different ppm columns because ppm can be interpreted in several ways, depending on the manufacturer of the ppm meter/probe. This can be a great source of confusion for new hydroponic growers trying to target a recommended ppm because they might be unsure whether their meter is measuring ppm using the same interpretation as the recommended ppm. To avoid this confusion, I recommend using an EC meter. That said, the reason there are so many different ppm interpretations is very interesting. As mentioned previously, EC measures how well a nutrient solution conducts electricity and EC increases as fertilizer is added to a solution, but all fertilizers do not increase the EC equally. Some nutrients have little impact on EC while others have a very significant impact. For example, an EC reading of 1 mS/cm could mean there is 400 ppm calcium or it could mean there is 620 ppm phosphorus. Nutrients are present in the nutrient solution as ions and some ions are better conductors of electricity. Almost all ppm meters measure a solution's EC and then convert that number into ppm by multiplying the EC by a conversion factor that the manufacturer suggests as an approximation for ppm. This means the manufacturer has to predict which nutrients will be used in the nutrient solution in order to determine how their meter should convert the original EC reading into ppm. Again, to avoid this confusion, please use an EC meter if given an option between EC and ppm.

KEY:
EC Electrical conductivity
CF Conductivity factor
TDS Total dissolved solids
PPM Parts per million

EC (mS/cm)	CF	ppm 500 (TDS)	ppm 700	EC (mS/cm)	CF	ppm 500 (TDS)	ppm 700
0.1	1	50	70	1.6	16	800	1120
0.2	2	100	140	1.7	17	850	1190
0.3	3	150	210	1.8	18	900	1260
0.4	4	200	280	1.9	19	950	1330
0.5	5	250	350	2	20	1000	1400
0.6	6	300	420	2.1	21	1050	1470
0.7	7	350	490	2.2	22	1100	1540
0.8	8	400	560	2.3	23	1150	1610
0.9	9	450	630	2.4	24	1200	1680
1	10	500	700	2.5	25	1250	1750
1.1	11	550	770	3	30	1500	2100
1.2	12	600	840	3.5	35	1750	2450
1.3	13	650	910	4	40	2000	2800
1.4	14	700	980	4.5	45	2250	3150
1.5	15	750	1050	5	50	2500	3500

6

SYSTEM MAINTENANCE

AT SOME POINT, EVEN THE most basic hydroponic gardens will require some upkeep. Hydroponic system maintenance includes everything from monitoring and adjusting nutrient concentrations to regularly flushing the system, and even the occasional scrubbing of pots and reservoirs.

MANAGING THE NUTRIENT SOLUTION

There are several ways to manage a hydroponic nutrient solution. Choosing the management strategy for your hydroponic garden will depend on crop selection, reservoir size, garden design, and personal preference. I often choose the option that requires the least amount of time even if that might slightly affect growth rate or crop quality, but you may wish to manage your nutrients more closely to optimize growth. The following management techniques are organized by the effort they require.

LEAST EFFORT: SET AND FORGET

Build the reservoir with the recommended fertilizer rate per gallon listed on the fertilizer bag/bottle. Adjust the pH if it is far outside of the target range, or don't. Allow the crop to grow until it is ready to harvest or until the water level is too low for plants to access the nutrient solution. This method can work great for leafy greens in floating raft systems and may work in other systems if they have a large enough reservoir relative to the number of plants growing. I've grown a surprising number of wonderful-looking crops using this minimal effort strategy. This management style can have issues when used with crops that have long growth cycles, such as tomatoes, peppers, cucumbers, and other flowering crops. If you wish to use minimal effort and grow crops that have a longer time until maturity, try the top off method.

LITTLE EFFORT: TOP OFF

This method is similar to set and forget, but as the water level drops the grower simply adds water to maintain the original level. Over time this method will dilute the nutrient concentration in the reservoir and nutrient deficiencies may appear on the crop. This method can work for fast-growing crops with low nutrient demands like microgreens, leafy greens, and some herbs. This method sometimes works for some larger crops depending on the system, but there is some risk of overdiluting the nutrient solution, especially when using a small reservoir.

SOME EFFORT: TOP OFF AND AMEND

The most common method for maintaining a nutrient solution in a hydroponic garden is to top off the reservoir as mentioned in the previous method, then add more fertilizer to the reservoir to maintain a target EC. Please see the appendix for example target ECs for common hydroponic crops. After adding fertilizer to reach the target EC, the grower adjusts the pH of the nutrient solution using either an acid (pH down) or base (pH up). There are many easy-to-use pH down and pH up products available in grow stores, and there are DIY options that are often less optimal but definitely usable. For pH down, some hydroponic gardeners use vinegar or lemon juice and for pH up some use baking soda.

To top off and amend the solution in your system, you will need an EC meter, hydroponic fertilizer, a measuring cup, a pH meter, pH down and pH up amendments, and a pipette (eyedropper).

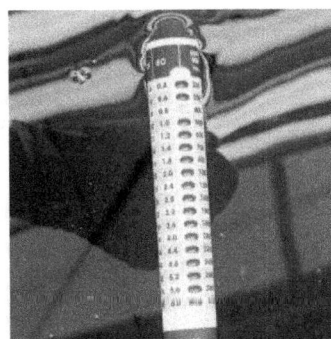

Measure the starting EC after adding water to the reservoir.

Mix dry fertilizers in a separate container before adding to the reservoir. It is important to fully dissolve dry fertilizers before adding them to the reservoir.

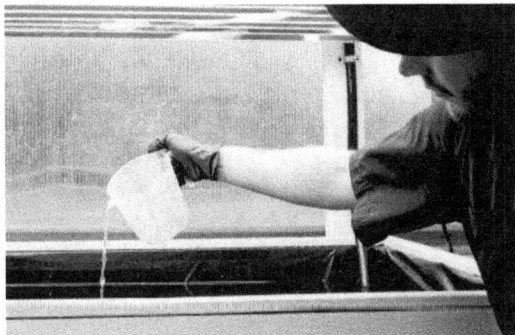

Add fertilizer in small increments to avoid overfertilizing.

Stir the reservoir by hand or use a pump to circulate the nutrient solution to disperse the concentrated fertilizer after each addition.

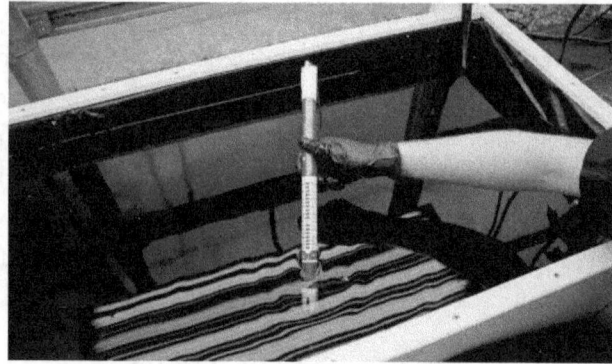

Check the EC after adding fertilizer and continue adding small amounts of fertilizer until the target EC is reached.

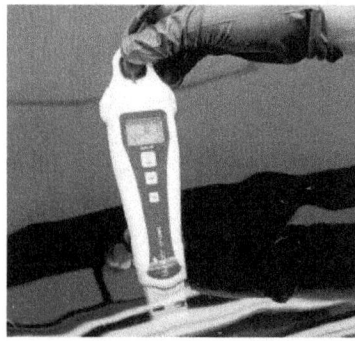

Measure the pH after reaching the target EC.

Any pH up and pH down products should always be handled with caution. Avoid skin contact and follow all safety recommendations on the product label.

Add pH down or pH up in small increments.

Thoroughly mix in additions before retesting the pH.

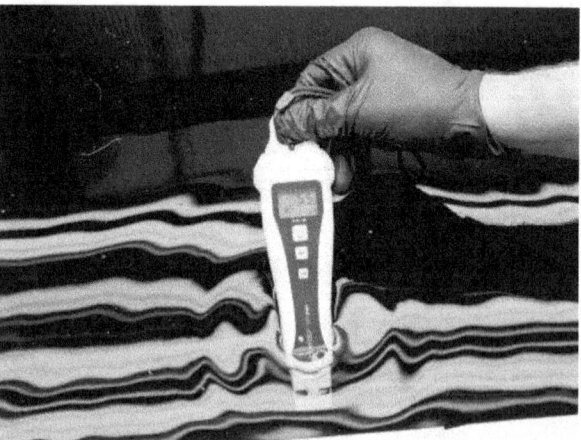

Slowly adjust the pH until the meter readings are within the target range.

SYSTEM MAINTENANCE

The flushed hydroponic nutrient solution can be used to fertilize a traditional soil garden.

FLUSHING

EC is a great general reference for nutrient content in a hydroponic reservoir, but unfortunately it does not tell the whole story. Not all nutrients are taken up by plants at the same rate. Over time, some nutrients will accumulate and others will be rapidly depleted, resulting in an imbalanced nutrient solution. Large commercial hydroponic farms send out water samples to testing facilities to get exact quantities of each nutrient in the reservoir and the grower then adjusts the fertilizer inputs accordingly. To perform these fertilizer adjustments requires complex chemistry and a deep understanding of a crop's specific nutrient requirements. The far-easier alternative is to periodically flush a hydroponic system. Flushing is the process of removing the existing nutrient solution and refilling the system with fresh water and then adding new fertilizer. The frequency of flushing is dependent on many factors, including crop, environment, system, fertilizer, and water quality. Most gardeners find success using the following rule of thumb to figure out flush frequency: "Flush a reservoir when the quantity of water added to top off a reservoir is equivalent to the size of the reservoir."

Example. A 40-gallon reservoir loses 5 gallons a day to evapotranspiration (plant transpiration and reservoir evaporation). The grower adds 5 gallons to the reservoir daily to top off the reservoir for water loss. After 8 days the grower adds a total of 40 gallons (8 days × 5 gallons = 40 gallons), the same volume of water as the original reservoir size. The grower should flush the reservoir every 8 days.

This rule of thumb is very conservative and many growers can flush less frequently when using traditional hydroponic fertilizers. This rule is useful, however, for getting a general guideline. The water flushed from a hydroponic system does not need to be put down the drain. Many gardeners use the old nutrient solution to water their potted plants, raised beds, lawn, or trees. A traditional garden is a great companion to a hydroponic garden, and it can be a home for old nutrient solutions, composted plants, and substrates.

CLEANING

Hydroponic growers can use a variety of products to sanitize their gardens. The safest and easiest option is usually dish soap. Some additional options available to hobby hydroponic growers include household bleach (use ½ to 1 ounce per gallon of water), isopropyl alcohol (70 percent or stronger), and hydrogen peroxide (3 percent is generally sufficient; stronger concentrations are available but they must be handled with care, so read and follow product labels).

Remove all substrate and plant material from the hydroponic garden before cleaning.

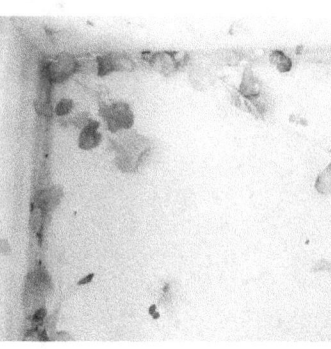

It is best to clean a hydroponic garden while it is still wet. Stains, plant roots, and leaves are more difficult to remove when dry.

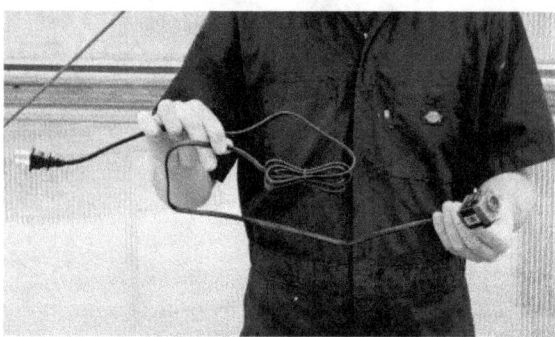

If possible, disconnect any pumps or air stones to clean independently from the reservoir.

Rinse the growing tray and reservoir to remove any plant debris.

Dish soap is often sufficient for cleaning most hydroponic gardens.

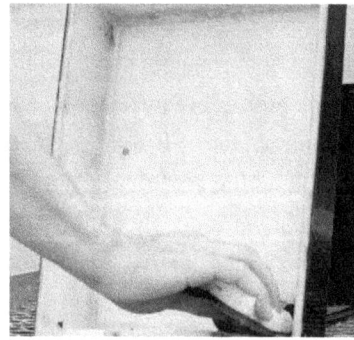

Scrub the growing area and reservoir with a soft sponge that won't scratch the plastic surfaces.

Fertilizer residue can accumulate on the pump and sections of the power cord that are submerged in the nutrient solution. Use a sponge to clean off any buildup.

Hand dry or air-dry the garden after a final rinse.

SYSTEM MAINTENANCE 161

7

COMMON PROBLEMS and TROUBLESHOOTING

NOW THAT YOU HAVE LEARNED to be a system builder, an indoor gardener, and a maintenance worker, it is time to learn to be a doctor. Here is a brief primer on how to diagnose and troubleshoot your hydroponic growing system.

NUTRIENT DEFICIENCIES

Traditional nutrient deficiency and toxicity identification guides show a single leaf with symptoms, but these can easily lead a gardener to overcorrect a problem or correct a problem incorrectly. Very often a nutrient toxicity or deficiency is due to nutrient solution/substrate pH, environmental conditions, crop age, or the presence of a pathogen. Before assuming the problem is nutrient related, check to see if:

- All plants of the same variety show similar symptoms.
- The pH is in the target range for the crop and not low (below 5.0) or high (above 6.5).
- The EC is in the target range for the crop.
- The air temperature is within the target range for the crop.
- The water temperature is within an ideal range for the crop, not below 55°F or above 85°F.
- The entire crop is receiving decent airflow. The leaves should be visibly moving.
- The crop is pest free.
- The light levels are within target range.
- The nutrient solution is created using a fertilizer designed for hydroponic gardens.

If the answer is yes to all these conditions, it is likely the problem is nutrient related. Often, nutrient-related issues can be remedied by dumping out the nutrient solution and restarting the system.

CHLOROSIS AND NECROSIS

Chlorosis is the loss of the chlorophyll, the green pigment in plants. Chlorosis can be used to describe leaf yellowing from many causes, including nutrient deficiencies or pest damage. Necrosis is plant tissue death. Plant diseases or nutrient deficiencies often start with signs of chlorosis that lead to necrosis.

Interveinal Chlorosis on New Growth

Interveinal chlorosis on new growth often indicates an iron deficiency or another micronutrient deficiency. Most hydroponic fertilizers provide plenty of iron, so the problem is rarely the presence of iron. Iron deficiencies generally occur because the pH is too high. Some crops are "iron-inefficient" and struggle to uptake iron. Basil is one of the common examples for an iron-inefficient plant. If basil is grown in a nutrient solution with a high pH, sometimes just over 6, it can show interveinal chlorosis on new growth indicative of an iron deficiency. The leaves showing this type of interveinal chlorosis will not recover but future growth can return to normal if the pH is adjusted and/or iron is supplemented to the nutrient solution.

Chlorosis on Older Leaves

Chlorosis on older leaves can be the result of a few different scenarios:

Nitrogen deficiency Nitrogen is a major component of chlorophyll, the green pigment in leaves. Plants are able to take the nitrogen from chlorophyll and move it throughout the plant as needed. When the plant detects a nitrogen

Healthy, chlorotic, and necrotic sage leaves

Chlorotic fig leaf with necrotic leaf edges

Interveinal chlorosis on new growth

Chlorosis on lower older leaves can indicate a nutrient deficiency, or it can be the natural senescence of older leaves.

deficiency, it will relocate the nitrogen in its older leaves to its new growth. Nitrogen deficiencies can appear when crops are grown at a low EC. New aquaponic gardens will sometimes have issues with nitrogen deficiencies.

Natural senescence Senescence is the natural dying of leaves due to old age. In mature plants, it is not uncommon to see some lower leaves die from natural senescence. If the hydroponic garden has both young and old plants, check to see if only the older plants are showing chlorosis on older leaves; this would indicate natural senescence.

Magnesium deficiency This looks similar to a nitrogen deficiency with older leaves showing chlorosis, but a magnesium deficiency will have interveinal chlorosis with necrotic spots and/or necrotic leaf edges. Most magnesium deficiencies can be remedied with magnesium sulfate (Epsom salt) at a rate of ½ to 1 teaspoon per gallon.

TIP BURN

Tip burn is technically a calcium deficiency, but very often it appears even when there is calcium present in the nutrient solution. Calcium is critical for the formation of plant cell walls. The plant's calcium uptake can sometimes struggle to keep up with the formation of new cells when a plant is growing fast in an environment with intense light and warm conditions. There are several ways to remedy this issue.

- Try a different variety. Some varieties are very sensitive to tip burn while others may grow fine in the existing conditions.
- Increase airflow on the crop to increase transpiration and speed up calcium uptake.
- Use a fertilizer with less nitrogen to slow down growth.
- Give the crop less light by adding shade or moving a grow light to slow down growth.
- Increase calcium. Sometimes this helps, but most hydroponic fertilizers provide sufficient calcium.

Tip burn on butterhead lettuce

Algae on the edge of a floating raft

INFESTATIONS

ALGAE

Algae growth is usually not an issue, but it can lead to other problems. Algae will steal some nutrients from the nutrient solution, but this is usually not a significant issue. The major concern is algae can act as a food source for fungus gnats and shore flies. To control algae growth, minimize the exposure of sunlight to the nutrient solution. Algae growing on the surface of seedlings is often a sign of overwatering, but it usually is not an issue that will significantly affect plant growth.

FUNGUS GNATS AND SHORE FLIES

Fungus gnats feed on fungi, algae, and plant tissue. The adult fungus gnats generally do not pose a threat, but the larvae can damage crops. The larvae feed on plant roots, creating wounds that make the plant susceptible to pathogens like *Pythium* and *Fusarium*. Shore flies are very similar to fungus gnats in looks but their larvae do not feed on plant roots. Shore flies do not damage crops, but they can definitely be annoying. Fungus gnats have a mosquito-like body shape with long legs. Shore flies look more like a fruit fly than a mosquito. There are many ways to control fungus gnats and shore flies; the following are just a few strategies.

Shore flies lay eggs in algal scum. The shore fly larvae feed on algae.

- Remove algae and decaying plant matter from growing area.
- Introduce beneficial nematodes like *Steinernema feltiae*.
- Use pest-control products containing the bacterium *Bacillus thuringiensis israelensis* (Bti).
- Use organic pesticides that contain azadirachtin.
- Use organic pesticides that contain pyrethrum/pyrethrin.

Aphids on mint

APHIDS

Aphids usually do not kill plants, but they can damage crops by distorting growth or by spreading viruses. The most common sign of aphids is a sticky honeydew on leaves. This honeydew can attract ants or be a site for fungus growth. Insecticidal soaps are great for controlling aphids. Products containing azadirachtin or pyrethrum/pyrethrin are very effective.

THRIPS

There can be many thrips or a single thrips. The word *thrips* is both the singular and the plural form. Thrips damage usually appears as spots on leaves, deformed flower growth, and/or distorted new leaf growth. Thrips can be a difficult pest to control. It is often easiest to find crops or crop varieties that are less attractive to thrips. A variety of biological pest-management techniques can be used, such as the introduction of predatory insects like green lacewings, predatory mites, parasitic wasps, and minute pirate bugs. Organic insecticides containing spinosad can be very effective on thrips. Additional options include insecticides that contain azadirachtin or pyrethrin, or an insecticidal soap.

Thrips damage and a small yellow thrips

SPIDER MITES

The most common mite found in gardens is the two-spotted spider mite. It is primarily a problem with flowering crops, including tomatoes, eggplants, cucumbers, and strawberries. Early damage generally shows as a speckled dull appearance on the top surface of leaves. This can progress to leaf chlorosis and leaf drop. Bad infestations have visible webbing on leaves. Very often spider mites attack the upper leaves on a plant. Spider mites like dry weather and are attracted to crops that are heavily fertilized. Predatory insects can be very effective when used preventively. The predatory mites *Phytoseiulus persimilis* and *Amblyseius fallacis* are commonly used. Insecticidal soaps and Neem oil can also help control mite populations. When using an insecticide on mites, always do two applications about 5 to 7 days apart. Mites in the egg stage may not be controlled as effectively by insecticides, so spacing out applications helps to fully eradicate mites.

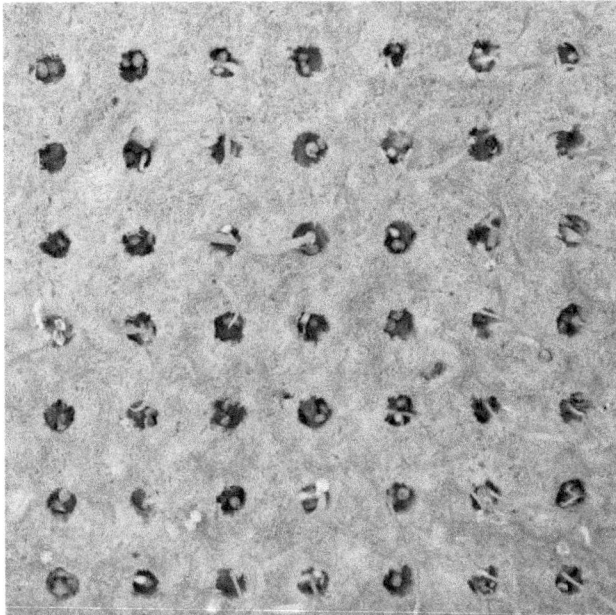

Poor spinach germination due to high temperatures

These basil seedlings are showing signs of stretch due to low light. These seedlings are still usable in this condition but they are on the edge of being unusable. Plants grown under low light will have weak stems and may not be able to support themselves.

SEEDLING PROBLEMS

Growing a healthy seedling can be one of the most challenging steps in the process for new hydroponic gardeners. Here are just a few of the reasons you may be having poor germination, seedling death, or poor seedling quality.

- Substrate is too wet and rotting the young seedlings (common with fine coco and heavy soil).
- Substrate is too dry.
- Seedlings have long, weak stems due to low light levels.
- Some seeds naturally have low germination rates.
- Some seeds are very sensitive to temperature.

WILTING

It is possible to overwater in some hydroponic systems. Letting the root zone dry out between irrigation cycles is beneficial to most crops. There are many techniques for determining when to water a crop, including the finger test, lift checks, and meters. The finger test is simply putting a finger through the surface of the substrate to check for moisture. Finger tests are less useful on large pots that can retain a lot of moisture deeper than a finger can test. A list test is more effective for large potted plants. Simply lift the pot to see if it is heavy with water weight. Water is very heavy and it will be noticeable when the pot is light and in need of water. There are a variety

Plants in NFT and aeroponic gardens can wilt quickly if there is a power outage or pump failure.

of moisture meters that can help too, but often a finger test and/or lift check is sufficient.

MUSHY BROWN ROOTS

Mushy brown roots are dead roots. The following are a few possible causes of root death:

- Low oxygen in the root zone due to overwatering in a heavy substrate, no aeration, and/or high water temperatures.
- Damage from very high EC or nutrient deficiency.
- Damage from very high or very low pH.
- Very warm water temperatures, often seen in hydroponic systems over 90°F.
- Damage from sanitizers used to clean system that were not fully rinsed before replanting.
- Root rot pathogens. There are many pathogens that are all clumped together under the same general name of root rot.

Remove plants that have dead roots. Very often it is necessary to fully clean out a system and sanitize it to remove the presence of pathogens. Try to remedy environmental conditions that are favorable to root rot before replanting. Increasing the flow rate in NFT can help. Increasing aeration in a floating raft garden can help. Burying the reservoir or adding a water chiller can also help.

GLOSSARY

Aeroponic: A hydroponic growing technique that suspends plant roots in the air and delivers nutrients in a fine mist.

Air pump: Aerates a nutrient solution when connected to air stones.

Air stone: Diffuses air into nutrient solution when connected to an air pump. Available in many shapes, including flat circles, cylinders, and flexible hoses.

Azadirachtin: A pesticide derived from the neem tree. Effective at disrupting insect molting for long-term pest management.

Beneficial microbes: Fungi and bacteria that can improve a plant's nutrient uptake, increase nutrient availability, provide protection against pests, or provide any other benefit in the growing environment.

Bloom: Often used to describe the flowering stage of growth. Bloom fertilizers are blended specifically for flowering crops that have different nutrient demands than leafy greens.

Ceramic metal halide: A high-intensity grow light with a blue dominant spectrum great for compact growth. Ceramic metal halides are more efficient than traditional metal halide grow lights.

CFL: See *compact fluorescent light*.

Clone: A rooted cutting.

CMH: See *ceramic metal halide*.

Coco coir: A growing substrate made from the husk of coconuts.

Compact fluorescent light: A beginner-friendly grow light that can be placed very close to plants. A compact fluorescent light may struggle to provide enough light for flowering crops.

Cut-and-come-again: A harvesting technique that allows for multiple harvests when used on specific crops. Plant is harvested by trimming back growth but leaving enough stem/leaves to allow the plant to regrow.

Cutting: Removing a section of stem and leaves from a "mother" plant with the goal of asexually reproducing a new plant.

Deep water culture: A hydroponic growing technique often associated with floating rafts or bubble buckets. Plants are suspended over a nutrient solution and roots grow freely into the solution.

Dissolved oxygen: A measure of the amount of oxygen present in a nutrient solution, often measured in parts per million (ppm).

DO: See *dissolved oxygen*.

Drain-to-waste: A hydroponic growing technique that does not recirculate the nutrient solution. The nutrient solution makes one pass through the growing substrate and does not return to the reservoir.

Dutch bucket: A pot commonly used in top drip hydroponics. The pot has a single drainage site that connects to a main drain line that returns nutrient solution to the reservoir.

DWC: See *deep water culture*.

Ebb and flow: Another name for flood and drain. See *flood and drain*.

EC: See *electrical conductivity*.

Electrical conductivity: A measure of a material's ability to transport an electrical current. The conductivity of a nutrient solution can be used as an estimate of fertilizer concentration.

Evapotranspiration: The cumulative water loss from surface evaporation and plant transpiration.

Expanded clay pellets: A growing substrate made of clay. It is pH neutral, inert, and quick draining.

Fertigation: The delivery of water-soluble fertilizers to crop using an irrigation delivery system. Simply a mix of fertilizing and irrigating.

Fertilizer: A broad term for anything natural or synthetic that can provide essential nutrients for plant growth.

Floating raft: A version of the deep water culture hydroponic technique that uses rafts to support plants floating in a nutrient solution.

Flood and drain: A hydroponic growing technique that waters plants from the bottom using periodic "flood" events in a grow tray. After a "flood" event, the nutrient solution drains back into the reservoir.

Flood tray: A general term for a watertight growing area with raised walls. Flood trays can be used in a variety of hydroponic growing techniques, including media beds, wicking beds, top drip, floating rafts/DWC, and flood and drain.

Flowering crop: Any plant that is grown specifically for flowers and/or fruits. *Flowering crop* is often used as a general term in hydroponics for a crop that has several growth stages and requires high light levels. Tomatoes, peppers, and cucumbers are some of the most common flowering crops grown in hydroponics.

Flush: Dumping out the nutrient solution from a hydroponic garden.

Germination: The beginning stage of starting a plant from seed. Seed germination is generally triggered by moisture and warmth.

High-pressure sodium: A high-intensity grow light that produces a yellow/orange light. High-pressure sodium lights are often used indoors for flowering crops and in greenhouses as a supplemental light source.

HPS: See *high-pressure sodium*.

Kratky method: A hydroponic growing technique similar to deep water culture. The Kratky method uses no pumps to circulate the nutrient solution; instead, it uses a static, noncirculating nutrient solution.

Leafy greens: A broad term for any crop grown for harvestable leaves. Typically used to describe lettuce, kale, chard, and herbs.

Light meter: A broad term for a variety of tools capable of measuring light intensity.

Lux: A unit used to measure light intensity. Lux is based on light intensity as perceived by the human eye.

Media/medium: Another term for a growing substrate. See *substrate*.

Media bed: A hydroponic growing technique that uses a flood tray filled with a loose, quick-draining substrate such as expanded clay pellets. Media beds use a similar irrigation design as flood and drain.

Metal halide: A high-intensity grow light with a blue dominant spectrum great for compact growth.

MH: See *metal halide*.

NFT: See nutrient film technique.

Nutrient film technique: A hydroponic growing technique that irrigates plants with a shallow stream of nutrient solution flowing through a growing channel.

Nutrient solution: Fertilizer dissolved in water.

Parts per million: The unit used by total dissolved solids (TDS) meters to measure fertilizer concentration.

Peat: A growing substrate made from partially decayed plant matter harvested from bogs. Often called sphagnum peat or sphagnum peat moss.

pH: A scale used to measure the acidity or basicity of a solution.

Photoperiod: Day length.

Photosynthetic photon flux density: A measure of the number of photons of light, measured in micromoles (μmol), within the 400nm–700nm wavelength range that are available per square meter (m2) per second (s).

PPFD: See *photosynthetic photon flux density*.

PPM: See *parts per million*.

Predatory insect: An insect that feeds on other insects. Predatory insects are often used to manage pest populations.

Pyrethrin: An organic pesticide derived from the pyrethrum chrysanthemum flower. One of the most powerful organic pesticides, it is capable of quickly killing most insects when applied at a strong concentration. Pyrethrins may potentially kill beneficial insects too.

Recirculating: Used to describe hydroponic systems that capture and reuse the nutrient solution after irrigating the crop.

Rock wool: Another term for stone wool.

Solution: A liquid mixture.

Stock solution: Fertilizer dissolved in water at a highly concentrated rate, often 50x–200x the strength of a nutrient solution.

Stone wool: A growing substrate made by melting basaltic rocks and spinning the "rock lava" into fibers.

Substrate: A material used to support plant roots. Common hydroponic substrates include stone wool, coco coir, perlite, and expanded clay pellets.

T5 fluorescent: A skinny tube-shaped fluorescent grow light that generally comes in lengths of 1, 2, and 4 feet. A great beginner-friendly grow light.

Top drip: A hydroponic growing technique that delivers irrigation to the top of the growing substrate, generally through ¼-inch irrigation lines.

Vegetative: Often used to describe a stage of crop growth focused on leaf production. Vegetative fertilizers are blended specifically for herbs, leafy greens, and early stage flowering crops. Vegetative fertilizers can be used for flowering crops, but they may not deliver the optimal nutrient recipe to maximize reproductive growth.

Venturi: An attachment used to aerate a nutrient solution. A venturi can connect directly to a pump or be installed inline in a section of tubing. Venturis take advantage of a phenomenon called the Venturi effect, which occurs when a liquid or gas flowing through a pipe moves through a constricted section, resulting in increased velocity and decreased static pressure. The venturi pump attachments have an intake tube positioned in the area of lower pressure. The decreased pressure creates a suction that is used to pull air into the pipe.

Wicking bed: A hydroponic growing technique that takes advantage of capillary action to deliver a nutrient solution to crops.

APPENDIX
CROP SELECTION CHARTS

KEY
Recommended
DIY System
- **B** Bottle Hydroponics
- **F** Floating Rafts
- **W** Wicking Bed
- **N** NFT
- **T** Top Drip
- **M** Media Beds
- **FD** Flood and Drain
- **A** Aeroponics
- **V** Vertical Gutter Garden

Rex butterhead lettuce

LETTUCE

- **Recommended DIY Systems:** Lettuce can grow in any of the hydroponic systems mentioned in this book.
- **Germination Temperatures:** Ideal germination temperature is 60–70°F, but germination will occur in much wider temperature range.
- **Water Temperatures:** Ideal water temperature is 65–70°F, but healthy lettuce crops have been observed in 55–90°F water.
- **EC:** Healthy crops have been observed growing in nutrient solutions with ECs in the range of 0.7–2.8. The exact target EC will depend on light levels, water source, environment, and crop age, but in general an EC of 1.8–2.3 will produce a healthy crop.
- **pH:** Healthy crops have been observed growing in nutrient solutions with pHs in the range of 5.2–7. Best growth has been observed at pH of 5.5–6.0.
- **Air Temperatures:** Ideal air temperature is 65–75°F, but healthy lettuce has been observed growing in temperatures 50–95°F.

Variety Name	Leaf Type or Color	Recommended DIY Systems	Seeds/ Cube	Notes
MIXES				
Allstar Gourmet Lettuce Mix	Mixed	B, F, W, N, T, M, FD, A, V	3–6	Great color, fast growing, and easy to grow. Includes green oakleaf, red oakleaf, green romaine, red romaine, lollo rossa, and red leaf lettuce.
Five Star Greenhouse Lettuce Mix	Mixed	B, F, W, N, T, M, FD, A, V	3–6	Green oakleaf, red oakleaf, red romaine, green leaf, and red leaf lettuce.
Wildfire Lettuce Mix	Mixed	B, F, W, N, T, M, FD, A, V	3–6	Green oakleaf, red oakleaf, green romaine, red romaine, and red leaf lettuce.
Elegance Greens Mix	Mixed	B, F, W, N, T, M, FD, A, V	3–6	Great spicy mix that includes pac choi, red mustard, mizuna, and leaf broccoli.
Premium Greens Mix	Mixed	B, F, W, N, T, M, FD, A, V	3–6	A decent mix but sometimes the cabbage grows poorly. Mix includes red mustard, green mustard, Chinese cabbage, pac choi, and tatsoi.
BUTTERHEAD				
Rex	Green	B, F, W, N, T, M, FD, A, V	1	The standard for hydroponic lettuce. Great tasting and heavy yields.
Flandria	Green	B, F, W, N, T, M, FD, A, V	1	
Salanova Green Butter	Green	B, F, W, N, T, M, FD, A, V	1	A green butterhead that does not form a dense core. Lower yields and smaller leaves than Rex.
Salanova Red Butter	Red	B, F, W, N, T, M, FD, A, V	1	Does not form a dense core like other butterheads, but still delivers a great yield. Leaves can range from light red to dark red depending on lighting.
Skyphos	Red	B, F, W, N, T, M, FD, A, V	1	If given enough light, this butterhead can grow huge. The leaves are generally not deep red, but they do taste great.
OAKLEAF				
Salanova Red Oakleaf	Red	B, F, W, N, T, M, FD, A, V	1	Good yields but be careful not to overgrow this crop. Leaves have a tendency for tip burn when grown too long.
Salanova Green Oakleaf	Green	B, F, W, N, T, M, FD, A, V	1	Similar to red oakleaf but fewer issues when growing larger heads.
Panisse	Green	B, F, W, N, T, M, FD, A, V	1	Huge, fluffy, green oakleaf. Great for high light conditions, not great for low light.
Rouxai	Red	B, F, W, N, T, M, FD, A, V	1	Grows well in a variety of environments and will generally produce leaves with deep red color.
Oscarde	Red	B, F, W, N, T, M, FD, A, V	1	Similar to Rouxai. Depending on environment, Rouxai or Oscarde may perform best.

Variety Name	Leaf Type or Color	Recommended DIY Systems	Seeds/Cube	Notes
LOLLO				
Dark Red Lollo Rossa	Red	B, F, W, N, T, M, FD, A, V	1–2	Generally low yielding.
Livigna	Green	B, F, W, N, T, M, FD, A, V	1–2	
ROMAINE/COS				
Green Star	Green	B, F, W, N, T, M, FD, A, V	1	Generally lanky and fragile, may not be optimal romaine for hydroponics.
Tropicana	Green	B, F, W, N, T, M, FD, A, V	1	Good resistance to tip burn when grown in intense summer light. Depending on environment, Tropicana or Coastal Star may be best.
Coastal Star	Green	B, F, W, N, T, M, FD, A, V	1	Susceptible to tip burn. Depending on environment, Tropicana or Coastal Star may be best.
Red Rosie	Red	B, F, W, N, T, M, FD, A, V	1	Some susceptibility to tip burn, performs best under shade or low light.
Breen	Red	B, F, W, N, T, M, FD, A, V	1–3	Won't yield much, but this miniature red romaine is beautiful and great tasting. Susceptible to tip burn when grown under high intensity light.
Thurinus	Red	B, F, W, N, T, M, FD, A, V	1	Similar color and shape as Breen, but much larger. Leaves are a little thicker than Breen too. Susceptible to tip burn when grown under high intensity light.
Flashy Trout Back	Mixed	B, F, W, N, T, M, FD, A, V	1–3	Very delicate leaves should be used immediately. This lettuce does not keep well.
Speckles	Mixed	B, F, W, N, T, M, FD, A, V	1	Similar to Flashy Trout Back.
Outredgeous	Red	B, F, W, N, T, M, FD, A, V	1	Quicker to bolt than other red romaines. Susceptible to tip burn.
LOOSE LEAF VARIETIES				
Salanova Green Sweet Crisp	Green	B, F, W, N, T, M, FD, A, V	1	Good yields but can be very fragile. Grows well under LEDs.
Salanova Red Sweet Crisp	Red	B, F, W, N, T, M, FD, A, V	1	Good yields but can be very fragile. Grows well under LEDs.
Salanova Red Incised	Red	B, F, W, N, T, M, FD, A, V	1	Good yields but can be very fragile. Grows well under LEDs.
Salanova Green Incised	Green	B, F, W, N, T, M, FD, A, V	1	Good yields but can be very fragile. Grows well under LEDs.
SUMMER CRISP/BATAVIA				
Muir	Green	B, F, W, N, T, M, FD, A, V	1	More tolerant of hot weather than other varieties. Plants look like a mix of romaine and oakleaf.
Cherokee	Red	B, F, W, N, T, M, FD, A, V	1	

HERBS

Variety Name	Recommended DIY Systems	Germination	EC	pH	Notes
Greek Oregano	W, T, M, FD, V	Sprinkle seeds on top of the growing medium; seeds require light to germinate.	1.2–2.3	5.5–6.5	Strong oregano aroma and flavor; great for pizza and Italian cooking. Characteristic dark green leaves with white flowers.
Italian Oregano	W, T, M, FD, V		1.2–2.3	5.5–6.5	
Rosemary	W, T, M, FD, V	Can be difficult to grow from seed; easier to grow from cuttings.	1.2–2.3	5.5–6.5	
Creeping Thyme	W, T, M, FD, V		1.2–2.3	5.5–6.5	Prefers drier conditions than provided in most hydroponic systems but still grows okay.
Summer Thyme	W, T, M, FD, V		1.2–2.3	5.5–6.5	Prefers drier conditions than provided in most hydroponic systems but still grows okay.
Sage (Extrakta)	W, T, M, FD, V		1.2–2.3	5.5–6.5	Great sage variety for hydroponics.
Calypso Cilantro	B, F, W, N, T, M, FD, A, V	55–75°F	1.0–1.8	5.5–6.0	Can be tricky to grow and susceptible to tip burn. Split seed for best germination.
Santo Monogerm Cilantro	B, F, W, N, T, M, FD, A, V	55–75°F	1.0–1.8	5.5–6.0	Monogerm cilantro is much easier to germinate than tradition cilantro seed. This variety is one of the easier cilantro varieties to grow in hydroponics, but cilantro is notoriously difficult to grow in hydroponics.
Tarragon	F, W, N, T, M, FD, V		1.2–2.3	5.5–6.5	
Watercress	B, F, W, N, T, M, FD, A, V	65–75°F	1.8–2.3	5.5–6.5	Loves wet conditions. Vigorous grower. Flavor is similar to arugula. Great addition to hydroponic fairy garden.
Flat-Leaf Parsley	B, F, W, N, T, M, FD, A, V		1.2–2.3	5.5–6.5	
Parsley Triple Curled	B, F, W, N, T, M, FD, A, V		1.2–2.3	5.5–6.5	
Chervil	B, F, W, N, T, M, FD, A, V		1.2–2.3	5.5–6.5	Anise flavor, grows similar to parsley.
Dill Bouquet	B, F, W, N, T, M, FD, A, V		1.2–2.3	5.5–6.5	
Fernleaf Dill	B, F, W, N, T, M, FD, A, V		1.2–2.3	5.5–6.5	
Green Fennel	B, F, W, N, T, M, FD, A, V	70–80°F	1.2–2.3	5.5–6.5	Prefers air temperatures around 60°F but capable of growing in a wide range of conditions.
Chives (Variety Staro)	F, W, N, T, M, FD, A, V		1.2–2.3	5.5–6.5	Great for rafts. Harvest as a cut-and-come-again crop. Plants can grow for years.
Tokyo Bunching Green Onion	F, W, N, T, M, FD, V	50–85°F	1.2–2.3	5.5–6.5	Very tasty. May be tricky to establish, but great once established.

(continued)

Variety Name	Recommended DIY Systems	Germination	EC	pH	Notes
Munstead Lavender	F, W, N, T, M, FD, V		1.2–2.3	5.5–6.5	Slow growing but produces beautiful flowers.
Corsican Mint Mini	B, F, W, N, T, M, FD, A, V		1.8–2.3	5.5–6.0	Partial shade to full sun. Keep roots moist. Very intense flavor. Small compact leaves.
Wrigley's Spearmint	B, F, W, N, T, M, FD, A, V		1.8–2.3	5.5–6.0	Partial shade to full sun. Keep roots moist.
Scotch Spearmint	B, F, W, N, T, M, FD, A, V		1.8–2.3	5.5–6.0	Partial shade to full sun. Keep roots moist.
Mojito Mint	B, F, W, N, T, M, FD, A, V	55–65°F	1.8–2.3	5.5–6.0	Partial shade to full sun. Keep roots moist. Great-tasting mint.
Chocolate Mint	B, F, W, N, T, M, FD, A, V		1.8–2.3	5.5–6.0	Partial shade to full sun. Keep roots moist. Unique flavor, definitely a mix of mint and chocolate.

Mint is generally grown from cuttings, but plants can be started from seed too.

BASIL

Note: Basil often grows best when densely seeded. Try using five to eight seeds per plug and do not thin out the seedlings after germination. Some of the plants will grow tall while others may stay short, creating a dense canopy of basil.

- **Recommended DIY Systems:** Basil can grow in any of the hydroponic systems mentioned in this book.
- **Germination Temperatures:** Ideal germination temperature is 65–75°F, but germination will occur in much wider temperature range.
- **Water Temperatures:** Ideal water temperature is 70–75°F, but healthy basil crops have been observed in 60–95°F water.
- **EC:** Healthy crops have been observed growing in nutrient solutions with ECs in the range of 0.7–2.8. The exact target EC will depend on light levels, water source, environment, and crop age, but in general an EC of 1.8–2.3 will produce a healthy crop.
- **pH:** Healthy crops have been observed growing in nutrient solutions with pHs in the range of 5.2–7. Best growth has been observed at pH of 5.5–6.0.
- **Air Temperatures:** Ideal air temperature is 70–80°F, but healthy basil has been observed growing in temperatures 55–100°F.

Variety Name	Type	Notes
Italian Large Leaf	Large leaf	Often the cheapest seed, this standard basil can yield more than most varieties.
Napoletano	Lettuce leaf	Huge leaves that are usually 5–6" long but can get to nearly 1' long. Great for making basil wraps. Do not seed densely like other varieties.
Mrs. Burns' Lemon	Citrus	One of the fastest-growing basil varieties. Great taste too. Try making a lemon basil pesto. Very sensitive to high pH, will quickly show iron deficiency. Keep pH at 5.5–5.8.
Aroma 2	Genovese	A favorite among hydroponic growers. Tends to perform great in situations where other varieties might struggle. Resistant to *Fusarium* (root rot).
Red Rubin	Purple	Great purple basil variety.
Genovese	Genovese	

(continued)

Variety Name	Type	Notes
Siam Queen	Thai	Favorite Thai basil. Grows huge, beautiful flowers that also taste great. Leaves are larger than traditional Thai basil.
Sweet Thai	Thai	Traditional Thai basil.
Thai Red Stem	Thai	Traditional Thai basil.
Purple Basil Amethyst Improved	Purple	Small but pretty basil variety.
Dark Opal	Purple	One of the best purple basil varieties.
Purple Ruffles	Purple frill	Beautiful frilly purple leaves.
Purple Delight	Purple	

PEPPERS

Note: Plants should generally be spaced 18 to 25 inches apart. All require high oxygen root zone environment. Prefer to dry out between irrigations. Peppers do well with 16 hours light, 8 hours dark when grown indoors.

- **Germination Temperatures:** Ideal germination temperature is 75–85°F, but germination will occur in much wider temperature range.
- **Water Temperatures:** Ideal water temperature is 65–70°F, but healthy pepper crops have been observed in 55–85°F water.
- **EC:** Healthy crops have been observed growing in nutrient solutions with ECs in the range of 0.7–2.5, but most peppers will respond well to an EC in the range of 1.4–1.8.
- **pH:** Healthy crops have been observed growing in nutrient solutions with pHs in the range of 5.0–7. Best growth has been observed at pH of 5.5–5.8.
- **Air Temperatures:** Ideal average air temperature over 75°F, but healthy pepper plants have been observed growing in temperatures 55–100°F.

Variety Name	Heat, Scoville	Recommended DIY Systems	Days to Harvest	Notes
Fatalii Jigsaw Gourmet	125,000–325,000	W, T, M, FD	120–180	Fruity flavor with intense heat.
Red Datil	100,000–300,000	W, T, M, FD		Solid variety for hydroponics.
Bulgarian Carrot	5,000–30,000	W, T, M, FD	75	Great for drying. Plant stays very short.
Anaheim Chile	500–1,000	W, T, M, FD	80–85	Long peppers (6–10") with a little bit of heat. Primarily picked green.
Scotch Bonnet Orange	100,000–350,000	W, T, M, FD	95–100	Grows 2 2½' tall. Very hot. Can be more finicky than other pepper varieties.
Tam Jalapeño	1,000–1,500	W, T, M, FD	70–75	Stays relatively short, around 3' tall.
Serrano Chile (*Capsicum annuum*)	6,000–20,000	W, T, M, FD	75–80	Stays relatively short, around 3' tall.
Bird's Eye Chile/ Thai Chile	100,000–225,000	W, T, M, FD		Grows well in very hot climates. Peppers dry fast and make very hot pepper flakes. Plants can grow 5' tall.
Peter Pepper	10,000–23,000	W, T, M, FD		Known for its unusually shaped fruit. Can be difficult to grow compared to other pepper varieties.
Relleno	1,000–1,500	W, T, M, FD	100–120	Goes from green to orange to red. Can be harvested at any stage. Popular for stuffing and frying.
Habanada	Almost 0	W, T, M, FD	70 green, 90 orange	A heatless habanero. Amazing fruity flavor without the heat. Slow to start but easy to grow once established.

TOMATOES

Most tomato varieties can be grown in hydroponics, I encourage you to try any varieties, especially if you already have a favorite tomato variety. The varieties below are some of my favorite tomato varieties I've tried in hydroponics.

Tomatoes are generally grown in full sun but many can grow well in partial shade.

Most seed packets will instruct gardeners to grow tomatoes at 60 to 75°F, if possible. Many of these varieties do great at higher temperatures, especially cherry tomatoes. Cherry tomatoes can tolerate temperatures over 90°F.

Variety Name	Type	Recommended DIY Systems	Germination Temperatures	Days Until Fruit	Air Temperaturess	EC
Tasmanian Chocolate	Dark red/purple oblate	T, FD	75–90°F	85	60–75°F	1.2–1.6
Dwarf Golden Heart	Yellow heart shaped	T, FD	75–90°F	70	60–75°F	1.2–1.6
Sarandipity	Round striped	T, FD	75–90°F	65	60–75°F	1.2–1.6
Dwarf Purple Heart	Purple heart shaped	T, FD	75–90°F	70	60–75°F	1.2–1.6
Sun Gold	Orange cherry	T	75–80°F	60	60–75°F	1.6–2.5
Juliet F1	Saladette and sauce	T	75–90°F	60	60–75°F	1.6–2.5
Sakura	Red cherry	T	75–80°F	55	60–75°F	1.6–2.5
Black Cherry	Black cherry	T	75–90°F	65	60–75°F	1.6–2.5
Yellow Pear	Yellow pear cherry	T	75–80°F	70	60–75°F	1.6–2.5
Green Zebra	Round, striped	T	75–90°F	75	60–75°F	1.2–1.8
Red Robin	Miniature cherry	F, W, T, M, FD, V	68–77°F	65	60–75°F	1.2–2.5

Green Zebra tomatoes

Sun Gold tomatoes

pH	Growth	Yield	Notes
5.5–6.0	Remains short, could be grown indoors.	Good	Great flavor, huge fruit. Plants grow to about 4' tall.
5.5–6.0	Remains short, could be grown indoors.	Great	Large yellow tomatoes have excellent flavor, one of the best-tasting dwarf heirloom varieties. Texture is not ideal for sandwiches, as tomato is very juicy.
5.5–6.0	Remains short, could be grown indoors.	Low	Mild flavor, great-looking fruit. Plant stays short (no more than 3' tall) with minimal branching.
5.5–6.0	Remains short, could be grown indoors.	Great	Large purple tomatoes that are great for sandwiches. Mild flavor, good texture.
5.5–6.0	Large sprawling growth. Best for greenhouse or outdoors.	Good	Amazing sweet flavor. Sweetest cherry tomato I've ever had. Hardy and easy to grow.
5.5–6.0	Large sprawling growth. Best for greenhouse or outdoors.	Great	One of the most prolific tomato plants, amazing yields. Flavor is good.
5.5–6.0	Large sprawling growth. Best for greenhouse or outdoors.	Great	Hardy red cherry tomato plant that can tolerate warm weather and has great disease resistance.
5.5–6.0	Large sprawling growth. Best for greenhouse or outdoors.	Good	Flavor is similar to large heirloom tomatoes, very unique for a cherry tomato. Tolerates warm weather. Great cherry tomato to complement Sun Golds in a garden.
5.5–6.0	Large sprawling growth. Best for greenhouse or outdoors.	Good	Flavor is mild. Great addition to a cherry mix to create a diverse mix of colors.
5.5–6.0	Medium size, could be grown indoors but would be best in greenhouse or outdoors.	Okay	Amazing flavor.
5.5–6.0	Very short, generally a maximum of 1' tall.	Low	Flavor is good but best feature is the height of this tomato. Mature plant remains very short, less than 1' tall.

STRAWBERRIES

Note: It is very important to keep the crown of a strawberry above the surface of the substrate. If the crown gets too wet, the plant will rot and die.

- **Recommended DIY Systems:** Strawberries can be grown in all of the systems mentioned in this book except bottle hydroponics.
- **Germination Temperatures:** Strawberries can be started from seed but it is more common to purchase bare-root plants ready to transplant. Ideal germination temperature for seeds is around 70°F.
- **Water Temperatures:** 60–75°F
- **EC:** 0.8–1.2. Can tolerate higher ECs even up to 2.5.
- **pH:** 5.5–6.0
- **Air Temperatures:** 60–80°F

Variety Name	Notes
Delizz	Good variety to grow from seed.
Jewel	
Earliglow	Good flavor, but mild compared to Evie.
Sparkle	
Evie	Very good flavor.
Pineberry	Requires cross-pollination to develop fruit. Produces a white strawberry with decent flavor. Flavor is supposed to taste like a mix of strawberry and pineapple; I only taste strawberry, though.
Mara Des Bois	Not a very robust variety in hydroponics.
Eversweet	
Seascape	A very popular variety for hydroponics, flavor is okay.
Sweet Charlie	Strong grower, great for hydroponics. Flavor is almost as good as Evie.

Various strawberry varieties grown in vertical towers

Various strawberry varieties grown in a DIY vertical garden

Borage flowers

Nasturium

Red-veined sorrel

RARE AND UNUSUAL

Variety Name	Recommended DIY Systems	Germination Temperatures	Air Temperatures	Water Temperatures	EC	pH
Iceplant	B, F, W, N, T, M, FD, A, V	70–75°F	65–75°F	65–75°F	1.8–2.3	5.5–6.5
	Notes: Thick succulent leaves that taste like a mild lettuce. The leaves are covered in trichomes, giving them a sparkly appearance.					
Green Sorrel	B, F, W, N, T, M, FD, A, V	65–70°F	65–85°F	65–85°F	1.2–2.3	5.5–6.5
	Notes: Naturally grows black roots. The best tasting part of the crop is often the stem. Green sorrel generally has more flavor than red-veined sorrel. Citrusy flavor.					
Red-Veined Sorrel	B, F, W, N, T, M, FD, A, V	65–70°F	65–85°F	60–80°F	1.2–2.3	5.5–6.0
	Notes: Leaf quality is best when shade grown. Older mature leaves can get leathery.					
Tangerine Gem Marigold	B, F, W, N, T, M, FD, A, V	75–80°F	65–85°F	65–85°F	1.2–2.3	5.5–6.5
	Notes: Not great tasting, but definitely edible. The plant is beautiful.					
Borage	F, W, N, T, M, FD, A, V	60–75°F	65–85°F	65–75°F	1.2–2.3	5.5–6.0
	Notes: The flowers taste great, just like cucumber. Grow in partial sun.					
Wasabi Arugula	B, F, W, N, T, M, FD, A, V	65–75°F	65–85°F	65–75°F	1.2–1.8	5.5–6.5
	Notes: Intense wasabi flavor. Slow-growing crop that has a tendency to flower quickly. Trim off flowers to keep plant producing leaves. Flowers are also edible. Full sun to partial shade.					
Mimosa Pudica	W, M, FD	65–75°F	65–95°F	65–80°F	1.2–1.8	5.5–6.5
	Notes: Known by many names, including Touch-Me-Not and Sensitive Plant, this plant quickly responds to touch by folding in its leaves. It can be sensitive to overwatering when young but it is tolerant once established. It grows best in warm environments with lots of light.					
Nasturtium Jewel's Mix	B, F, W, N, T, M, FD, A, V	60–65°F	65–95°F	65–75°F	1.2–2.3	5.5–6.5
	Notes: Great-tasting leaves and flowers. Intense watercress-like flavor. Tastes great with goat cheese. Produces flowers when stressed. Let the plant roots dry out to force flowering.					
Hibiscus Roselle (*Hibiscus sabdariffa*)	W, T, M, FD	70–80°F	65–95°F	65–75°F	1.2–2.0	5.5–6.5
	Notes: Young flowers have strong citrus/cranberry flavor. Very popular for making tea. Grows well in a chunky, fast-draining coco coir. Full sun, warm weather.					
Purslane	B, F, W, N, T, M, FD, A, V	70–80°F	65–75°F	65–75°F	1.2–2.3	5.5–6.5
	Notes: Fairly easy to grow in hydroponics. Great addition to a hydroponic fairy garden.					

(continued)

Variety Name	Recommended DIY Systems	Germination Temperatures	Air Temperatures	Water Temperatures	EC	pH
Red Callaloo	B, F, W, N, T, M, FD, A, V	65–75°F	65–95°F	65–75°F	1.2–2.3	5.5–6.5
	Notes: Leafy green that tolerates hot environments.					
Sugarcane	W, T, M	Start from cane/root stock/ratoon	70–95°F	65–80°F	1.2–2.3	5.5–6.5
	Notes: Grows well in coco coir and loose substrates.					
Celeriac	F, W, N, T, M, FD, A, V	70–75°F	55–85°F	65–75°F	1.8–2.3	5.5–6.5
	Notes: Grows well with partial sun to full sun. Can be cut and harvested multiple times.					
Stevia	B, F, W, N, T, M, FD, A, V	68–75°F	55–85°F	65–75°F	1.2–2.3	5.5–6.5
	Notes: Sensitive to overwatering when young but can grow great in floating rafts if transplanted when mature. Partial shade to full sun. Trim to harvest.					
Toothache Plant	B, F, W, N, T, M, FD, A, V	70–75°F	70–95°F	65–90°F	1.2–2.3	5.5–6.5
	Notes: The flowers don't taste great but they create a numbing/tingling sensation when chewed. Sensation is similar to pop-rocks candy.					

KALE

Days to harvest is 10 to 15 for microgreens, 20 to 25 for baby leaf, and 35 to 60 for mature leaves. Kale for salads is best harvested at baby leaf or microgreen stage. Mature leaves are great for cooking. Cold weather often improves the color and flavor of kale.

Variety Name	Recommended DIY Systems	Germination Temperatures	Air Temperatures	Water Temperatures	EC	pH
Red Russian	B, F, W, N, T, M, FD, A, V	75–85°F	60–90°F	60–75°F	1.2–2.3	5.5–6.5
	Notes: Okay color, unique leaf shape/texture. One of the highest yielding kale varieties.					
Toscano (aka Dinosaur, Italian, or Lacinato)	B, F, W, N, T, M, FD, A, V	75–85°F	60–90°F	60–75°F	1.2–2.3	5.5–6.5
	Notes: Not the fastest grower, but leaves make great kale chips.					
Red Kale	B, F, W, N, T, M, FD, A, V	75–85°F	60–90°F	60–75°F	1.2–2.3	5.5–6.5
	Notes: Great color. Good yield.					
Scarlet Kale	B, F, W, N, T, M, FD, A, V	75–85°F	60–90°F	60–75°F	1.2–2.3	5.5–6.5
Nash's Green	B, F, W, N, T, M, FD, A, V	75–85°F	60–90°F	60–75°F	1.2–2.3	5.5–6.5
	Fast-growing kale.					
Scarlet	B, F, W, N, T, M, FD, A, V	75–85°F	60–90°F	60–75°F	1.2–2.3	5.5–6.5
Darkibor F1	B, F, W, N, T, M, FD, A, V	75–85°F	60–90°F	60–75°F	1.2–2.3	5.5–6.5
Siberian	B, F, W, N, T, M, FD, A, V	75–85°F	60–90°F	60–75°F	1.2–2.3	5.5–6.5
Starbor F1	B, F, W, N, T, M, FD, A, V	75–85°F	60–90°F	60–75°F	1.2–2.3	5.5–6.5
Olympic Red	B, F, W, N, T, M, FD, A, V	75–85°F	60–90°F	60–75°F	1.2–2.3	5.5–6.5
Dwarf Blue Curled	B, F, W, N, T, M, FD, A, V	75–85°F	60–90°F	60–75°F	1.2–2.3	5.5–6.5
	Great compact curly blue-green kale.					

Mix of red kale and Toscano kale

Bright Lights Swiss chard

ADDITIONAL LEAFY GREENS

Variety Name	Recommended DIY Systems	Germination Temperatures	Air Temperatures	Water Temperatures	EC	pH
Ruby Red Swiss Chard	B, F, W, N, T, M, FD, A, V	75–90°F	55–95°F	60–85°F	1.2–2.3	5.5–6.5
	Note: Full sun.					
Bright Lights Decorticated Chard	B, F, W, N, T, M, FD, A, V	75–90°F	55–95°F	60–85°F	1.2–2.3	5.5–6.5
	Notes: Very fun crop. The root color matches the stem color. Full sun.					
Amara Mustard	F, W, N, T, M, FD, A, V	75–85°F	60–85°F	65–80°F	1.2–2.3	5.5–6.5
	Notes: Huge fast growth.					
Scarlet Frills Mustard	B, F, W, N, T, M, FD, A, V	75–85°F	60–85°F	65–80°F	1.2–2.3	5.5–6.5
	Notes: Vigorous growth, good color, strong flavor.					
Mizuna	B, F, W, N, T, M, FD, A, V	75–85°F	60–85°F	65–80°F	1.2–2.3	5.5–6.5
	Notes: Fast growing and beautiful.					
Astro Arugula	W, N, T, M, FD, A, V	65–75°F	60–75°F	65–75°F	1.0–1.8	5.5–6.0
	Notes: Some tolerance to heat, but still can be difficult to grow in hydroponics. This is a good variety for arugula microgreens.					
Sylvetta Arugula	W, N, T, M, FD, A, V	65–75°F	60–75°F	65–75°F	1.0–1.8	5.5–6.0
	Notes: Slow growing but great taste. Difficult crop to grow in hydroponics.					
Celery (Variety Conquistador)	F, W, N, T, M, FD, A, V	70–75°F	60–70°F	65–80°F	1.2–2.3	5.5–6.5
	Notes: Tastes great and can be harvested multiple times.					
Upland Cress	B, F, W, N, T, M, FD, A, V	55–75°F	60–85°F	65–75°F	1.2–2.3	5.5–6.0
	Notes: Fast growing. Taste is similar to arugula.					

ASIAN GREENS

Variety Name	Recommended DIY Systems	Germination Temperatures	Air Temperatures	Water Temperatures	EC	pH
Toy Choi	B, F, W, N, T, M, FD, A, V	75–85°F	60–80°F	65–75°F	1.2–2.3	5.5–6.5
	Notes: Great-tasting miniature bok choi.					
Joi Choi	F, W, N, T, M, FD, A, V	75–85°F	60–80°F	65–75°F	1.2–2.3	5.5–6.5
	Notes: Fastest and biggest bok choi I've grown.					
Red Choi F1	F, W, N, T, M, FD, A, V	75–85°F	60–80°F	65–75°F	1.2–2.3	5.5–6.5
	Notes: Fast-growing red bok choi.					
Purple Choi	F, W, N, T, M, FD, A, V	75–85°F	60–80°F	65–75°F	1.2–2.3	5.5–6.5
Da Hong Summer	F, W, N, T, M, FD, A, V	75–85°F	60–80°F	65–75°F	1.2–2.3	5.5–6.5
	Notes: Deep purple color.					
Tatsoi	F, W, N, T, M, FD, A, V	75–85°F	60–80°F	65–76°F	1.2–2.3	5.5–6.5

SPINACH

- **Recommended DIY Systems:** It is possible to grow spinach in any of the systems mentioned in this book but it is almost always a difficult crop to grow hydroponically.
- **Germination Temperatures:** Best at 45–65°F. Germination is very sensitive to high temperatures, so avoid germination conditions over 80°F.
- **Water Temperatures:** 50–70°F
- **EC:** Healthy crops have been observed growing in nutrient solutions with ECs in the range of 0.7–2.3.
- **pH:** 5.5–6.0
- **Air Temperatures:** 65–75°F

Variety Name	Notes
Kookaburra F1	Good variety for hydroponics. Decent resistance to root rot. Plant stays compact with large leaves.
Bloomsdale	Not great for hydroponics.
Space F1	Big leaves, some resistance to root diseases. Slow to bolt and stays short.
New Zealand	Very slow to germinate compared to other spinach varieties. Has a thick leaf. Very unique spinach.
Monstrueux de Viroflay	Some resistance to root diseases. Huge leaves. Okay growth in hydroponics.
Giant Noble	Susceptible to root diseases.
Avon	Good variety for hydroponics. Very big mature leaves, slow to bolt.
Catalina	Grows slower than other varieties. Susceptible to root diseases.
Gigante de Invierno	Not great for hydroponics, very susceptible to pythium.
Red Kitten F1	Spinach with red stem. Decent growth in hydroponic systems, but slower growing than most green varieties.
Carmel F1	Good variety for hydroponics.
Reflect F1	Not great.
Emperor F1	Not great.
Chinese Spinach	Okay in hydroponics.
Corvair F1	Not great.
Woodpecker F1	Not great.
Flamingo F1	Not great.

Spring mix, spicy mix, and arugula microgreens. Some microgreens can be harvested multiple times if cut above the lowest leaves.

MICROGREENS

- **Germination Temperatures:** 70–80°F for most varieties
- **Water Temperatures:** 60–75°F
- **EC:** 0.7–2.5. Microgreens generally do not need much fertilizer but many of them can be grown successfully at higher ECs.
- **pH:** 5.5–6.0
- **Air Temperatures:** 60–75°F

Variety Name	Days to Harvest	Teaspoons per Square Foot	Notes
Cilantro	14–28	14.0	Use split seeds for better germination. Cilantro can be difficult to grow.
Purple Kohlrabi	10–14	4.0	Awesome color with mild cabbage flavor.
Red Rambo Radish	10–14	5.0	Pretty and a little spicy.
Astro Arugula	14–28	3.0	Can be harvested multiple times.
Mizuna	10–14	3.0	Several varieties available, some spicier than others. Generally very easy to grow.
Scarlet Frills Mustard	10–21	3.0	Several varieties available, some spicier than others. Generally very easy to grow.
Citrus Basil	14–35	2.5	Very sensitive to high pH, keep pH close to 5.5. Great flavor.
Opal Basil	14–35	2.5	Flavor similar to Italian basil. Grows slower than other basil varieties.
Italian Basil	14–35	2.5	Great topping on pizza and pasta.
Carrot	28–35	7.0	Tastes like a carrot without the crunch.
Kale	10–21	5.5	Flavor is mild compared to mature kale leaves. Great mixed into a salad.

METRIC CONVERSIONS

Converting Measurements

To Convert:	To:	Multiply by:
Inches	Millimeters	25.4
Inches	Centimeters	2.54
Feet	Meters	0.305
Yards	Meters	0.914
Miles	Kilometers	1.609
Square inches	Square centimeters	6.45
Square feet	Square meters	0.093
Square yards	Square meters	0.836
Cubic inches	Cubic centimeters	16.4
Cubic feet	Cubic meters	0.0283
Cubic yards	Cubic meters	0.765
Pints (US)	Liters	0.473 (Imp. 0.568)
Quarts (US)	Liters	0.946 (Imp. 1.136)
Gallons (US)	Liters	3.785 (Imp. 4.546)
Ounces	Grams	28.4
Pounds	Kilograms	0.454
Tons	Metric tons	0.907

To Convert:	To:	Multiply by:
Millimeters	Inches	0.039
Centimeters	Inches	0.394
Meters	Feet	3.28
Meters	Yards	1.09
Kilometers	Miles	0.621
Square centimeters	Square inches	0.155
Square meters	Square feet	10.8
Square meters	Square yards	1.2
Cubic centimeters	Cubic inches	0.061
Cubic meters	Cubic feet	35.3
Cubic meters	Cubic yards	1.31
Liters	Pints (US)	2.114 (Imp. 1.76)
Liters	Quarts (US)	1.057 (Imp. 0.88)
Liters	Gallons (US)	0.264 (Imp. 0.22)
Grams	Ounces	0.035
Kilograms	Pounds	2.2
Metric tons	Tons	1.1

Converting Temperatures

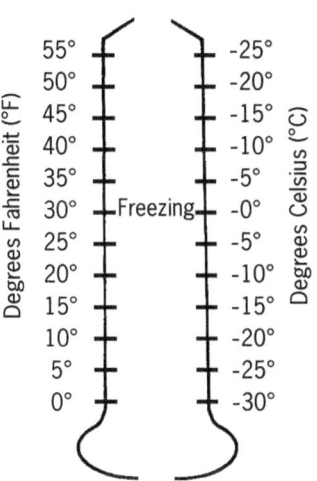

Metric Equivalent

Inches (in.)	1/64	1/32	1/25	1/16	1/8	1/4	3/8	2/5	1/2	5/8	3/4	7/8	1
Feet (ft.)													
Yards (yd.)													
Millimeters (mm)	0.40	0.79	1	1.59	3.18	6.35	9.53	10	12.7	15.9	19.1	22.2	25.4
Centimeters (cm)							0.95	1	1.27	1.59	1.91	2.22	2.54
Meters (m)													

Inches (in.)	2	3	4	5	6	7	8	9	10	11	12	36	39.4
Feet (ft.)											1	3	3½
Yards (yd.)												1	1½
Millimeters (mm)	50.8	76.2	101.6	127	152	178	203	229	254	279	305	914	1,000
Centimeters (cm)	5.08	7.62	10.16	12.7	15.2	17.8	20.3	22.9	25.4	27.9	30.5	91.4	100
Meters (m)											.30	.91	1.00

°F to °C: Subtract 32 from the Fahrenheit temperature reading. Then mulitply that number by 5/9.
For example, 77°F − 32 = 45. 45 × 5/9 = 25°C.

°C to °F: Multiply the Celsius temperature reading by 9/5, then add 32.
For example, 25°C × 9/5 = 45. 45 + 32 = 77°F.

INDEX

A

add-on fertilizer products, 153
advantages, 8–13
aeration, 42–43, 51, 57
aeroponic towers, 107, 116–117
aeroponics
    building instructions, 108–114
    crops for, 106
    difficulty of, 107
    locations for, 107
    overview of, 106
agricultural runoff, 10
air pumps, 20–21
air stones, 21
airflow, 29
algae, 21–22, 56, 70, 87, 101, 109, 166
aphids, 167
aquaponic media beds, 93
aquaponics, 13
Arnon, Daniel, 13
Asian greens, 184
automation, 12
Azadirachtin, 34

B

Bacillus thuringiensis (Bt), 34
Bacillus thuringiensis israelensis (Bti), 34
basil, 176–177
beneficial insects, 33
beneficial microbes, 7–8, 34, 93
bottle hydroponics
    building instructions, 45–48
    crops for, 43–44
    lighting for, 49
    locations for, 44
    maintenance of, 48
    options for, 49
    overview of, 42–43
    troubleshooting, 49
Bt (*Bacillus thuringiensis*), 34
Bti (*Bacillus thuringiensis israelensis*), 34

C

calcium deficiency, 165
ceramic metal halide (CMH) lights, 30–31
channels, 70
chlorosis, 164–165
cleaning, system, 161
cleanliness, 11–12, 14
climate control equipment, 29
CMH (ceramic metal halide) lights, 30–31
coco chips, 26
coco peat, 26
coconut coir, 25–26
conventional fertilizers, 153–154
crops
    contamination of, 12–13
    and growing system selection, 39–40
    growth of, 8, 11
    in the hydroponic system, 14
    nutrient content of, 10–11
    for specific systems, 43–44, 50–51, 61, 70, 84, 92–93, 99, 106
    See also specific types
cuttings, 141, 142–145, 146. *See also* transplanting

D

daily light integral (DLI), 36–37
daily light integral (DLI) meters, 36–37
deep water culture (DWC), 50
delivery height, water, 19
difficulty, level of, 41
dissolved oxygen *see* oxygen
DLI (daily light integral), 36–37
DLI (daily light integral) meters, 155
double bucket systems, 84
drain-to-waste systems, 16
drip towers, 117
dry fertilizers, 153
Dutch bucket gardens *see* top drip systems
DWC (deep water culture), 50

E

ebb and flow *see* flood and drain systems
electrical conductivity (EC), 154, 155, 158
essential nutrients, 7, 8, 153
essential oils, 33
expanded clay pellets, 27, 96

F

fairy garden, 94–98
Ferris wheel systems, 118–119
fertilizer concentration, 154–155
fertilizer storage, 155
fertilizers, 15–17, 152–155. *See also* nutrient solution
fittings, 22
floating rafts

188 **DIY HYDROPONIC GARDENS**

building instructions, 52–58
crops for, 50–51
locations for, 51
maintenance of, 58
options for, 58–59
overview of, 50
sizing of, 51
troubleshooting, 59
flood and drain grow racks, 117
flood and drain systems
building instructions, 102–104
crops for, 99
locations for, 99
overview of, 99
planting options, 105
variations of, 100–101, 117–118
flood trays, 24
flow rates, 19–20, 71
flowering crops, 50, 177–182
fluorescent lights, 29–30
flushing, 10, 160
fungus gnats, 166–167

G

Gericke, William Frederick, 13
germination, 137
grow lights, 29–31
grow tents, 28
growing area, 14
growing media *see* substrates
growing season, 8
growing space, 8
growing systems, 39–41. *See also specific systems*
growth, plant, 24

H

heavy metals, 12–13
herbicides, 9
herbs, 174–176
high pressure sodium (HPS) lights, 30
history of modern hydroponics, 13
Hoagland, Dennis, 13
Hoagland solution, 10
HPS (high pressure sodium), 30
humidity monitoring equipment, 37
hydroponics methods, 16, 50
hygrometers, 37

I

indoor growing equipment, 28–31
infestations, 166–167
interveinal chlorosis, 164
irrigation equipment, 19–22

K

kale, 182
Kratky method, 42–43

L

leafy greens, 172–174, 182–185
LEDs (light emitting diodes), 31
lettuce, 172–174
light emitting diodes (LEDs), 31
light intensity meters, 35–36
light meters, 35–37
lighting, 15, 29–31, 49, 135
lighting accessories, 31–32
liquid fertilizers, 153
location
flexibility in, 9
and growing system selection, 40
for specific systems, 44, 51, 61, 70, 84, 93, 99, 106
lux, 35–36
lux meters, 36

M

magnesium deficiency, 165
maintenance, 40–41, 48, 157–161
manure, 12, 16, 151, 152
media beds
building instructions, 94–98
crops for, 92–93
irrigation methods for, 93
locations for, 93
overview of, 92
substrates for, 93
media/medium *see* substrates
metal halide (MH) lights, 30–31
meters, 35–37
MH (metal halide) lights, 31
microgreens, 185
multi-part fertilizers, 153–154
mushy brown roots, 169

N

natural fertilizers, 16
natural senescence, 165
necrosis, 164
neem oil, 33
negative pressure grow room, 29
NFT (nutrient film technique) *see* nutrient film technique (NFT)
nitrogen deficiency, 164–165
nutrient content, crop, 10–11
nutrient deficiencies, 163–165
nutrient film technique (NFT)

building instructions, 72–82
channels for, 70
crops for, 70
flow rates in, 71
locations for, 70
overview of, 69
transplanting in, 82
troubleshooting, 82
variations of, 119
nutrient solution, 13, 35, 152, 155, 157–159, 160. See also fertilizers; water
nutrient sources, 13
nutrient uptake, 151–152
nutrients, 151–152
nutrition, 151–155

O
one-part fertilizers, 153
organic fertilizers, 16–17, 152–153
oxygen, 8, 19, 20–21, 24–25

P
PAR (photosynthetically active radiation) meters, 36
parts per million measurement, 155
pathogens, 12
peat, 27
peppers, 177
perlite, 27
pest infestations, 10, 166–167
pest management, 32–34
pesticides, 10
pH, 35, 158, 164
pH meters, 35
photosynthetic photon flux density (PPFD), 36
photosynthetically active radiation (PAR) meters, 36
positive pressure grow rooms, 29
potassium bicarbonate, 34
pots, 23–24
power outages, 71
PPFD (photosynthetic photon flux density), 36
predatory insects, 33, 167
pump failure, 71
pumps, 19–21
pyrethrins, 34

R
rafts, 55
rain gutter systems
    building instructions, 122–133
    options for, 134–135
    overview of, 120–121
    planting, 134
    troubleshooting, 135
    See also vertical gardens
rare plants, 181–182
recirculating hydroponics, 16
reservoirs
    and maintenance, 40–41, 160–161
    overview of, 13, 24
    in specific systems, 53–55, 69, 72, 86, 95, 103, 109, 134
rock wool see stone wool
root death, 169
root rugs, 101
rotating/Ferris wheel systems, 118–119

S
sanitizer, 161
seeds, starting, 137–141, 168–169. See also transplanting
set and forget method, 157
shore flies, 166–167
single bucket systems, 84
soap, 34, 161, 167
sodium bicarbonate, 34
soil quality, 8
soilborne pathogens, 12
space, growing, 8
spider mites, 167
spinach, 184
Spinosad, 34
sticky traps, 33
stock solutions, 152
stone wool, 25, 137, 138–141
strawberries, 180
Streptomyces lydicus, 34
substrates
    overview of, 15, 24–27
    for specific systems, 57–58, 61, 66–67, 93, 100–101
synthetic fertilizers, 16
system features, 13–17

T
TDS (total dissolved solids) meters, 155
thermometers, 37
thrips, 167
tip burn, 165
tomatoes, 178–179
top drip systems
    building instructions, 85–91
    crops for, 84
    locations for, 84
    overview of, 83

top off and amend method, 158–159
top off method, 158
total dissolved solids (TDS) meters, 155
toxicity, 163
transplanting, 47, 57–58, 148–149. *See also* cuttings; seeds, starting
trays, 24
troubleshooting, 163–169
true hydroponics, 16
tubing, 21–22

U
unusual plants, 181–182

V
vacuums, 33
venturi pumps, 21
vertical gardens, 115–119. *See also* rain gutter systems

W
water, 8, 9, 12–13, 14, 16, 19, 24–25, 154–155. *See also* nutrient solution
water delivery height, 19
water pumps, 19–20, 71
water temperature, 37
wicking bed
  building instructions, 62–68
  crops for, 61
  locations for, 61
  overview of, 60–61
  transplanting into, 67
  variations of, 61
wicking strips, 48
wilting, 168